ARMED PEGASUS
THE EARLY YEARS

In Greek mythology, Pegasus was a winged Horse, sired by Poseidon in his role as the Horse God, and foaled by Gorfon Medusa.

ARMED PEGASUS
THE EARLY YEARS

Somnath Sapru

KNOWLEDGE WORLD

KW Publishers Pvt Ltd
New Delhi

in association with

Centre for Air Power Studies
New Delhi

The **Centre for Air Power Studies** is an independent, non-profit, academic research institution established in 2002 under a registered Trust to undertake and promote policy-related research, study and discussion on the trends and developments in defence and military issues, especially air power and the aerospace arena, for civil and military purposes. Its publications seek to expand and deepen the understanding of defence, military power, air power and aerospace issues without necessarily reflecting the views of any institution or individuals except those of the authors.

Jasjit Singh
Director
Centre for Air Power Studies
P-284, Arjan Path
Subroto Park
New Delhi 110010

Tele: (91-11) 25699131
E-mail: diroffice@aerospaceindia.org

Published in India by
Kalpana Shukla
KW Publishers Pvt Ltd
4676/21, First Floor, Ansari Road, Daryaganj, New Delhi 110002
T: +91.11.23263498 / 43528107 E: mail@kwpub.in / knowledgeworld@vsnl.net
www.kwpub.com

ISBN 978-93-80502-91-5

Printed and bound in India

Contents

Introduction

Any work, manuscript or narrative based research needs to explain the "why" of it. Why write such a book? Does it have any relevance today? The answer to this is a very big "YES", and it needs an explanation. Unlike the Army or the Navy, the Air Force came to India initially as a result of World War I, and thereby hangs a tale.

Right from 1838, the British had slowly but surely inched their way into the North-West Frontier Pathan tribal territory to control the activities of the inhabitants whose major source of income and enjoyment was raiding, from the unadministered areas into the settled districts, for arms, money and ransom. This went on for decades with the Army coming out of the cantonments to punish the guilty whenever disorder spread and anarchy prevailed. By the turn of the century, Lord Curzon, the Viceroy, decided to separate the Frontier from the control of Punjab into a separate province named North-West Frontier Province (NWFP) with its capital at Peshawar headed initially by a Lieutenant Governor and later a Governor.

When World War I broke out in Europe, the initial thrust of the German Army sent the French and the British Expeditionary Force (BEF) reeling back. There were no spare troops that could be sent to the front. It was this desperate situation that forced the British Government to send an Army Corps comprising infantry and cavalry divisions of the Indian Army to Europe. To accomplish this, they had to withdraw battle-hardened troops from the NWFP and send them to France.

This was the first time that the Indian Army fought in Europe. This development resulted in very few troops being available for Frontier duty. That became the catalyst and justification for the Viceroy of India to ask the British government to send units of the Royal Flying

Corps (RFC) to India in 1915 to help the Army on the ground to police the area by helping with aerial reconnaissance. That is how military aviation, in an organised form, came to India.

The Early Years

Since the RFC was new to India, and back at Home it was still treated as a distant country cousin, not welcomed, but tolerated, the first military aviation unit (later called a squadron), was billeted with the Army. The ground technicians and pilots were young and felt totally alien in a foreign land. How they felt and how they acclimatised themselves later to the contours of the Frontier is also dealt with in this narrative.

The scene at the beginning of 1916 was such that developments were taking place in the air war on the battlefields of Europe. Initially, the RFC was required only to provide aerial reconnaissance reports – to see the other side of the hill which is generally denied to the ground forces in the absence of higher ground. As the war progressed, aircraft were used for photography. When guns were fitted in the aircraft, ground attacks commenced. Apart from that, new experiments were carried out for directing artillery fire. By the time the war got over, wireless had developed sufficiently for air-to-ground and ground-to-air communication. The same was followed in the Frontier areas. As happened in Europe during the retreat from Marne, when aerial reconnaissance proved invaluable to the Army commander on the ground, so it did on the Frontier when Squadron No. 31 provided valuable intelligence in 1916. On the ground, at the local level, the Army commander was extremely satisfied, and said so in official reports.

The Third Dimension

Every organisation has its own history to look back at and the armed forces of a nation are no exception to this practice. In India, we had no tradition of keeping written records and most knowledge came either through palm leaf manuscripts or through the oral tradition of passing knowledge and information from generation to generation.

Written records, catalogued scientifically were introduced in the Western format to conform to the British system. Britain was the paramount power in India for close to 300 years.

Today (2010), if one were to ask as to who actually organised and founded the Indian Army as a military force in the modern sense, the records kept meticulously over the centuries would tell us that it was Major Stringer Lawrence, as a precursor to the organisation, and setting up, of the three separate Presidency Armies.

For practically 2,000 years, conflicts between states broke out either on land or on the sea. Thus, sailors and soldiers were the first identified symbols of the Navy and the Army.

From the time of Leonardo da Vinci, the quest for the conquest of the air began in Europe although flying as an activity has been mentioned in ancient Hindu sacred books and legends and even folklore in Europe and the Middle East. In 1783, the Montgolfier Brothers launched the first balloon in France. Thereafter, in many countries, inventors, visionaries and scientists worked on producing a device that could fly. Initially, soon after the dependence on wind was almost done away with, Armies began to use balloons for reconnaissance. Until then, Armies faced each other at a lateral level and the balloon added the third dimension to it. The use of the balloon as an observer for the artillery soon gained acceptance though problems of controlling the balloon remained.

Simultaneously with this, the quest for a heavier than air machine driven by an internal combustion engine began and after years of trial and error, the Wright Brothers produced a machine that indeed flew on December 17, 1903, at Kitty Hawk, North Carolina, USA.

This heralded the air age and with it came, by stages, military aviation. How India entered the air age is a story mainly of aviation and then, of military aviation. First, a machine that could fly, then a pilot who could fly the machine safely and then fly with weapons, either to defend himself and his machine or to attack a similarly equipped enemy machine. And that brings us to military aviation.

Military aviation in India today (2010) is almost a century old and is represented by the Indian Air Force (IAF). Its history has been written and though the available literature on the IAF is not much, quite a bit is known about the Service since its birth on October 8, 1932. What is not known is what happened before 1932 in terms of the development of military aviation in India. And thereby hangs a tale.

In the first decade of the 20th century, before the aeroplane made its appearance, the railways and the motorcar had already become the modes of transport for the ordinary people and the affluent ones respectively. However, the rulers, in their wisdom, did not credit the 'natives' with the ability to handle machinery. True, Indians did not have exposure to machines, but they were, and are, fast learners.

Meanwhile, even aeroplanes began to make occasional appearances in the Indian skies. The first organised attempt was made by two British companies and one Belgian company in December 1910. They gave demonstration flights in the hope that aviation could make a dent in the vast Indian market. Only one of these companies had an eye on the military application of the aeroplane for aerial reconnaissance. The result was that the world's first ever military air reconnaissance took place during Army manoeuvres in western India on January 15, 1911.

This proved conclusively that the air element would be of great use to the Army in India.

Steady Transformation

Between 1916 and 1939, a timespan of 23 years, many innovations and developments as also aerial tactics that developed on the Western

Front were adopted and adapted by the RFC/ RAF (Royal Air Force) in India. The numbers went up slowly from one squadron in 1916 to eight squadrons by 1928. This period saw, especially after the RAF came into being on April 1, 1918, and the end of the war, a number of innovations backed by war-time experiences which were tried out on the Frontier. While the guns, including the aerial ones, may have fallen silent on the Western Front, aerial policing and constant vigil had to be maintained at all times on the Frontier right up to 1947.

One has to recall how military aviation developed and evolved in Britain. First, it was the balloon, then the dirigible and then the airship or Zeppelin as it was then called. A beginning was made by setting up the balloon section as a part of the Royal Engineers. Soon, it was felt that that was not enough. From 1912, when the Royal Flying Corps (RFC) was set up with aeroplanes, it was hoped that it would fulfil the need for an aviation service. While it did well in the beginning, controversy dogged the corps as both the Army and the Navy wanted to control it as a part of their own service. With all these difficulties, the RFC did go to war as part of the British Expeditionary Force (BEF) to fight, although the Royal Navy, not to be left behind, also sent units of the Royal Naval Air Service (RNAS) to the front.

Back in India, the lessons learnt in the skies and grounds of Europe were incorporated in the rules and regulations, which eventually reached the RAF on the frontier of India. First, let us look at the organisation. In the Army, the smallest unit is a section of about eight to ten men, a platoon comprises about 30, and a company about 150-180. Four companies comprise a battalion. This was in a sense copied. The basic fighting unit in the Air Force is a squadron. This word comes from both the Army and the Navy. You had a squadron of cavalry then, now a squadron of tanks. You also have a squadron of ships. The East Indies Squadron of the Royal Navy was responsible for defending the shores of India.

The smallest fighting unit in the Air Force is a section. Several sections make a flight and several flights make a squadron, usually 12 aircraft, with four extra machines as war reserve. When the first squadrons went to France, they were grouped into wings — 2–4 squadrons into a wing. When it came to the next echelon, they had no answer, but they needed a structured organisation that would perform and be responsible for, or attached to, some Army formations. Being innovative, they borrowed from the Army. Several wings were put together in a brigade. Each brigade was assigned to a field Army which, in turn, would assign individual squadrons to various corps and further down, to various divisions.

This system was adopted in India. But in India, with three wings, it was called the India Group initially and later RAF Command (India). After the war, in Britain, the next echelon was created, namely the group and above it was the command such as Fighter, Bomber and Coastal Commands. During World War II, these groups fought in the Battle of Britain.

England was the first country in the world to set up an Air Force completely independent of the Army and the Navy and absolutely equal in status with the other two services. Britain created history when it set up the Air Ministry on January 2, 1918, to look after and administer the Royal Air Force (RAF).

To help differentiate the airman from the Army soldier or the Navy sailor, a new uniform was designed through trial and error and, finally, the present blue uniform was decided upon. Along with this came rank names and badges of rank. This too took time and effort in the form of prolonged discussions, and, finally, the uniform too was settled upon, and then the rank names and badges of rank in the form of rings/ tapes.

The most revolutionary change was the introduction of double wings to identify the pilot from the others. This, the RAF owes to the Army Order of 1913.

Practices and Innovations

The following are briefly the innovations and practices introduced over a span of over 20 years by the RAF in India:

- **Ghooley Chits:** Banking on human greed, these chits declared that if a pilot, who may have crashed in the mountainous tribal areas, was rescued unharmed and returned to the authorities, a reward in cash would be given to the tribal with no questions asked. This practice was later employed in the occupied Europe during World War II where pilots and air crew needed to be protected from capture by the German armed forces.
- **Squadron Identification:** In the Army, the regiment has a name and a number. While no names were initially given, numbers were assigned and, in some cases, even the role of the squadron. This was to give an identity to the unit and inculcate pride among the air crew and ground staff.
- **Service Ensign:** From 1918 to 1921, the RAF had no service ensign to identify it. This came into force in 1921.
- **The Service Motto:** *Per Adua ad Astra* (By Work to the Stars). This motto was suggested by General Jack Cowan at the War Office and was promptly accepted. Years later, when the Indian Air Force was formed, it also got a motto: "*Ittehad me shakti hai*" (in unity there is strength). After independence, it was changed.
- **Puff Shoots:** In the airmen's language, this referred to directing artillery fire from an aircraft. Initially, there was no communication system except the one that was developed by the RAF on the Frontier. This was a metal message box that would be thrown out of an aircraft informing the ground troops about the enemy disposition facing them. The same box was used to tell the gunners whether their shells were falling on the target or short of it or over it. This was used to reach the pilot without wireless. The same message box with a hook was dangled on a rope between two bayonets held upright, about 20 ft apart. The aircraft would

come in a shallow dive, fly over and and with the hook fitted on its underside, pick up the rope holding the message box, then take it into the aircraft, open it and read the contents of the message.

- **Transporting Troops and Supplies:** After the war was over, a few of the bigger bomber aircraft like the Vickers Valencia were used for carrying a few passengers. This was the beginning of developing troop and cargo carrying capacity. Experiments were made in supply dropping, initially ending in failure, but over a period of time, experience was gained and expertise developed. When emergency situations arose, as in 1919 and 1928 and on several occasions in Mesopotamia, Aden and Palestine, troops were rushed by air. Later on, during World War II, this experience got expanded into full-fledged troop carriers like the Curtiss Commandos and airlifting large numbers of troops from one part of the front to another. Added to this was supply dropping for troops behind enemy lines as was done for the two Chindits operations.
- **Importance of Ground Staff:** It took quite some time for policy-makers both in the UK and in India to realise that the Air Force was a highly technical service. According to a battle-hardened pilot on the Frontier, "As pilots, we can get a plenty, but getting good fitters is damn difficult." After the war, during peace-time, the RAF specially set up a school to train young technicians at Halton (UK) and sent out to India a mixture of the young and older experienced mechanics who guided the young ones in the practical field of servicing, repair and maintenance.

During operations on the Frontier, by trial and error, aircraft were designed and designated for specific tasks. Even in the official records, a squadron number would be followed by its role number, for example, No. 27 (Bomber), and others as Fighter, and on the Frontier particularly, AC (Army Cooperation). In official despatches during World War II, Indian Air Force Hurricane squadrons were classified as AC-Army cooperation and the two Vengeance squadrons as Bombers.

In the beginning, there were no air gunners on the Frontier and the fitter who maintained the aircraft would fly in the rear cockpit as an air gunner. Gradually, training was given and a speciality was created: the air gunners, and a special badge was given to them. This was officially sanctioned in 1923. Similarly, in multi-engined service aircraft, especially for maritime reconnaissance, observers were separately trained. They also got a single wing with the letter "O" at the top of the wing.

To give the new service a complete identity totally separate from the Army and the Navy, gallantry awards equivalent to those current in the two services were introduced – the DFC (Distinguished Flying Cross) equivalent to the Military Cross/ Distinguished Service Cross of the Navy, and the Air Force Cross (AFC).

Although a technically oriented service, the RAF was certainly a military organisation and as such, parades were necessary and were regularly held. A band was in attendance. But, initially, in India, it depended on the Army for a band to provide music for marching. The RAF theme music was composed later and played on formal occasions.

All regulations about physical attributes and minimum requirements for the service were gradually formalised as was the minimum number of flying hours, both dual and solo, before a pilot could get his 'wings'. Apart from that, a proper discussion was initiated about who would make a good pilot. One of myths which floated in Britain, before 1914, was that a good horse rider would make a fine pilot. It is, however, true that quite a few cavalry and artillery officers who became pilots did come from the Army where horse riding was compulsory.

There was, however, one aspect of the medical examination of new entrants that somehow escaped the RAF. It was left to one of the six Indians who had been selected for training as pilots at Cranwell to point out the lacuna. It was the height requirement of the future pilots. Flight Cadet T N Tandon was found to be too short and not able to use his feet when flying in 1931. He was taken off flying and commissioned as an Equipment Officer. After this incident, a minimum height was prescribed by the RAF.

The Past is a Guide

An oft-quoted quotation goes: "The farther you look back into the past, the further you can look into the future." One might justifiably ask: why do we need to know what the RAF did in India from 1916 to 1933 and from that date through the war to 1947.

There is every possibility that today (2010), the seniormost officers of the IAF would not know about the circumstances that surrounded the introduction of the double wing as a part of the uniform of a pilot: when it came into force and by whose order, which was the first military plane to fly in the Indian skies, who was the pilot, which squadron has the motto "First in the Indian Skies"? There are many other related things, practices, rules and regulations that the successor IAF inherited. We have to concede that the RAF brought the planes to India as well as the people to run and maintain them. Many senior officers of the Air Force will be surprised to know that the basic and advanced flying schools they attended at Ambala and Walton (Lahore) around 1940-42 were, in fact, RAF squadrons converted practically overnight into a training establishment – No. 27 Squadron, RAF. All these are part of the tradition and lore that the infant Indian Air Force absorbed and even bettered.

We, in India, especially the Air Force, and even the Navy, cannot forget that unlike other dominions in the British Commonwealth, India was the only one where the Air Force and the Navy were subordinate to, and under the control of, the Commander-in-Chief (C-in-C) of the Indian Army. How and when did the Air Force attain its position as equal to the Army?

Free India's First Air Chief

For that, we have to turn to what Air Marshal Sir Thomas Elmhirst, who became the first C-in-C and the Chief of Air Staff of the Indian Air Force, penned about himself.

On August 15, 1947, when the Union Jack was lowered from the ramparts of the Red Fort and in its place was unfurled the tricolour, the Indian Air Force was in a peculiar position. There were not enough senior officers to take on the policy-making and controlling roles. On Prime Minister Nehru's advice, it was decided that in the initial stage, we would retain British RAF officers, both at the level of Chief of Staff, head of the service and other technical services.

Thus, it came about that Air Marshal Sir Thomas Elmhirst took over as Commander-in-Chief of the IAF. It needs to be stressed that during the British rule, both the Navy and the Air Force (earlier, before 1933, only the RAF and later, the IAF as well) were under the control of the Army Commander-in-Chief. This was a situation very much like that of Britain where both the War Office and the Admiralty Office tried very hard to absorb the Air Force as a subordinate in their respective services. A long struggle followed but eventually the Air Force emerged as a separate, independent service, equal in every way to the Army and the Navy.

Thus, for the IAF to come up on its own and grow substantially, the soothing balm of being an independent service within the democratic set-up was essential. Equality with the other services was the need of the hour and this was provided by Air Marshal Elmhirst when he was offered the assignment.

At the time of Partition in 1947, neither India nor Pakistan had enough experienced senior Air Force officers to head the service. Both Pandit Nehru and M A Jinnah, requested Lord Mountbatten to select the service heads for them. His recommendations were accepted by both sides. However, there was an exception in the case of the selection of the Indian Air Force. Air Marshal Sir Thomas

Elmhirst was, at that time, holding the appointment of Chief of Inter-Services Administration at General Headquarters, Delhi. Air Marshal Elmhirst recalls the sequence of events of his appointment as head of the IAF.

"It was the first week in August 1947 and I was closing my office at GHQ Delhi, preparing to leave India before the Independence Day on the 15th of the month, and return to London, with an RAF appointment in Washington in view. The phone rang, 'The Viceroy wishes to speak to you.' 'Dickie' Mountbatten spoke, 'Tommy, I hear that you are about to depart, do not go until you have seen me, my staff will fix an appointment later today.'

"I walked across the Vice Regal Palace that afternoon and saw the Viceroy. He told me that it was his job in the next few days to find six officers to command the three services of the two new dominions about to come into being. He said he had asked the new Prime Ministers-to-be, Nehru and Jinnah, to put forward names but both said that they would leave it to him, except in the case of the new Indian Air Force-to-be for which Nehru had put forward my name as its commander.

"I had not, till then, met Pandit Nehru, but I later learnt that my elder brother was a friend of his. Mountbatten went on to say that he would like me to take the job and stay and help India as he intended to do as Governor General for a short time after the Independence Day.

"But he said, 'Make your own contract with Nehru, I will fix for you to have an interview with him tomorrow.' That evening, I pondered over three terms of a possible contract. The RAF in India, together with its small IAF contingent, had always been under the Army Commander-in-Chief in India. The first requirement in any contract I made with Nehru was that the IAF would be an independent fighting service under me as its Commander-in-Chief, being subordinate to his Minister of Defence and then to him only as Prime Minister.

"The second point I must be sure on was that I must have the right to choose from the RAF in England, half a dozen senior staff officers on the technical side to help me in the first two years. My third point would be that I must have the right to appeal to him personally if I have difficulty with any of his subordinates, political or civil service.

"I saw Mr Nehru the next morning. We talked for half an hour. He accepted my independent Air Force requirement and my right to appeal to him. The other points were small and could easily be adjusted. There was no contract. He was prepared to accept me and I was prepared to accept the job. We shook hands."

Elmhirst was the first among three RAF officers who headed the Indian Air Force, until Air Marshal Subroto Mukherjee became the first Indian to head the IAF in 1954.

— Air Marshal Bharat Kumar,
An Incredible War

Elmhirst's role has been summed up by another contemporary as: "It was the organising capability of Air Marshal Sir Thomas Elmhirst which gathered the scattered and unbalanced units of the IAF over the next three years (1947-50) and blended them together to make them into a formidable service which would develop into a force most powerful in the region."

— Air Marshal M S Chaturvedi, IAF (Retd)

Air Marshal Sir Thomas Elmhirst relinquished his office as the first C-in-C and Chief of the Air Staff (CAS) of the Indian Air Force after India became independent in 1947, on February 22, 1950. In January 1973, he paid a nine-day official visit to India and had the pleasure of seeing first-hand the growing edifice whose foundation he had laid 23 years earlier. His host at that time was Air Chief Marshal P

C Lal, CAS, Indian Air Force. Air Marshal Elmhirst was an honorary Air Marshal of the Indian Air Force.

Knowledge and Experience

The following pages underline an attempt to describe the emergence of military aviation in 1901 on the Indian soil. Not many in this country know that as in the UK, in India too, military aviation began with balloons. The Bengal Engineer Group was the first that was handed the balloons by the Royal Engineers who brought them to India and initially tried using them on the Frontier. From 1901 to 1910, balloons were held on the strength of the Army. Soon, the powered aeroplane arrived and attention shifted to this new vehicle of the air.

Soon after, with the war going on in Europe, the first military aviation unit landed in India and was initially posted at Naushera on the Frontier. This was No. 31 Squadron of the Royal Flying Corps (RFC). Soon there were two, and from two in the Twenties, it went to six squadrons. Eventually it became an eight squadron force largely concentrated in the Frontier Province.

The arrival of a Boxkite plane heralded in a small way the beginning of military aviation in India. In January 1911, it was demonstrated that aeroplanes are ideal for reconnaissance. Events in England influenced the proposal to set up a flying school in India for for the Indian Army officers to learn to fly in Indian conditions. The school was set up but the war intervened and all the pilots were sent either to the UK or Mesopotamia (Iraq) or Egypt.

Then came the creation under war-time conditions of an 'Indian Flying Corps' in Iraq. True, all its pilots were English from the Indian Army. This small group had their initiation in war-time flying, but such was the prejudice against anything having an 'Indian' identity, that this miniscule flying corps was ordered by the RFC to be merged with No. 30 Squadron, RFC, in Mesopotamia.

As the war raged in Europe, there was a great need for more pilots and the colour bar on Indians and other non-European candidates was temporarily relaxed. Five Indians qualified as pilots, of whom four went to war, two were killed, one was taken prisoner and one survived. This officer, Lieutenant Hardit Singh Malik, who after the war joined the Indian Civil Services (ICS), was the lone Air Force witness before the Skeen Committee who testified that Indians had the ability to become officers in the RAF.

Immediately after the war, demobilisation commenced and Lieutenant Malik too was demobilised. Major General Sir Sefton Brancker, who had served in the Indian Army and learnt to fly in India, visited No. 11 Squadron at Neville (Malik's last posting in France). Meeting Malik, he asked him what he would do now that the war was over. "Some leave first, Sir, to go home. Then continue in the RAF in India."

"Good show," said the monocled General. He was kind enough to arrange eight months leave for Malik and then sent him to Marseilles and by the P & O liner to India.

On board the ship en route to India, Malik had an interesting experience as the war was over. There was an English officer, Captain Keen, from the 28th Punjabis of the Indian Army. Pleasant and friendly, they dined and talked many times together during the voyage. One evening while talking about the Indian Army, he asked Malik what his plans were. He said he would join the RAF in India.

"Oh, Malik, don't do that."

"Why not?" Malik asked, annoyed at this unsolicited advice.

"You know, we don't want Indians in the RAF. You will find one fine day, that you will go up and your plane will break up in the air."

He persisted and tried to convince Malik that he meant what he said.

— Somnath Sapru,
Skyhawks

Colour Bar and Prejudice

This should convince anyone that the RAF did not want Indians as officers in their service. Archival material, recently made public, tells us that the War Office and even the Air Ministry had decreed that no British soldier or airman would agree to serve under an "Indian or half-caste or non-European officer."

The Indian Air Force was the result of a compromise arrived at between Lord Trenchard, Chief of the Air Staff, RAF, and the Air Officer Commanding (AOC) India, Air Vice Marshal Sir W Geoffrey H Salmond, who served in India from 1927 to 1930. This is evident from the correspondence reproduced in this book between the two. There were, at that time, political compulsions and the compromise formula would result in a mini Air Force which would remain subordinate to the English officers of the RAF.

The Indian Air Force, when it came into being, faced discrimination at both officer and technician levels. But the pioneers of the service, like the mechanics and other ground staff, braved all criticism and eventually blunted it by the sterling worth of their work. It is interesting in retrospect to dwell on an incident that took place after an accident in which about a dozen soldiers were killed by an aircraft piloted by an Indian officer. After this incident, the AOC India, Sir John Steel declared that he would wind up the Indian Air Force.

If World War II had not taken place, the IAF would have remained a tiny part of the RAF, on paper, separate, but in practice, a subordinate. Even before the war, the single flight of No. 1 Squadron IAF proved what it could do in the Frontier area. And the crowning irony is that the Indians, whom the British officers would not allow to enter the hangars and the workshops in 1933, left the defence of their biggest aircraft park and depot in Karachi to the IAF in 1942, when RAF squadrons were sent for service elsewhere.

All this and much more is a part of our history. It should be penned so that future generations may know what the RAF brought to India and what the Indians did on the Frontier and later in the skies over war-torn Burma. That part of the IAF's history has been dealt with by others, and this narrative is an effort to understand in the right perspective the emergence of military aviation and its arrival and growth in India.

I crave the indulgence of the reader and hope he will enjoy reading the book as much as I enjoyed writing it, in spite of lack of material pertaining to the period 1916-33. I, as the author, am responsible for any mistakes that may have occurred in writing this book.

Bangalore

Somnath Sapru

ssapru21@yahoo.com

Acknowledgements

While researching for my earlier book *Skyhawks*, I found out through the memoirs of the late Air Vice Marshal Harjinder Singh, edited by Air Commodore Amrit Lal Saigal, what the RAF was like in the Thirties of the 20th century. Learning new technology, getting used to military discipline and at the end of the day (literally) delivering the goods was a new life for young Indian officers and airmen. I was curious to know how the British managed in the early days of their arrival in India, especially on the Frontier.

The following is the result of that and more than that. The RFC/ RAF was, in fact, even in Europe, a growing organisation. Improvisation, innovation and competition in some areas with the Army were some of the problems they faced. Added to that, for the RAF in India, were the alien surroundings, the language barrier and an inherent colour prejudice that surfaced later.

The catalyst in my undertaking this project was an elderly, long since retired airman, Mathew Clarke, in the UK, who served as a fitter and wireless operator in the RAF in India on the Frontier in the Twenties and Thirties. After returning to England, he sought out his old comrades and they began corresponding with one another and even producing a small newsletter which they circulated among themselves. The theme was always service on the Frontier. I was admitted as an honorary member though I was far younger than most of them, they being in their seventies. Reading through their letters, I got to know what it was like then. All this took place in the Seventies.

So, I would like to thank them – most of them are no more. All that is left are newsletters written on faded paper describing the ‘far away and long ago' of service life. Beginning with Mathew Clarke who served in Lahore, Ambala, Peshawar, Risalpur, Kohat and even Fort Sandeman, there were others, such as Flight Sergeant G H Hayles (No. 5 Squadron), Wing Commander H L Millyard, Wing Commander H Hampshire, L H Smith (No. 5 Squadron), G S Dumble, Charles Holdway, S H Michinson, Bill Brighton, Sergeant F Beaumont, G F McDonnel (HQ 2, Indian Wing, Risalpur), A Evenett (No. 31 Squadron), Dick Field (Australian), Sergeant Pilot Syd Chapman, Harry Lawton, W M Cox (AOC Flight, New Delhi).

To John Ross goes a big 'thank you' for having published his memoirs as an erk and later as an officer in the RFC and RAF. Thanks are due to Chaz Bowyer who spent his entire working life in the RAF and has penned very well researched books and articles on the service and written an entire book on his squadron — No. 27 Squadron, RAF. Before getting to know Chaz Bowyer, I was introduced, nearly thirty years ago, to the *Cross and Cockade (C&C)*, the research journal on World War I aviation. The *C&C* was also good enough to publish two of my articles on I L Roy and H S Malik, two of the four Indians who served during World War I as pilots in the RFC.

Due to lack of archival material in India, I had to approach the RAF Museum in the UK. To Peter Devitt, I owe a debt of gratitude as he provided me with many links to the happenings in the RAF in India during the Twenties and the Thirties and the political and racial overtones towards the demand for Indians to be recruited as pilots and officers in the RAF. To Lieutenant Colonel Dinkar Verma (Retd) of the Corps of Engineers (MEG), Indian Army, heartfelt thanks for the information on the setting up of the balloon section of the Indian Army in 1901.

For getting an idea of the difficulties the RAF in India had in the initial stages, one can refer to the most comprehensive history of the very first squadron to fly in the Indian skies (No. 31 Squadron, RFC/RAF) written by another veteran, Norman L R Franks.

I would like to place on record my thanks to Peter Subbu (P Subramanyam) based in the UK, an old classmate and friend for 56 years, who has helped me a lot with research into early British aviation. To Ms Jayanthi Krishnamachary, my thanks for responding very generously to my questions about facts, figures and computerese.

And next, thanks to *The Sainik Samachar* (earlier *Fauji Akhbar*) for faithfully recording the events in the life of the armed forces, which helped me to identify people and places correctly.

Since I belong to the pre-computer era and am completely ignorant of the mysteries of the computer, I placed my problems before Mr K Pushparaj and his wife Mrs Rathna K Pushparaj. They are running the computer firm 'Computron' and have generously given their time to help me. I owe a debt of gratitude to them and would like to thank them.

The engine is the heart of an aeroplane
but the pilot is its soul!!

– Walter Raleigh

The Fledgling Years

Military Aviation Comes to India — 1901

Military aviation came to India when the then Government of India through the Commander-in-Chief, Indian Army, decided to use the air arm, then still in its infancy in England, in the tribal, lawless regions of the North-West Frontier Province (NWFP), to assist the Indian Army in reconnaissance from the air.

The first military aviators to fly in India employed balloons. Balloons had already figured in the British plans from the late 19th century. In England, the British military authorities began experiments with balloons in 1878 and balloon detachments took part in the Army manoeuvres in 1880 and 1882. Two years later, a balloon unit attached to the Royal Engineers took part in the Bechuanaland Expedition and created a considerable impression.

In 1885, the unit saw service in Sudan. By then, a balloon depot and factory had been in existence for two years. In 1892, it was given permanent quarters at Aldershot, where a school of ballooning was founded. In 1883, the factory began to work but soon had difficulties to contend with. Nevertheless, under the energetic direction of Major J L B Templer, it began to forge ahead and was soon doing excellent work. Balloons made in it played a part in the South African War, notably at the battle of Magersfontein and the siege of Ladysmith.

The balloons appeared to have seriously disquieted the Boers and on more than one occasion, to have saved British forces from ambushes and ambuscades. Malta also had her first experience of an Air Force. Balloons from Aldershot paid a prolonged visit to the island in 1904 but found conditions difficult.

Captive balloons came fully into their own in the Four Years War, in which the work of the observers, who swung precariously in baskets below their swelling forms, was of the highest value.

It was at the turn of the century that many Indian Army officers, including among them, Captain Sefton Brancker, later a great votary of air power, felt that if balloons could be used in Africa, surely India could also provide an opportunity to utilise them for aerial reconnaissance in the troublesome, lawless mountain areas of the NWFP and help in subduing the rebellious tribes.

Accordingly, it was decided by the Army to bring a balloon unit to India. In 1901, Captain A H B Hume, Royal Engineers, and six Non-Commissioned Officers (NCOs) and Sappers from the 4th Balloon Section, RE, arrived in India in order to establish an experimental balloon section at Rawalpindi as part of the Bengal Sappers and Miners.

"The first commander of this experimental section was Captain W A Stokes, RE, and during its brief history, it would further have four commanders, all drawn from the Royal Engineers. They were Captain G C B Loch, RE, Lieutenant P W L Broke Smith, RE, Captain T H Spaight, RE, and Lieutenant C E Colbeck, RE."

Brigadier P W L Broke Smith CIE, DSO, OBE,
"The History of British Military Aeronautics,"
Royal Engineers Journal, 1952, reprinted by
the Library Association 1968, p. 19.

In his account, Brigadier Broke Smith noted that "Considerable proficiency was reached in the handling of balloons"; the section developed a good technique, and successfully practised direction of artillery fire at the Hutti (in modern Karnataka) artillery practice camp.

However, the performance of the section was hampered both by the effects of the Indian climate on the balloons which deteriorated rapidly unless treated with glycerine and by shortages of transport, facilities and equipment. For eight long years, the men of the section did good, dedicated work, but time was against them. The aeroplane had come.

In 1908, though no aeroplanes were on the Frontier, the section was shifted from Rawalpindi to Roorkee in the United Provinces (UP), the regimental centre of the Bengal Sappers and Miners. The section continued its training at Roorkee and it was finally decided to wind up the section completely in 1911. Ironically, it was in January 1911 that aeroplanes were first seen in the Indian skies.

Broke Smith attributed the limited opportunities available for the balloon section to deploy other arms "partly to the disabilities of the section and partly to the general lack of interest in balloons, which was finally accentuated by the prospects of the suppression of balloons by aeroplanes."

While early aeronautical development in India lagged some way behind that in the UK, by 1909, sufficient interest had been engendered in aviation to enable the co-founder of the Aerial League of the British Empire, Colonel Harry Stanley Massey, to establish an Indian branch of the society; its first President being the Commander-in-Chief of the Indian Army, Sir O'Moore Creagh.

Other officers in India, at this time, had begun to look to the aeroplane as an instrument of war. As early as January 1910, Captain Walter Mervyn St. George Kirke (Royal Artillery) noted in the *Journal of the United Service Institution of India* that "from a military point of view, such high speed machines would be valuable for offensive and defensive purposes, particularly against other flying machines but also to fulfil their main role with a field Army in reconnaissance."

The Indian military establishment also considered the viability of using airships to secure India's borders. In July 1914, the Director of Air Department in the Admiralty, Captain Murray F Sueter, replied to a request from Colonel Wyndham Knight of the General Staff, "for information regarding the employment of airships on the Indian frontier."

The 'technical remarks' forwarded with Sueter's letter, outlining suitable designs for such an airship and the supporting infrastructure that it would require, cautioned that "it should be clearly understood that no satisfactory results are likely to be obtained without the expenditure of a large sum of money. Airships cannot be run on the cheap." Although Sueter undertook to provide full details of the ship, sheds and all accessory requirements for work of a somewhat similar character, with the outbreak of war, this proposal would seem to have fallen by the wayside.

Deployment of the Balloon Section

One of the assignments recorded was the deployment of the section in Burma as part of an Indian contingent, consisting of an infantry brigade and a cavalry regiment under Brigadier General J Hudson which was included in General Graham's Division, and with it was the F Company, Madras Sappers and Miners under Captain C B Wilkieson, RE, with Captain F J Romilly and Lieutenant E M B Newman, RE, and two telegraph sections and a balloon section.

This was, perhaps, the only occasion when the balloon section was sent out of India as part of a contingent in Burma. These working balloons were described as being part of "Balloonatics". The officers and men of the Bengal Sappers and Miners who composed the personnel of the balloon section stationed at Rawalpindi for employment on the North-West Frontier were never actually used in war.

In August 1901, once the decision to have an experimental balloon section had been taken the previous year, seven men of the 4th Balloon Section who had served in the Third China War were sent to Rawalpindi. The remainder of this section was sent back to Aldershot, UK.

Captain W A Stokes took charge of the experimental unit soon after its arrival and was joined by Lieutenant G C B Loch, RE. A detachment of 28 men of the Bengal Sappers and Miners under Company Sergeant Major E Dawkins was sent from Roorkee and with eight Non-Commissioned Officers (NCOs), completed the original establishment.

Hydrogen was manufactured in Rawalpindi and carried (compressed) in long steel cylinders loaded on wagons. The first experiment with the balloon Venus (11,000 cu ft) in the Murree foothills showed the risk of damage from trees and rocks though some useful observation was carried out.

Lieutenant F C Molesworth, RE, joined the section in June 1902, when Stokes handed over command to G C B Loch. In November, the unit was in Delhi for the Coronation Durbar and afterwards the balloon Achilles (13,000 cu ft) was used to transport troops across a canal.

Larger balloons, made of cotton fabric, were supplied in 1904, but their valves were defective and they gave much trouble. By this time, the strength of the unit had mounted to 51 in all ranks. Molesworth left the section and Lieutenant T H L Spaight, RE, joined it early in 1905.

A demonstration was given in 1907 at Agra for the benefit of the Army of Afghanistan.

Lieutenant P W L Broke Smith, RE, joined the establishment in 1907. Experiments by Broke Smith near Murree at an altitude of 7,000 ft proved that the available balloons were too small for use at such a height and were consequently unsuitable for Frontier warfare.

How did the balloon section fit into the Indian Army's scheme of things? While enthusiasts in the Army were keen on using the air element for reconnaissance from the third dimension, the reliability of the balloon as an instrument of military steadfastness left much to be desired. Some of the experiences in the Indian context are given below:

"Someone describing an ascent said he saw the officer in the car shouting down the telephone with one hand and being dreadfully sick with the other.

"When the ceasefire was sounded on certain manoeuvres in 1902, all units were ordered to march on the balloon which appeared to be stationary at a height of 1,000 ft. Unfortunately, however, it was actually being towed along at a smart pace and the confusion which ensued among the sweating troops may be left to the imagination.

"The last occasion on which a captive balloon was used in field exercises was in 1909, when the Commandant Lieutenant Colonel G M Heath, RE, and his Adjutant Lieutenant E H Kelly, RE, tried to manoeuvre a balloon at night towards some trenches below the Shivaliks and were ignonimously captured by the 4th Company.

"Some three years later, the next Commandant, Lieutenant Colonel T G Twining, RE, was ordered to prepare a few small signal balloons for manoeuvres and was told that arrangements had been made with the North-Western Railway at Saharanpur to fill them with gas. He replied briefly that coal gas is heavier than air. Nevertheless, he was directed to 'experiment' and consequently sent a Warrant Officer to Saharanpur to watch the inflation of a balloon which could never leave the ground and, subsequently, to prepare a suitable report for transmission to Simla (the summer headquarters of the Government of India).

"In 1908, a deathblow was given to the prospects of the balloon section by recent developments in aeroplanes. Loch and Broke Smith having left the unit, Spaight took it to Roorkee as the Government was contemplating its abolition. Lieutenant C E Colbeck, RE, assumed charge and afterwards Lieutenant L Evans, RE, and at the end of 1910, the balloon section ceased to exist.

"The men rejoined their companies and most of the equipment was sold by auction, with the balloon envelopes, which had cost hundreds of pounds, fetching only a few annas.

"Such was India's introduction to the third dimension in warfare. Soon, in December 1910, aeroplanes descended on India and just five years later, as the Great War was on in Europe, the first military aeroplane flew in the Indian skies."

— Lieutenant Colonel E W C Sandes,
The Indian Sappers and Miners
(Institution of Royal Engineers, Chatham, England, 1948)

Metal Birds in Indian Skies – 1911

"One bright sunny morning in December 1910, I was sitting in my office in Fort William, Calcutta, when one of my Sergeant Majors came and said, 'Beg pardon, Sir, they have just disembarked some aeroplanes at the docks'.

"I was up, and as quick as I could go, I arrived at the docks to find an expedition dispatched by the British & Colonial Aeroplane Company half way ashore. The party consisted of Farnall Thurstan as leader, Henri Jullerot, a well known French pilot, and two British mechanics with three aeroplanes of the 'Boxkite' variety.

"They had come to demonstrate the possibilities for aviation in India, but their instructions were vague and they knew nothing about the country. Naturally, such unexpected enterprise was treated with profound suspicion by those local authorities with whom they came into touch, but I have always enjoyed being one of the fools who step in where angels fear to tread and so took them under my wing with a will which certainly deflected a good deal of energy from my more legitimate duties."

These are the words of Captain Sefton Brancker, who had been commissioned in the Royal Artillery from the Military Academy, Woolwich, saw active service in the Boer War in South Africa, was wounded in action and later chosen for staff duties in India where he served in the artillery regiments from 1903 to 1912.

During this period, he was posted in the Calcutta Brigade as

Deputy Assistant Adjutant (DAA) and Quarter Master General (QMG) in January 1909 and stationed at Fort William.

"The first problem was to find a suitable aerodrome for the initial demonstration. We soon realised that the only feasible spot was the Race Course on the Calcutta Maidan. It took a little tact and persuasion to induce the Calcutta Turf Club authorities to agree to such an unusual and doubtful use of their beautifully kept enclosure — but after some discussion, they gave us leave for a one-day demonstration on the understanding that we should charge entrance fee to the race stands and give the proceeds to a local military charity.

"There was a somewhat stunted tree in the middle of the race course and under it the two mechanics sat to work to erect the first of their machines. On January 6, 1911, a vast crowd assembled. The pilot, Jullerot, made an effective flight and landed amidst tremendous enthusiasm."

The Bristol Boxkite was one of the earliest aeroplanes to be manufactured in fairly large numbers before the onset of World War I. The Bristol Company had decided to design its own aeroplane and had appointed G H Challenger as the chief engineer and designer. The first product from his drawing board was based on a French design — the Henri Farman pusher bi-plane. Nicknamed 'the Boxkite', assembly of the machine was completed at Larkhill, Salisbury Plain, on July 29, 1910, and it made its first proving flight the following day.

This type was used at the newly formed Bristol Flying School at Brooklands which functioned under M Edmund. The idea of manufacturing aeroplanes came to Sir George White, the Chairman of the parent company Bristol Tramway & Carriage Company, when he was on a holiday at Cannes where he saw French aeroplanes flying and decided that he would also build aeroplanes.

The Pioneer newspaper reported in its columns, on January 8, about the flight by the powered aeroplane in Indian skies as:

"M Jullerot, aviator of the Colonial Aeroplane Company gave a flying display in the afternoon on January 6, 1911, in a Bristol

Boxkite bi-plane that is considered specially suitable for military requirements.

"The whole space, within the railings which make the concourse, was kept clear by troops and police. An immense crowd gathered on the adjacent roads and lined the railings throughout their entire length. There seldom has been a larger gathering on the maidan. The race stands were reserved and a number of ladies and gentlemen watched the display.

"Sir O'Moore Creagh, C-in-C of the Indian Army and Lady Creagh, Lady Barrow, Sir Douglas Haig and the principal military officers were present. Her Excellency, Lady Hardinge, with a party from the Government House, drove to the Race Course at 1.30 pm and the bi-plane then ascended.

"After a short run on the ground, M Jullerot ran 300 metres so as to be clear of the trees and took off. He circled around, passing over the race stands, three times. His steering was admirable. The bi-plane rose and fell, turned and altered its course gracefully. There was a roar of applause from the crowd and the spectators on the stands as the machine sailed along. A light breeze was blowing.

"The aviator descended after a flight lasting six minutes, the machine bumping slightly as it touched the ground. One of the straps of the ailerons was broken and thus the bi-plane was crippled, so far as further flights were concerned. The proceeds of the performance will be made over to Lady Creagh for the soldiers' and sailors' families' association.

"It was a thrilling event, the first in Calcutta. While, the Bristol company officials were elated at the success of the flight, Captain Brancker was ecstatic. He soon came down to earth and faced the problem: how to continue his association with the Bristol party's flying operations?"

If one was to chronicle the coincidences that history has thrown up, one would point to the link that India developed with the world of aviation.

On December 17, 1903, the Wright Brothers flew the first aeroplane, Kitty Hawk, in North Carolina, USA.

Exactly seven years later, on December 17, 1910, the world's first air-mail post was delivered from Allahabad to Naini, six miles away.

Aviation and the Empire — 1903-11

The seven years that followed the Wright Brothers' epoch-making flight in December 1903, saw frantic activity in the field of making 'the aeroplane' more reliable and safe in the air.

In Britain, the entire effort was private. Any new product or service needs a user, who, if convinced, will certainly buy it. Three private firms, one Belgian and the other two British, felt that it was time to take their new products to the farthest corners of the Empire. The land route from Europe led to the Middle East and to reach Australia and New Zealand one had to cross the Indian subcontinent. Also, after the opening of the Suez Canal in 1867, transport of goods and people took far less time than it did earlier.

Thus, it was that the three private companies sent their marketing teams to India in December 1910. They brought with them different types of aeroplanes to demonstrate this new vehicle of the air that held tremendous possibilities for the future in a vast country like India.

The first firm's group arrived in early December. This was the Humber Company of Coventry. The team was led by Captain Walter George Windham and two pilots namely, Henri Pequet, a Frenchman, and Keith Davis, an Englishman. Two technicians, Haffkin, an Englishman, and Billion, a Frenchman, comprised the ground technical crew.

They arrived by ship, the SS *Persia*, in Bombay and the crates containing the aeroplanes were loaded on a train to Allahabad, UP, where they intended to give demonstration flights. At that time, for the first time in the 20th century, an industrial and agricultural exhibition was planned to be held at Allahabad (as this was thought to be a suitable venue to showcase their products).

The group reached Allahabad on December 5, 1910, and the aeroplanes were assembled at the polo field adjacent to the exhibition ground.

The head of the second group was Baron de Caters, the Belgian aeronaut and pilot who was already a name in aviation. He was assisted by Jules Tyck, a pilot, and reached Calcutta on December 12. His stock in trade included four bi-planes and two mono-planes, which had earlier been shipped to India. Their objective was to start their campaign by giving demonstration flights in Calcutta before moving to other parts of India.

The third group, which arrived last, was the Bristol & Colonial Aeroplane Company, whose mention has been made earlier.

According to a December 21, 1910, report in the *Statesman* newspaper of Calcutta, the first flight in India was made in Allahabad on December 10, 1910, by Keith Davis. This was actually a test flight, but it certainly was the first. The *Statesman* reported that "this aeroplane was a Bleriot mono-plane which was assembled on the polo ground and was taken up for a test flight. The first actual flight was successfully attained by Mr Davies in a Bleriot. He circled the polo ground at a height of 25-30 ft."

"Thus, Allahabad has had the distinction of giving the lead not only to India but also to the whole of the Asian continent in connection with the latest of scientific wonders," added the *Statesman*.

The first official flight was, however, made by Henri Pequet, the other pilot of the Humber Company, in Allahabad, on December 17, 1910, with the machine flying over Jumna and Ganges and around the Allahabad Fort in a bi-plane. This was exactly seven years after the Wright Brothers' flight. Pequet also carried the first passenger on this flight, the son of the Maharaja of Benares. His distinction is that he was India's first air passenger.

The *Statesman* reported on December 21, 1910, that the second flight in India was made at Tollygunge, a Calcutta suburb, after Baron de Caters' Bleriot mono-plane was assembled. His pilot, Jules Tyck made a 12-minute test flight at the Tollygunge Club on December 20. Among those who witnessed the flight at Tollygunge were Thurstan and Jullerot who had just arrived from Bombay. On December 21, 1910, Baron de Caters took off with a lady passenger, Mrs N C Sen, who became the first lady passenger to fly in India. She was the daughter-in-law of the great social reformer Keshav Chandra Sen; her husband was at one time the First Secretary at the High Commission of pre-independent India in Britain.

On December 28, Baron de Caters organised an air rally which was attended by thousands of Calcuttans. The Baron was the first to fly and he took a number of passengers in his Henri Farman plane — the first passenger was General Mahon of the Indian Army followed by two lady passengers, Mrs O'Brien and Miss Hewett. The next day, his pilot, Jules Tyck, ascended in his Bleriot mono-plane from Tollygunge Club grounds at 4.30 pm and flew over the city of Calcutta, passing directly over the Government House and returning to Tollygunge and alighting at 10 minutes to 5 pm — the first aviator to fly over the city of Calcutta. One more distinction was that Tyck reached and flew at a height of 7,000 ft, which was perhaps the first aerial height record for India.

The three months, from December 1910 to March 1911 were full of news about the new science of aviation. By then, the English language press, which many educated Indians had begun reading, was full of enthusiasm about the tremendous possibilities of aviation. In this, the lead was given by the Englishmen who were either businessmen or teachers or engineers, especially in India. The use of the aeroplane was seen as initially carrying mail, taking the analogy of the Pony

Express and the railways further in the 20th century. Suggestions were made to experiment with aeroplanes carrying mail.

When this was put to the Government, they welcomed it. In fact, with the UP exhibition in mind, the Humber Company was approached to carry mail bags from Allahabad to Naini, six miles away, across the Jumna river. Accordingly, plans were made for first day covers to be issued and advance publicity given so that people could participate in this venture.

On February 18, 1911, Henri Pequet flew the world's first aerial mail from Allahabad, across the Jumna, to Naini and back to Allahabad. The *Statesman* of February 21 reported the event, "Letters posted for the first aerial post from Allahabad on Saturday were delivered in Calcutta yesterday (Monday). The impress on the stamp was circular and bore the inscription 'First Aerial Post — UP Exhibition 1911'."

Of the three groups, that of Baron de Caters and Humber Company toured India from north to south and from east to west to demonstrate the possibilities of aviation. Quite a few Indians were interested in aviation and the lead given by the Maharaja of Patiala was followed by others. In fact, till date, the contribution made by Princely India to the growth of aviation has not been recorded. In World War II, they helped the Indian Air Force to grow by donating their planes and indirectly helping the war effort.

The Bristol Company was the only one that took the military route for which Sefton Brancker was mainly responsible. He had foreseen that the third dimension of air could be useful both for the advancing force and for the retreating force in any future war. In fact, just three years later, the first military aviation units flew from Dover as part of the British Expeditionary Force to France in August 1914.

Those Magnificent Men

While aeroplanes were flying in the Indian skies beginning in December 1910, a great deal was happening in England led by men of vision and ability. A look back will help one understand how a single person's dream became a reality after so much sweat was expended by him. The unknown people who struggled against physical, financial and even weather odds and succeeded in later years, became world famous and part and parcel of aviation history and lore.

Ever since 1783, the word 'aviation' had entered the vocabulary and balloons and airships were added to it. Even after 1903, the aeroplane was seen as an adjunct to the airship. The terminology also underwent a gradual change. Taking off was going up and landing was coming down. Even Henri Jullerot, writing in his diary about his aerial reconnaissance, called the joystick the control lever. It was a period of transition and historically speaking, aviation, both civil and military, grew at the fastest rate when compared to the other two services.

Being the brightest jewel in the British Empire's Crown, all events pertaining to aviation in Britain had their fallout on India. Even the formation of a military aviation service was preceded by the stationing of British military aviation units in India as also their civilian counterparts such as the flying clubs and the regulating body, the Directorate of Civil Aviation.

The Royal Aero Club of the United Kingdom was established in 1901, acknowledging thereby that aviation, whichever form it was to take, had come to stay. Soon it became an examining body to issue flying licences to those who qualified after completing a course that the club prescribed. The first aviator's certificate — the term was not pilot — that was to come as the first decade of the century progressed — was issued to J T C Moore Brabazon in March 1910.

But scepticism about the new invention remained. Prior to this, in 1906, the Engineering Supplement of the *Times* dated January 24, 1906, contained a letter from Alliot Verdon Roe stating, "The writer's absolute belief in the claim made by the American Brothers Orville and Wilbur Wright, to have flown 20 miles and adding that if he were to construct a full-sized machine on the lines of the model which he had already made and successfully flown, it would be possible for him to perform the same feat."

The comment of the Editor was definite enough, "It is not to be supposed that we can in any way adopt the writer's estimate of his undertaking, being of the opinion, indeed, that all attempts at artificial aviation on the basis he describes, are not only dangerous to human life, but foredoomed to failure from an engineering standpoint."

Today, after nearly a century, we know who Roe was. Who can forget the stream of aircraft, both civil and military, that have come out of the Avro stable. The Avro planes flew in the skies of the Empire in peace and war, whether it was the Avro Lancaster or the Avro Vulcan or the Avro 748 which flew in India in the post 1947 period.

Roe lived a simple life and continued with his experiments and at last, on June 8, 1908, he took to the air, the first Englishman to fly in an all-British-built machine. The distance flown was 150 ft. This took place at Brooklands where Roe had constructed a temporary shed but was all the time facing the threat of eviction by the owner who had constructed a motor racing track at Brooklands.

During this period, Colonel S F Cody, an American, who subsequently became a British citizen, was employed at the balloon factory at Farnborough, but his interests lay with aeroplanes. He was working on a bi-plane of his own design. Despite odds, he persevered and flew his plane over Laffan's Plain in Wiltshire. He continued flying and was killed in August 1913 by the breaking up of his machine in mid-air.

Another pioneer who added to the collective knowledge of aviation was Captain J W Dunne of the Wiltshire Regiment. He was encouraged in his efforts by H G Wells and Sir Hiram Maxim. He produced several machines for the War Office. In 1908, he produced a glider and was killed while flying it.

At this point of time, the official thinking, both at the War Office and the Admiralty, was that of grudging tolerance of this new vehicle of the air. Since the technology of aviation was in its infancy, and failures were frequent, the War Office was unwilling to finance any more experiments. This is best illustrated by the letter that the War Office wrote to both Cody and Dunne saying, "It had decided to cease making any experiments with aeroplanes as the cost had proved too great." The cost had amounted to Pounds Sterling 2,500. During that period, Germany was spending four hundred thousand pounds on military aeronautics.

In Britain of that era, the Army Council was its highest decision-making body. Dunne, the inventor, had a talk with two leading members of the Council. To his statement that aeroplanes could not maintain themselves in the air at speeds less than forty miles an hour, one of the two replied that it was impossible for anyone moving at such a pace to see anything at all. The other, thumping the table said, "That is exactly my opinion."

At that point, Major Lindsay Lloyd, the manager of Brooklands, from where he had threatened to evict A V Roe, decided to convert the motor racing track into an aerodrome. It took some time for British opinion to crystallise in favour of aviation. "The English, who usually start late, but who have a habit of finishing well in front, were, at last, beginning to take interest in aviation," says Hillary St. George Saunders in his complete survey of British air power and its development till 1939.

In retrospect, one recalls how Brooklands, now an aerodrome, influenced a young Gunner Subaltern to learn flying and join the newly started Flying Corps. And this young man grew up in the new service — Royal Air Force (RAF), and retired as Air Chief Marshal Sir Philip Joubert de la Ferte.

There was envy when the British saw what the Europeans were doing in the field of aviation. Inspired by this, by the spring of 1910, the British were making their own aeroplanes and flying them — all this was in the domain of private endeavour. Apart from Bristol & Colonial Aeroplane Company, Martin Handasyde, Scottish Aviation Company, J V Neal, D G Gilmore and F P Raynham set up their factories to produce a proper British flying machine. Added to this, Mrs Hewlett, the wife of the novelist Maurice Hewlett set up an aviation school at Brooklands and taught her son to fly.

Soon such like-minded people began to meet and what best place to congregate in than a traditional English pub. This was the 'Bluebird Restaurant' where such people met to discuss the latest developments in aviation. "Their efforts were fostered by the Aero Club which had been founded in 1901 by F S Hedges, assisted by Hon C S Rolls, an early aviation pioneer and the founder of the Rolls Royce Company, whose engines helped to win the Battle of Britain, 30 years later," says Hilary St. George Saunders. From 1910, the Aero Club began issuing flying certificates, which the British recognised as certificates of proficiency in flying.

Among the initial lot of aviators, who were granted licences, were T O M Sopwith and Geoffrey de Havilland, two names that soon became bywords in aviation circles. From the Sopwith stable came the 'Tabloid', 'Pup', 'Camel' and 'Snipe' which contributed substantially to help the Royal Flying Corps (RFC) gain mastery of the air during World War I. Before World War II, he gave Britain the Hawker Hurricane without which Britain would have been severely handicapped during the Battle of Britain. The Hurricane did splendidly as the 'eyes and ears' of the XIV Army in the Burma theatre of war and was flown extensively by the pilots of the Indian Air Force during World War II.

Geoffrey de Havilland built his first machine in 1910. He was responsible for making the DH4 and the DH9 which did yeoman service and 20 years later gave Britain the famous 'Mosquito'. Besides him and others, the Short Brothers who were makers of motor boats, produced seaplanes for the Royal Naval Air Service (RNAS). One was the 'Stirling' and the other the famous Sunderland flying-boat.

While Europe was making giant strides in aviation, official Britain was still indifferent. In 1909, several European countries, led by France, Germany, Italy and even Russia held an aviation meeting at Rheims in Germany where every country except Britain sent an official delegation. It was left to that intrepid aviation enthusiast G B Cockburn to represent England at Rheims. He did so in his personal capacity.

To this brave pioneer goes the credit of training four commissioned officers as fliers. They were Lieutenants C R Samson, R Gregory and A M Longmore of the Royal Navy and Captain E L Gerrard of the Royal Marine Light Infantry. Service officers were getting more and more interested in aviation. Brooklands became a centre as did Hendon, developed by Holt Thomas and Larkhill on Salisbury Plain. While the Navy had already started its flying school at Eastchurch, Larkhill became the centre for the military. All this was accompanied by the swift setting up of factories to fabricate and manufacture aeroplanes. And this was still on private initiative.

At last, the Government woke up and by an order issued on February 28, 1911, created the Air Battalion of the Royal Engineers. Hence, "flying was no longer a hobby but a part of the Army." This battalion was put under the command of Sir Alexander Bannerman who divided it into two companies — the first one to look after and operate airships, including balloons; and the second one to look after aeroplanes.

It is curious but the dates bear out the reality and irony of it — that the Air Battalion should have been created and set up just one and a half months after the world's first military air reconnaissance at Aurangabad, India, on January 15, 1911, which proved that aviation would, in the coming years, become an integral part of a nation's military establishment. Not to be left behind, the Admiralty set up its separate Naval Flying School at Eastchurch, adjacent to the Royal Aero Club, in December 1911. From such small beginnings, grew the two services of the Royal Flying Corps (RFC) and the Royal Naval Air Service (RNAS). And eventually the amalgamation of these produced the Royal Air Force (RAF). Indeed, they were the parents of the third service.

For any sea-faring nation, especially island nation, the sea is omnipresent and, thus, over the centuries, England developed a strong maritime tradition and the Navy was in the forefront. In fact, in the order of precedence, the Royal Navy came first, followed by the Army and last by the RAF. The Navy's pre-eminent position can be gauged by the fact that although the British created the RAF by amalgamating the RFC and the RNAS, the Admiralty was not reconciled to it and continued opposing it. This state of affairs continued right through the Twenties and Thirties of the 20th century, until 1938, when the British government finally conceded the Navy's demand to have its own air component. Thus, came the birth of the Fleet Air Arm (FAA) as a part of the Royal Navy, which continues even now, and all the dominions of the Commonwealth too have an FAA as part of their Navies (India, Canada, Australia, New Zealand and South Africa).

The growth of naval aviation was marked by the autonomy that the Navy enjoyed. Unlike the Army, the Admiralty had shown great faith in the Short Brothers and the Sopwith Company to produce and supply planes that were designed specially for the Navy's use for landing and taking off both from the surface of the sea and from the deck of a ship, giving, thereby, birth to the idea of an aircraft carrier that later came onto its own in World War II.

These developments generated enthusiasm, and in 1911, Lieutenant C R Samson of the Royal Navy made the first successful flight from the deck of a warship in December by taking off from HMS *Africa* and landing in the sea, where his machine was successfully supported by air-bags. In March 1912, the Short Brothers produced the first seaplane which was successfully flown by Lieutenant Samson. Meanwhile, the Sopwith Company constructed the first flying boat. The Short Brothers' names will forever be associated with the 'Stirling' and later with the most famous flying boat in history — the Sunderland Flying Boat.

Meanwhile, the Government appointed a committee in late 1911, which recommended the creation of the British Aeronautical Service to be known as the Flying Corps. It was to have two wings, one naval and the other military, with one common flying school. Thus, the Royal Flying Corps (RFC) was constituted by a Royal Warrant on April 13, 1912, and soon after, the Air Battalion was absorbed into it.

Initially, no country in Europe took aviation seriously and even after it was clear that aviation had come to stay, the powers felt that due to the technical nature of the service, it should become a part of the Royal Engineers. And that is how the Air Battalion came into being as part of the Engineering Corps. It is curious that even in the US, aviation was first promoted under the umbrella of the Signal Corps. Only in Germany did they constitute the aviation activity as a separate service under the name of the Imperial German Air Service.

Thus, with the RFC as a part of the Army, the British Expeditionary Force crossed the Strait of Dover to fight on the European mainland, what the future historians would call the Great War. Along with it, went the fledgling RFC with 37 frail aeroplanes.

Balloons in Military Aviation — 1783-1914

Aviation has been described as the third dimension, the other two being land and sea. When land or sea battles were fought, it was on a lateral plane, with both the opponents being at the same level, able to see only for a limited distance even with the help of binoculars. It was the use of artillery that provoked men to search for height — a high ground or a hill from where forward observation officers could direct the fire and check its accuracy in terms of hitting the target.

It was in 1783 that the Montgolfier Brothers proved that being able to look down from a moving flying contraption, one could see in a complete 360 degree circle the position of both the sides in a conflict. The Montgolfier balloons were the forerunners of the powered flying machines that could be steered direction-wise and could take-off and land at will.

When airships such as the Zeppelins made their appearance, three factors stood out that limited their use — one was the large amount of inflammable gas, the second being the mechanism to steer it at the desired speed and the third was the lack of motive power and total dependence on the wind. When the British Airship R101 crashed, experts remarked that it was necessary for controls to be installed before one could utilise such a craft for flying.

When Sefton Brancker was commissioned in the Royal Artillery in July 1896, he was barely 19 years old. But by then, there were many new inventions in transport and communication that the media brought before the public. One of them was aviation. Brancker had no link with aviation. He had become a gunner and got his posting to an Artillery Regiment.

The word 'aviation' began to gain currency after the Montgolfier Brothers successfully released a balloon in Paris in 1783. Thereafter, for nearly a century, balloons were exhibited and flown by a few daring aviators, but their use as observation platforms in the sky began when the French Revolutionary Army used captive balloons at the Battle of Fleurus and at the siege of Maubeuge. During the French Revolution, in the beginning of 1789, reports about events were smuggled in balloons and sent to England and some English newspapers were also dropped from balloons in Paris. At the Battle of Fleurus in June 1794, the French Republican Army used a captive balloon for observation work. However, the sightings of Captain Coutelle were not apparently of much consequence.

Balloons filled with hydrogen were first used effectively for reconnaissance during the American Civil War (1861-65). Three freelance aeronauts, T S C Lowe, with James Allen and John la Mountain, were employed by the Union Army. This team made many reconnaissance flights with considerable success.

During the Franco-Prussian War of 1870-71, balloons were used during the siege of Paris to convey messages and, sometimes, people in and out of the city. A special lightweight edition of the *Times* newspaper was produced for conveyance by balloons and was fairly regularly available in Paris.

It was in 1878 that the first use of balloons was made during Lord Napier's campaign in Abyssinia, when the British Army deployed a balloon for observation of the enemy's position and its composition.

In serious application of aviation for military purposes, Italy was the first in the field. The Italian Army had set up an aeronautical section in 1884 and had used balloons successfully for reconnaissance during the Eritrean War of 1887-88.

The next attempt by the British Army to utilise the balloon in a military operation was during the Boer War in South Africa in 1900. Balloons of that era were of the spherical type which, when anchored to the earth, swayed in the direction of the prevailing wind.

In 1897, Brancker, an enthusiastic Subaltern, had his first brush with aviation. While posted at Lydd, he went up in one of the old spherical captive balloons, belonging to the Royal Engineers, during some experiments in observing artillery fire. "The captive balloon at once revealed to me the enormous possibilities of aerial observation," recalled Brancker.

This was a new thought and a new passion that held him throughout his career till 1930 when he was killed in the R101 crash. He was posted to M Battery, Royal Horse Artillery, which was sent to South Africa in July 1900. He served with distinction in the Boer War, was mentioned in dispatches and was promoted to Captain in

October 1901. He was wounded, and sent back to England and later sent to India in January 1903, where he served in artillery regiments until his posting to Fort William, Calcutta. In between, he underwent the Staff College Course at Deolali and graduated in December 1907. Coincidentally, at the Staff College, the student officers were asked to write an essay on the effect of aviation on war. That whetted Brancker's appetite further.

It was in South Africa that Brancker saw the balloon being used in military operations. A balloon was a part of the expedition headed by Lord Roberts when he advanced on Pretoria in 1900 and there again he saw, under field conditions, attempts at aerial reconnaissance. The Army used the balloon for reconnaissance, in order, as General Sir Edward Swinton put it, "To see the other side of the hill." The balloon unit, under the command of Colonel B J Templar, of the Balloon Factory at Farnborough, was mobile. By now, he had become an aviation enthusiast and watched with interest all the developments in this new field. In 1910, Brancker became a member of the Royal Aero Club.

By then, military aviation had entrenched itself in his psyche. When preparing to write the essay at the Staff College at Deolali in 1905, Brancker visualised the possibilities of 'stationary battle' with deployment of heavy artillery from long ranges, and the necessity of carrying out movements by night or during bad weather — all as a direct result of observation from the air.

On To Powered Flight

Thus, as a Staff Captain in Calcutta, Sir Sefton Brancker was desperate to be3 associated with the Bristol Boxkite team and tried to get his superiors to permit him to go as an official Indian Army observer. But, for this, he needed permission from the highest military authority in Calcutta. Fortunately for him, at that time General Mike Rimington was about to organise some large scale manoeuvres in Western India.

Unlike most hardbound top brass in any Army, who are wedded to tradition and practice, he was a man of courage and imagination. He agreed to let Brancker accompany the Bristol team and observe, but, not officially. He had told the Bristol team that they could send one aeroplane which he would permit to be used for aerial reconnaissance during the cavalry manoeuvres. Brancker was granted leave and told that if he wanted to fly, he must go on leave and do it at his own risk. At that time, it must be noted, the official establishments, at both the War Office and the Admiralty, did not think much of aviation as a future organised activity which may help the two services in any future conflict.

So, Brancker, for the time being, assumed the status of a civilian. The Boxkite was packed and the Bristol party, with an unofficial guide in the person of Brancker, proceeded by train to Aurangabad, 1,400 miles to the west. There was an open ground close to the railway station where the crate was unpacked and four Privates of the Dublin Fusiliers were set to work under Henri Jullerot's direction to erect the Boxkite.

"This machine made in 1910, was a mass of light spars, piano wire and fabric which responded to every change in temperature. As the nights were very cold, with heavy dew, while the sun by day was burning hot, we found ourselves up against all sorts of difficulties in rigging. The spar bowed, the wires stretched and contracted, the fabric sagged, the whole structure creaked and cracked as if it were going to fall to pieces," records Brancker in his diary.

He added, "We mounted the engine, a 50HP Gnome, but owing to faulty rigging, we broke two struts in the box-shaped tail when running it up. Then we found that the petrol provided was of inferior quality and had to telegraph for fresh supplies. But, in spite of everything, we were ready in the time given to us (48 hours) to make a trial flight in the afternoon before the manoeuvres started.

"These manoeuvres involved the concentration of four Cavalry Brigades and one Infantry Brigade, so we had a great crowd to see our maiden effort — a crowd which included twelve British Generals. Rumours had gone around the countryside that someone was going to fly and thousands of local inhabitants came in from all sides and camped along the railway line in order to see the latest madness of the Sahibs."

Further, adds Brancker, "Since the Hindu religion definitely recognises the possibility of flying, these simple peasants were not-so incredulous as our own (British) villagers had been. Their attitude was more of intelligent interest than of surprise."

The Proving Flight — 1911

"The Boxkite of that day was not a particularly comfortable conveyance. The pilot sat on the leading edge of the lower plane with his feet on the rudder bar which was supported by an outrigger through which he looked down between his knees into space. The observer sat behind somewhat higher than the pilot, with his legs round the latter's body and he also had a direct view down.

"Our only instruments were an oil-pulsating gauge which did not work and an aneroid barometer which I think I wore round my neck. I also provided myself with field glasses and an ordinary artist's drawing block which I tied on Jullerot's back for the writing of reports. I must admit that by the time we had the engine running, and were taxiing across our improvised aerodrome followed by an immense cloud of dust, I was thoroughly frightened but, as we rose gently and swiftly from the ground and I looked back and waved at the crowds vanishing below us, I experienced one of the most glorious moments of my life — one of my most precious dreams had come true (the day was January 14, 1911).

"We climbed to 1,000 ft and flew round for half an hour. Everything seemed very much as I had expected. Within a few minutes, I was making notes on the block on Jullerot's back and thoroughly enjoying myself watching the local inhabitants, cattle and poultry stampeding in every direction at the unwanted sight and sound. We made a perfect landing and full of glorious exhilaration, set to work to prepare for our first reconnaissance. I received a sealed envelope from the Commander, Sir Douglas Haig, containing orders for the first reconnaissance the next day.

"The troops at Aurangabad were supposed to be an advanced guard moving south who had lost touch with a hostile force which was retreating through Jalna. Our job was to locate the retiring force and bring back information regarding its strength and disposition. Our cavalry had not yet got in touch with the retreating enemy."

The World's First Military Air Reconnaissance

"We started soon after 6 am. It was a glorious Indian cold weather morning and the air was like champagne and as clear. Before we had been in the air for ten minutes, I saw heavy clouds of dust, away to the south, and pointed them out triumphantly to Jullerot.

"We headed for them at 1,100 ft, which was pretty near the ceiling of our old Boxkite with its rather sketchy rigging. We flew over them for about ten minutes, during which I located every company and section of the rear guard and recorded them on the drawing block. So good was the visibility that I could almost recognise a friend of mine who I knew was commanding the Horse Artillery.

"We then flew home, only to find our landing place occupied by a raiding party of hostile cavalry. However, we got down a little further on and under cover of a native hut, I made out my report. This was probably the first military air reconnaissance report that had ever been written in proper staff form.

"A large number of staff officers were present, including General Sir Edmund Barrow, commanding the Southern Army, Sir Douglas Haig and Lieutenant Colonel Hudson from Army Headquarters and also Generals Alderson, Grover, Wapshare and Rimington. We had been out for 45 minutes, covered 27 miles across country as the crow flies, and our GOC had a full report of the enemy's position within an hour and a quarter of our start — a great feat for aviation in those days, and entirely due to Jullerot's fine piloting.

"That evening (January 15, 1911) we received orders to move to Jalna, about 35 miles to the south, first thing to be done next morning."

The First Crash

"After this epoch-making flight, we had to face our first disaster. The previous day's flight had consumed all our good quality petrol. The engine refused to work properly. The morning broke beautifully fine and the air was dead still. We started off towards a belt of trees with what looked like plenty of room to get up. The altitude (between 2,000-3,000 ft) with the lack of wind and loss of power due to poor fuel, affected the life of the machine, and we got nearer and nearer to the trees without leaving the ground.

"Eventually, Jullerot decided to chance it — yanked it up about 60 ft, lost flying speed, side-slipped, turned sharp towards our point of departure and crashed. We were both a bit shaken, I had some skin knocked off, and the machine was a complete 'write-off'. Jullerot's skillful handling, when we side-slipped, saved us from a much worse smash. Just as we lost flying speed, I saw two scantily attired cultivators ploughing directly below us, and watched them start to run. By the time we had collected ourselves, they were over the horizon.

"The crash was a setback. The other two aeroplanes were in Calcutta and could not be obtained in time to take part in the manoeuvres."

A report in the newspaper *The Pioneer*, dated January 23, 1911, recalled that, "On January 21, just after the crash at Aurangabad, Captain Brancker who came specially to the manoeuvres at Jalna, seemed none the worse for his exciting fall on Tuesday last."

So Thurston and Jullerot went back to prepare another machine at Calcutta for the Presidency Brigade training which took place in February 1911, at Midnapore (Bengal), while Brancker spent ten days on General Rimington's staff with the cavalry. He rejoined the Bristol team near Calcutta in February.

"Here, we erected another machine under a tree, close to the polo ground which made a very good aerodrome. Our successful reconnaissance at Aurangabad had caused a considerable stir throughout military circles in India. An officer of the General Staff at Simla named Aspinall was now sent to report on our operations, with instructions that he was not to believe too much of what was told to him, and on no account was he to go into the air.

"After the machine was ready, we accomplished several trial flights near the temporary aerodrome on the polo ground but never worked properly with the troops again. Due to the crash, Jullerot got sick and further operations were abandoned.

"Thus, ended the first effort at military aviation in India."

— Norman Macmillan, *Sir Sefton Brancker*
Published by William Heinemann, 1935.

An Early Aeroplane Reconnaissance — Pilot Jullerot's Report

A clear record of events of importance helps to place such an event in its correct perspective in terms of its importance. Sefton Brancker, as an observer, flew with Henri Jullerot as the pilot on the world's first aerial reconnaissance and recorded his impressions in his diary which his biographer published after his death.

While Brancker's impressions have appeared earlier in this narrative, Jullerot's diary gives us for the first time a pilot's viewpoint. The following is an account extracted from the diary of Monsieur H M Jullerot, pilot of the aeroplane reconnaissance carried out by himself and Captain William Brancker (observer) during the Indian

Army manoeuvres of 1911. The flight took place on January 15, 1911, at Aurangabad in western India and the aeroplane was attached to the force of Sir Douglas Haig, which was in pursuit of the retreating 'enemy'.

"Today, we were out before daybreak and find the camp quite deserted — no troops anywhere. Colonel Watson, commanding the Cavalry Brigade, sends a message that he has lost contact with the enemy for five hours. Therefore, with the first gleams of the sun showing up the graceful form of the feathery palms on the eastern horizon, we are ready, and our machine rises softly from the ground and directly drives into the early rays of the Indian sun, which makes one of the most gorgeous sights I have so far beheld.

"Turning towards Aurangabad station, we pass over a group of officers who wave their topees to us. We learn afterwards that they were the staff of Sir Douglas Haig. Well, I look back to Captain Brancker, who seems to enjoy himself so far, and points a direction to me. We see clearly, on both sides of us, hill ranges, which provide us with the best landmarks one could wish.

"The wind is quite fresh and dead against us, so our progress is very slow. We see nothing in front of us except a wide deserted stretch of yellow land and dried-up vegetation. I look around to my left and perceive in the distance a small white speck, which I localise as the Mosque I visited the day before, and which looks like a tiny Taj Mahal.

"We pass over a small river, and our machine begins to wobble about in a very unpleasant manner. Captain Brancker puts his hand on top of mine on the control lever, and then we fly together for a while. Suddenly, we see far away to the north a little cloud of dust. I push my foot to the left to alter our course towards it. As we get nearer and nearer, I see distinctly on the ground below a track of wheels and horses. We follow it and it leads us to Chickaltana, which, from our point of observation, looks like a toy village.

"Quite distinctly, now I see the rear guard of the retreating forces, then a long line of bullock carts — at least 150 — we pass over, then a battery of horse gunners. It all looks like delightful playthings for dolls. Captain Brancker is writing all the time now. Could it be that he is making his will — it is only his second trip and he may well dislike the way the Bristol is now fighting with the bumps. Now we see plainly an infantry brigade deployed and facing west.

"Still we go on east to Karmad, just far enough to see the advance guard still moving east. Perhaps then the brigade was only deployed at Chickaltana to deceive us. Anyway, we are here to observe and not to draw conclusions. We circle a couple of times over the troops, wave good-bye to them for fun, and fly back to the troops for whom we were working.

"We are very fast now with the wind behind. It is quite amusing to watch our shadow sweeping along the ground at great speed. Captain Brancker is now controlling the machine with me. It is really bumpy now, and I feel quite relieved when I see in the distance the white towers of the Mosque. At the same moment, we see two squadrons of Native Lancers. I glide down in order to land and suddenly Captain Brancker shrieks in my ear to ascend again, as those are Poona Horse and belong to the other party, and seem to be in a great hurry, as they are galloping full-out.

"We then pass over a screen of trees and land safely in a kind of discarded polo ground, not very far from the advance party of our Army. Captain Brancker was highly delighted, both with his flight and success of his mission. 'I have had the time of my life' were his first words when he came again to his feet.

"The following day, when starting for Jalna some forty miles away, our engine refused to work as we had exhausted our supply of petrol and were then using some dirty stuff bought in a Hindu bazaar. Still we attempted to start, left the ground tail down, lost flying speed when trying to clear a tree, and crashed to the ground. We were both flung out, none the worse for it. My companion had scratched his face, but his eye-glass (monocle) was intact. He is most plucky, for he is planning to come up with me again, directly the second machine is erected."

— Hilary St. George Saunders,
Per Adua: The Rise of British Air Power (1911-1939)
University Press, Oxford, 1944.

Aerial League in India

"Colonel H S Massey, CB, arrived at Calcutta on December 10, 1909 and commenced a tour of India on behalf of the Aerial League, of which an Indian branch has just been formed, the presidency of it having been accepted by the Commander-in-Chief General Sir O'Moore Creagh. Several enthusiastic meetings have already been held, and Colonel Massey will also give lectures in the most important cities, including Bombay, Madras, Lahore, Allahabad and Peshawar."

— *The Flight Magazine*, January 8, 1910.

Plan for Indian Flying School

In the House of Commons on April 30, 1913, Sir J D Rees asked the Under Secretary of State for India whether the 15,500 and 4,100 Pounds Sterling, for forming a school of aeronautics and for aviation buildings respectively, represented all that was to be done in India in 1913-14 in respect of military aviation; whether officers of native regiments when on leave in England would be under some official disability, which prevented them from being appointed to the Royal Flying Corps; whether officers of British regiments serving in India could only join such corps on less favourable pecuniary terms than their brother officers serving in regiments at Home; whether an officer who was attached for a short period to the late Air Battalion had been appointed adviser on aviation to the Indian General Staff; why officers serving in India, which offered superior physical conditions for airship and aeroplane practices, to those obtaining in these islands, were not encouraged to perfect themselves in the art of aviation by being allowed to join the Royal Flying Corps on favourable terms; and whether the Secretary of State in Council would advise the Governor General in Council that provisions made in the Budget and the conditions under which officers serving in India could learn the art of aviation, were wholly inadequate to the importance this branch of warfare had attained.

Mr Montagu replied, "The Government of India intend to have their own school of military aviation, and have provided the sums mentioned by the honourable member to meet preliminary charges in the present year.

"The scheme will be under an officer trained in the Home Air Battalion here, and the future staff of instructors will be similarly trained at the cost of Indian revenues. In view of the facilities which will shortly exist in India, it is not considered necessary to insist that Indian officers of the Indian Army learn flying in this country, or to accept charges on account of the training here of officers of British regiments stationed in India. The Secretary of State has no reason to suppose that these arrangements will prove inadequate."

The Indian Army Flying School

"From India, it was announced that Captain S D Massey of the 29th Punjabis has been selected as the Commandant of the flying school which is to be organised in India, while the instructors will be Captain Hoare of 39th Central India Horse, Lieutenant Newall of the 2nd Gurkha Rifles and Lieutenant Reilly of the 82nd Punjabis.

"These officers were certified pilots, but they were coming to England in order to undergo a long period of training at the Central Flying School, Upavon, before taking up their new duties."

—*The Flight Magazine*, May 10, 1913.

Winds of Change — India

While public enthusiasm was aroused and further strengthened by the demonstration flights at Calcutta, Allahabad, Hyderabad, Madras and Bangalore by the pilots of the three groups, then touring India, the Indian Army was most interested in this new vehicle of the air. There were no facilities for training people to fly, nor were there any firms who could manufacture engines and other parts that go into an aeroplane.

Already, younger officers of the Army were enthused by the various pioneering flights and when Bleriot crossed the English Channel, he destroyed with that one feat the insularity of England which depended on the Navy to protect its shores. The third dimension had stepped into military thought and far-sighted experts saw that England would need a force that could become airborne and act as the eyes of the Army on the ground.

The then Government of India had already seen the possibilities — the Calcutta flight, and Allahabad for the exhibition and then the first airmail flight. Right across India, in Aurangabad, it had been demonstrated that military reconnaissance had been given a wider and new scope.

General O'Moore Creagh, then Commander-in-Chief of the Indian Army, fully understood the flying machine's vast possibilities and its future importance, but funds at his disposal were terribly limited and he was, therefore, unable to start an aviation unit at once as he desired. The Aurangabad-Jalna manoeuvres and the role of the aeroplane deeply impressed all the officers, especially from Army Headquarters, and had it not been for lack of resources, he would have started a flying organisation in India before the flying corps in England came into being.

Sir Sefton Brancker later recalled, "The English language press reported demonstration flights and the enthusiasm and interest they generated, among the 'natives' and British businessmen and the young

English Army officers of the Indian Army. India is fortunate in having among its visitors a number of enterprising spirits to introduce it to the art of aviation. Prominent among them is Baron Pierre de Caters, the best sportsmen from Belgium."

Official India was also interested in aviation and as public opinion among those who mattered, crystallised, suggestions from the public were considered. Even before the Aurangabad-Jalna manoeuvres took place, its mere announcement brought serious comment from *The Pioneer*.

"The use of the British aeroplane at the Jalna manoeuvres next week may have important results for the military authorities in India who have no intention of ignoring aviation now that they have before them the examples set in England and the Continent.

"A School of Military Aviation is a necessity in India as at Home and there will be no lack of officers anxious to become proficient in aerial reconnaissance. A good type of machine suitable to the climate and to the special internal conditions that prevail, say on the North-Western Frontier, has to be secured and then the work of instruction can begin.

"India can benefit to a large extent by the experience already gained in Western countries and, thus, save expenditure on mere experiments. The various flights that have taken place at Allahabad and Calcutta have proved that during the cold weather, flying in this country can be carried out under most satisfactory conditions."

— *The Pioneer*, Allahabad, January 14, 1911.

Aviation and War

An intense debate was already brewing up in the 'cantonment world' of official India that spilled over into the pages of the newspapers, beginning with the arrival of aeroplanes and the first use of the Bristol Boxkite for military reconnaissance.

H S Wildeblood, a true-blooded Englishman, who was a professional civil engineer in the UP Government's Public Works Department (PWD), stationed at Meerut, was a keen student of the latest developments in aviation.

Unconfirmed reports said that he had designed and fabricated a machine, the engine for which he had got from England. However, his proving flight was a failure and his machine, though it was airborne for some time, crashed after hitting a tree. Undaunted by failure, he began campaigning for aeroplanes to be initially brought from England and for the British officers of the Indian Army to learn to fly them and use them as the 'eyes' of the Army. For several years, his campaign through the columns of the newspapers bore fruit.

By that time (1910-14), India had become a part of the British psyche and those in India, wanted the best for India, the brightest jewel in the British Crown. In a letter to the Editor, Wildeblood wrote in *The Pioneer*, from Meerut, "Up to the present, we have not received much information regarding the uses to which aeroplanes have been put during a war, but it would not be safe to infer from this that they are not being, and will not be, utilised to any serious extent.

"I am aware that the feeling of my fellow countrymen in India is that the Air Forces of Europe have done, and are likely to do, very little in the coming war to justify their existence and that in any case India is powerless to help in this matter, but while acknowledging that appearances are at present against me, I appeal at least to men of scientific training to give their imagination a reasonable amount of rein and look a little into the future.

"Germany's ambition, I believe, is to obtain the command of the air as well as of the land in Europe and elsewhere and, thus, to nullify our command of the sea. The nation that obtains command of the air as well as of the land will be able to impose on other nations such terms as the total prohibition of building of aircraft and so will be able to strengthen her position considerably.

"I grant that we are heavily handicapped in the manufacture of aeroplanes and engines in India but, with the hearty cooperation of all concerned, the difficulties could be surmounted. Aeroplanes, though not the very best, we can certainly build and I believe that some of our iron and steel works could turn out fairly good aero-engines from some of the samples we have in this country.

"Magnetos, if unobtainable, could be replaced by dry-cell ignition. The training of pilots would present no difficulty. If it were only a question of a few weeks' war, as many imagined on the outbreak of hostilities, the matter would not be worth discussing, but it is to remain with us in one form or another for months and perhaps for years with possible intervals of peace for short duration, then it would be wise to put this part of our house in order with all the energy we possess.

"I do not say that we can do much, but we can help and even if our machines were not the very best obtainable, the foundation of an industry and the experience gained would be worth the expenditure.

"I shall be glad to hear from any firms in India, that are willing to help in the matter of engines if reasonable facilities are forthcoming."

NOTE: This letter was written on August 31, 1914, and published in *The Pioneer*, dated September 5, 1914, almost a month after World War I started. All this coming from an Englishman!

Public Debate and Decision — 1912

By 1912-13, the developments in aviation worldwide were being discussed and debated upon in England and its fallout on India was such that people began to urge the then Government of India to take some concrete steps lest India be left behind in this vital field.

This debate, articulated among the British in India and top echelons of the Indian Army, eventually reached the portals of the Council of the Viceroy of India. Meanwhile, with official blessings, four officers of the Indian Army were sent to the Central Flying School (CFS) at Upavon in England to learn to fly aeroplanes.

Commenting on this, *The Pioneer* newspaper of Allahabad wrote:

"The sending of four officers of the Indian Army to England for flying training shows that military aviation in India is receiving some attention. The school that will eventually be established will probably be at Sitapur in UP and we are told provision has been made in the budget for the current year for some of the buildings acquired and also for expenses under the heading 'Formation of a School of Aeronautics'. When Captain Massey and the other three instructors return to India, 'a course' can be instituted and then there will be no lack of officers anxious to get flying certificates.

"There will probably be officers of British regiments coming out who have qualified at Upavon, while others on leave at Home may think it worth their while to go through a course now that military aviation is being officially taken up out here. We have not heard what pattern of aeroplane is being adopted for India, but the best on the market should be secured. We do not want a machine for experiment, but for practical use, first for training purposes and later for employment at manoeuvres — possibly for war in case of any operations on our frontiers, though aeroplaning in hill and jungle territory presents great difficulty. The great thing, however, is that a start is being made and next cold weather we hope to see Sitapur at work with its classes."

— *The Pioneer*, May 7, 1913.

Author Walter Raleigh in his monumental work *The War in the Air*, Vol. 1, says, "There was, at Farnborough, at that time, a small group of officers belonging to the newly formed Indian Flying Corps.

They were led by Captain S D Massey, of the 29th Punjabis, an early pioneer pilot who had flown with the Air Battalion of the Royal Engineers in 1911, Captain C G Hoare and Lieutenant C L N Newall, Captain H L Reilly and Captain D Pitcher."

The general doubts about specific uses of aeroplanes for the Army were again highlighted by H S Wildeblood, who said, "At the present moment, when so much uncertainty exists as to the part which will be played by aeroplanes and airships in a war, the following, from *Aeronautic Journal,* is of great interest.

"Our Indian Flying Corps is unfortunately in the embryo stage, but I think it would be a wise move for the Government to put forward the construction of aeroplanes and training of pilots with every means in their power. No one can foresee where this war may lead us and it is certain that even if the war ended tomorrow, the struggle for supremacy in the air will go on and any work done in this direction of strengthening our position will not be wasted. There is bound to be enormous loss of pilots and aircraft in the present war and assistance from India might prove invaluable."

— August 6, 1914 (six days after the war was declared).

While the press and the public wanted a flying school, the biggest hurdle in the way was the parsimony of the Government of India and the next step was to make a provision in the Army budget for military aviation, which would be presented to the Council of the Governor General of India for consideration, debate and eventual approval.

Special Grant for Flying School — 1913

Under the heading of the overall defence expenditure proposed for the Army, the Gazette Extraordinary of India, dated March 20, 1913, says, in Para 214, that under new measures, a School of Aeronautics is to be set up at Sitapur in the United Provinces. A sum of Rs 2.33 lakh (Pounds Sterling 15,500) was earmarked for this purpose.

"Delivering the financial statement for 1913-14, the Hon'ble Sir Guy Fleetwood Wilson said, 'I rise to present the financial statement for the year 1913-14..'."

— Military Services, Para 28

"The schedule grant for 1913-14 shows an increase of Pounds 217,600 as compared with the figure adopted in the current year, but it includes Pounds 119,000 to meet the final payments on account of the extra rifles which are to be ordered this year and Pounds 106,700 for the acquisition of land and commencement of building operations in connection with the new military cantonment at Delhi. Provision is made on a modest scale for the inception of Military Aviation in India."

— Proceedings of the Council of the Governor General of India
March 1, 1913, Vol. II, Page 277, Para 28.

Debate on the Defence Budget

The Hon'ble Babu Surendra Nath Banerjee:

"Sir, we rejoice to find that the military expenditure is practically at a standstill. But Sir, there is an ominous note of warning in the speech of the Hon'ble Finance Minister. He says that a committee has been appointed to enquire into what he calls the Marine expenditure."

Malik Umar Hayat Khan:

"I advocated two years ago the necessity of moving towards forming aerial and naval fleets for the efficiency of the Army. I have only said it again because circumstances have since been entirely altered. At that time, the aircraft was in its infancy, while now it is an accomplished fact and I hope that if funds be available, they should be placed in the hands of the 'military authorities'.

"The advance can only be accomplished by the aid of the Finance Minister, because the increase of persons and efficiency in various forms, construction of better lines and Army's defence works, Navy and aircraft require funds.

"I hope that some regulations will also be framed in regard to the honorary ranks so that the officers newly appointed do not supersede those already holding commissions."

Mr Surendra Nath Banerjee:

"The Indian Army serves as an Imperial Reserve, it has been so used in the past and it will continue to be so used in the future. This point was pressed with great insistence upon the attention of the Welby Commission. As a matter of imperial justice, I think, the Imperial Government ought to pay for that portion of the Indian Army which is in excess of our requirements and which is in the nature of an Imperial Reserve."

Rai Sri Ram Bahadur:

"My Lord, there is another ground why this appeal for financial help should be responded to by the Home Government. That such is really the case was the view expressed on behalf of the India Office by their Financial Secretary in para 2 of a memorandum submitted by him in 1895 before the Royal Commission appointed to enquire into the question of expenditure in India. It runs as follows.

"That India is utilised as a reserve for England in a much truer sense than England is for India; that England not merely claims the services of British regiments for the time stationed in India, but that she frequently uses the Native Regiments towards the cost of which she has in no way contributed (page 1022-23); that it may, therefore, be reasonably urged that England ought to assist in the maintenance in India of so large a force upon which England does not hesitate to draw."

In the armed forces newsletter, *Fauji Akhbar*, which was printed initially in Urdu and Roman Urdu, the following announcement appeared on March 15, 1913:

"Aircraft Training School for the Indian Army: A sum of Rs 2,33,000 has been sanctioned in the budget to open an aircraft training school in the Indian Army and Rs 62,000 has been earmarked for the construction of its building in the QMG's funds."

Decades later (on July 20, 1976), the British Ministry of Defence put a seal of history on this announcement. In a letter to the author, the Air Historical Branch 5 (RAF), said, "It is confirmed that a Central Flying School was in the process of formation at Sitapur in the United Provinces, India, and the first course of instruction was to have been held in September 1914. On the outbreak of the war, however, the school was disbanded and its staff and aircraft and equipment were devoted to active services in the field."

The Indian Central Flying School — 1914

Even as the discussion on aviation expanded into a public debate, the Army authorities began a serious search for a place for locating the proposed flying school. Since official thinking favoured such a project, the choice narrowed down to a place which would be easily accessible. They found it in the Sitapur cantonment, about 500 km from Delhi.

The cantonment already had the main barracks and a fairly big parade ground and adjacent to it the playing fields for the troops. There were no troops in this cantonment and it was decided that it would be ideal for setting up the flying school there.

Getting possession was not difficult as the land already belonged to the Army. Meanwhile, the budget proposal that provided the funds was passed before June 1913, and the Army set about putting up the buildings and the runway and sheds for the aeroplanes.

The school started with three aeroplanes and four flying instructors. The Government of India's proposal in the initial scheme contemplated the establishment of a Squadron

Headquarters at Peshawar with two flights broken up into two groups of three machines (two active, one reserve) at various points from the Malakand through Peshawar down to Bannu and perhaps, Dera Ismael Khan — later Quetta. They were to be supported by an aircraft park somewhere centrally situated — a point like Rawalpindi, whence railway communication leads to aero-locations on the Frontier.

Besides this park, forming a depot at Sitapur was contemplated (the flying prior to the war) whence there were workshops and an aerodrome, and it was intended to have instructional flights here also. Besides that, it was intended to recruit Indian mechanics for maintaining the aeroplanes.

In the original proposal for setting up a flying school in India, it was held that the school would primarily be meant for officers of the Indian Army to learn to fly under Indian conditions. And so it was, since at that time all officers of the Indian Army were British and no Indian had as yet held the King's Commission. Although King George V had announced at the Delhi Durbar in 1911, that Indians would henceforth be selected for training to hold the King's Commission, the establishment in India and the British bureaucracy delayed implementation of their sovereign's command. The King also announced that henceforth Indians, irrespective of rank, would be eligible for the award of the Victoria Cross, which had hitherto been denied to them.

It took the pressure and other exigencies of World War I to wake up the authorities and the first course for officers' training was conducted at a war-time location, the Princes' college named Daly College, Indore, and the first commissioned officers of the Indian Army graduated in 1919, but by then the war was over.

Looking back nearly a century later, one needs to note that Captain Massey, who was appointed Commandant of the Central Flying School, was an infantry officer from the 29th Punjab Regiment and the other three were: Captain H Hoare from the cavalry from the Central India Horse (CIH), Lieutenant Colonel Newall from the 2nd Gurkha Rifles and the third, Captain H L Reilly, also an infantry officer, from 82nd Punjabis. Including the Commandant, there were four flying instructors.

After the buildings were ready, flying began in February 1914 and the first course for which applications had begun to arrive, was planned for September 1914. Keeping in view the prejudiced view that prevailed later that Indians were not good mechanics, it is interesting to note in retrospect that Indian mechanics were to have been employed had the school continued.

The school was formally inspected by the Commander-in-Chief of the Indian Army General Sir Beauchamp Duff on March 27, 1914, after which he was flown in one of the school's Maurice Farman bi-planes piloted by Captain Massey, the Commandant of the school.

However, despite its name, the Central Flying School was not charged initially with a training role. Replying to a question from Sir John Rees on April 7, 1914, in the House of Commons, the Parliamentary Under Secretary of State for India, Charles Robert stated: "There are three aeroplanes and five others have been ordered. The immediate object is to gain experience in aviation under Indian conditions, with a view to the eventual expansion of the school as a training establishment."

Although it was known that war was imminent, nobody could visualise how long it would last. Thus, when the war did actually break out in the first week of August 1914, the situation in France deteriorated so fast that for the first time, an Indian corps of two divisions was formed to strengthen the British Expeditionary Force and was sent to Europe.

Added to this was the major task of thwarting Turkish attacks on the Suez Canal. Here too, Indian troops were utilised and it was decided that all available pilots and aeroplanes should be sent to Iraq to provide air cover to the troops against the Turks who were already marching towards the Suez Canal. The group of five pilots, all from the Indian Army, formed the Indian Flying Unit which was sent to Egypt. Here, this unit performed valuable service with the Indian Expeditionary Force sent to Egypt in 1914. It flew reconnaissance missions in connection with the Turkish assault on the Suez Canal. After the failure of the Turkish attack, the Indian flying unit was relieved by an RFC squadron and its personnel were sent to Mesopotamia.

The nucleus of the Air Force required for the Mesopotamia Expeditionary Force consisted of an air contingent provided by the Commonwealth of Australia. This was supplemented partly by trained pilots from this Indian flying unit released from Egypt.

The Indian Flying Unit may be regarded as the embryo of the Royal Air Force in India. Just a year after the war began, the first RFC squadron, namely, No. 31, arrived in India in December 1915. Thus, the first course of flying training was cancelled and the school was closed down. In 1915, the instructors and aeroplanes and the technical staff were sent to Egypt. The unit thus formed may be regarded as the embryo of the RAF in India.

By the middle of 1915, according to the official history records, the Indian Flying Corps was disbanded as a separate body and was merged with the Royal Flying Corps (RFC). Meanwhile, Captain Massey and the other instructors were sent to the UK and soon after, were sent back to Egypt. In November 1914, when the Turks began their attack on the Suez Canal, a flight consisting of Captain Massey, Captain Reilly and Lieutenant S P Cockerell with three Maurice Farman machines was sent to give the Army aerial support. This small flight was the beginning of the Middle East Brigade under the command of Major General W G H Salmond, which played a great part in the campaigns of Mesopotomia and Palestine. One of the flying instructors, Cyril Newall, was sent to England and posted to a regular squadron. He rose to the rank of Air Chief Marshal and became the Chief of the Air Staff of the RAF.

In retrospect, it is ironical that since the war lasted more than four years, a flying school in India would provide pilots for service in the Middle East theatre of operations. But all the powers that be thought it would be a short war and, hence, every trained pilot would turn the tide in England's favour.

What Happened to the Flying School?

The flying school, which would have given India a foundation nursery for training pilots, was lost to the country due to the exigencies of war. After the war was over, the entire project was forgotten and the military barracks and the runway and buildings were handed over to the United Provinces Police and is today (2009) a workshop-cum-training centre where police vehicles are repaired and police personnel trained to become drivers and mechanics. From 1914 to 1945, the place was back to being an Army barracks and, subsequently, a motor driving school was started.

The buildings are there, the runway is there and only faded memories remind us of what it could have been. The Central Flying School (CFS) was a dream which came true but was snatched from our hands by the German Emperor, Kaiser Wilhelm.

Meanwhile, in view of the turbulent conditions prevailing in the North-West Frontier Province (NWFP), and open rebellion by the tribes, the Viceroy of India requested the Home Government to send a squadron of RFC to India to provide aerial cover to the Army in their operations against the hostiles.

The Operational Test

The Indian Flying Corps — 1914-16

Just after the first successful military aerial reconnaissance on January 15, 1911, the entire military establishment in India was all for military aviation to become part of the war doctrine of the Empire. Acquisition of aircraft was the hot topic of the day. Among the strongest votaries of military aviation were the Commander-in-Chief of the Indian Army Sir O'Moore Creagh and his Chief of General Staff Sir Douglas Haig.

The latter saw at first hand how aerial reconnaissance helped the Army at the Battle of Marne in 1914. Brancker, at the beginning of the war, was a comparatively junior officer but recorded that Creagh was convinced of aviation's vast possibilities and its future importance to the Indian Empire; but money for the Army was terribly short and he was unable to start an aeronautical organisation at once as he ardently desired.

Creagh's frustration was also reflected in a letter sent by Sir Douglas Haig to his successor as Director of Staff Duties at the War Office, Brigadier General Lancelot Kiggell in May 1911. Writing to Kiggell, Haig noted:

"We are considering here how best to start a school of instruction and a corps for air work. I should be greatly obliged if you could let me have any suggestions on the subject. Money, at present, is very tight here and we shall find it difficult to make a beginning even in a small way."

Meanwhile, Captain Seaton Dunham Massey of the 29th Punjabis became the first serving officer of the Indian Army to complete initial flying training and qualify as a pilot with the Royal Aero Club (RAC). Massey learnt to fly at the Bristol School of Aviation at Larkhill on Salisbury Plain and on May 9, 1911, he qualified for the RAC, Aviators Certificate No. 84.

He spent at least part of that year attached to the Air Battalion of the Royal Engineers. This unit had been formed on April 1, 1911, at Larkhill with the specific duty of training officers and men in the handling of all forms of aircraft and providing a small body of expert airmen from which air units for war could be formed for, in the words of the Commandant of the Air Battalion, Major Sir Alexander Bannerman, Bart, RE, "the mere taking of an Aero Club's aviator's certificate does not make a man a military flier."

By the end of the year, at least, four other Indian Army officers — Captain Duncan Le G Pitcher and Cuthbert Gurney Hoare (both from Central India Horse), Lieutenant Latham Valantine Stewart Blacker of the Queen's own Corps of Guides and Lieutenant Cyril Louis Norton Newall of the 2nd battalion of the 2nd Gurkha Rifles, had also gained their aviators certificates at Larkhill.

In September 1911, the commandant of the Air Battalion was requested to arrange for some officers of the Indian Army who had obtained pilot certificates to receive some further training in aeroplane work with the Air Battalion.

Advocates of military aviation in the Indian Army continued to press their case during the following year. In an article published in the *Journal of the United Service Institute of India* in October 1912, Captain Massey emphasised "the necessity of India having its Flying Corps and having it without delay....our requirements in aircraft will be large."

Although a small number of Indian Army officers continued to receive flying training to RAC certificate standard in UK civil schools between 1912 and 1914, given the limited flying training resources available to the British Army, it was clear that there would be little or no capacity to spare for the training of Indian officers for the foreseeable future.

As a first step towards creating an Indian Flying Corps, it would, therefore, be necessary to establish facilities in India capable of generating trained personnel for the new air arm. Massey spent the summer of 1912 at Army Headquarters in India working out the details of a scheme for introducing a School of Aeronautics in India.

In a letter to the War Office dated July 12, 1912, the Assistant Military Secretary at the India Office outlined the scope of the planned school. It was proposed that ten aeroplanes in active commission, and five complete but not erected spares would be acquired, together with all the tools and spares required to maintain them, and also to construct an erecting shop, a repair shop and a store at the chosen site for the school.

In response to a request to help establish the initial and ongoing monthly costs of such a school, the War Office forwarded an estimate in October 1912 that placed the cost of maintaining a school on the scale envisaged (not including the purchase of the aircraft themselves) at over Pounds Sterling 9,000.

In response to a question from Rt Hon Sir John Rees, MP, the Parliamentary Under Secretary of State for India, Edwin Montagu, confirmed in the House of Commons on April 30, 1913, "The Government of India intend to have their own school of military aviation. The scheme will be under an officer trained in the Home Air Battalion here, and the future staff of instructors will be similarly trained at the cost of Indian revenue."

In a separate announcement, the Government of India named Massey as the commandant of the new school and Hoare, Newall and Reilly of the 82nd Punjabis as the first instructors. A report on May 10, 1913, in *The Flight Magazine* noted, "These officers are certified pilots, but they are coming to England in order to undergo a long period of training at the Central Flying School (Upavon) before taking up their new duties."

Captain Massey was formally appointed to command the Indian Central Flying School on December 1, 1913. The site chosen for the school was at Sitapur in the United Provinces. The school was inspected by the new Commander-in-Chief of the Indian Army, Sir Beauchamp Duff, on March 27, 1914, after which he was flown in one of the school's Maurice Farman bi-planes, piloted by Massey.

Replying to a further question from Sir John Rees on April 7, 1914, Montagu's successor as Parliamentary Under Secretary of State for India, Charles Robert, stated, "There are three aeroplanes, and five others have been ordered. The immediate object is to gain experience in aviation under Indian conditions, with a view to the eventual expansion of the school as a training establishment."

Indian Army Air Operations During World War I — 1914-16

With the outbreak of war in August 1914, the Royal Flying Corps (RFC) deployed in the field en masse in support of the British Expeditionary Force in France. At least five Indian Army aviators — Captains Massey, Hoare, Reilly, Pitcher and Lieutenant Newall — were at Farnborough and all were caught up in this hurried mobilisation.

Reilly and Pitcher were attached to No. 4 Squadron, all but one flight of which left Dover en route to Amiens, in conjunction with Nos. 2 and 3 Squadron, on the morning of August 13, 1914. On August 21, 1914, Pitcher would appear to have become the first Indian Army officer to take part in an operational flight, serving as observer on board an aircraft piloted by Lieutenant W G S Mitchell during a reconnaissance sortie over Mons, Soignes, Roeulx, and La Louviere (all in France).

Of the remaining three Indian Army officers, in October 1914, Captain Massey was appointed in command of No. 1 Reserve

Aeroplane Squadron at Home (UK), the other two being made Flight Commanders in two other squadrons.

Although Indian Army officers flew initially on attachment to the RFC, by the end of 1914, personnel and equipment from the Indian Central Flying School (Sitapur) had been formed into an aviation detachment paid for by the Indian exchequer and used to support Indian Army operations in the field. These air operations did not take place in India itself.

The requirement to form an air detachment for expeditionary operations, some distance beyond India's own borders, reflected a marked shift in the policy that governed the deployment of the Indian Army.

In his 1919 London Gazette dispatch, examining the part played by India, including the Indian (Princely) states, in the prosecution of the war, the then Commander-in-Chief in India, Sir Charles Monro, stated, "In August 1914, the Army in India numbered some 77,000 British and 159,000 Indian ranks, exclusive of 38,000 volunteers and 35,000 Indian reservists."

However, despite its size, this force was in no sense a potential reserve to the armed forces of the British Empire. While acknowledging that there have been many precedents for the employment of small contingents from India in support of imperial interests in other parts of the world, Sir Charles emphasised, "It had never been the policy to maintain troops in India in excess of those actually required for the protection of her own interests."

As the Government of India was aware, the primary functions of the pre-war Army in India were two-fold, namely, the maintenance of order within and on the borders of British India, and, secondly, the provision of a field Army, capable, should the necessity arise, of undertaking a campaign beyond the border for the purposes of defence against external aggression. The Army in India was in no sense maintained for meeting external obligations of an imperial character.

During the summer of 1914, the prospect of Britain becoming embroiled in a major worldwide conflict led the Government of India to reappraise this stance. While it remained the case that no appreciable contingent could be furnished for employment overseas without involving considerable risk, it was nevertheless recognised that in the event of an emergency threatening the integrity of the Empire, the Government of India might be called upon to accept this risk with the objective of adding to our strength at the decisive point.

Immediately prior to the outbreak of the war, the Government of India, therefore, undertook for the first time to create and fund expeditionary forces for service beyond the Indian subcontinent.

One consequence of this change in policy was the deployment of Indian troops to Egypt. The entry of Turkey into the war in November 1914 in support of the Central Powers heightened concerns with regard to safeguarding the Suez Canal against attacks from the Ottoman Empire.

In response to the Turkish threat, an Indian Army contingent, under the command of Major General Sir Alexander Wilson, was dispatched to defend this vital line of communication. In addition, an RFC detachment, drawn from a small group of officers belonging to the newly formed Indian Central Flying School, was formed for cooperation in the defence of the canal.

The detachment sailed from the UK, aboard the SS *Beethoven* on November 4, 1914. Captain Massey was appointed to command the detachment and he was accompanied by Captain Reilly (now returned from No. 4 Squadron) and Lieutenant Samuel P Cockerell, a RFC Special Reserve Officer.

On arrival in Egypt, the detachment established itself at Camp Moascar, Ismalia, and here it was reinforced by officers from units in Egypt and the UK. Further reinforcements also arrived on December 21, 1914, from the Indian Central Flying School, including one officer (Lieutenant S C Parr), three civilian mechanics and three airframes –

a Royal Aircraft Factory BE2a and two Maurice Farman 'Longhorns' (1913 type), all without engines.

On November 27, 1914, the detachment flew its first reconnaissance sortie. It continued to patrol the area east of the canal defence zone for most of the following year, working in conjunction with French Navy seaplanes operating from seaplane carriers. Although, the Sinai Front remained quiet for most of this period, in January and February 1915, the detachment played an important role in locating and harassing Turkish forces attempting to cross the Suez Canal.

In his dispatch, describing the defence of the canal, Wilson expressed his high appreciation of the valuable work done by the pilots and observers of the French hydro-aeroplane squadron and the RFC detachment in the numerous reconnaissances carried out by them previous to, and during, the advance of the enemy. They were constantly under shrapnel and rifle fire and carried out their difficult and dangerous duties with courage, resourcefulness and success.

Aircraft National Markings

When the RFC decided to send aeroplanes to Egypt and Iraq, aircraft recognition for ground observers was almost unknown. But far away, on the Western Front, things were happening which resulted in improvements. Initially, aircraft of both the Allied and the German and Austrian sides, had nothing painted on the fuselage, but the infantryman on the ground was not worried as the task involved reconnaissance. When crude dogfights with revolvers and rifles started, both sides began to fit guns into the aircraft. An aerial gun platform became available to pilots and this evolved, in practice, a new role for the RFC in aid of the infantry.

By this time, the soldiers learnt about the lethal qualities of flying. So, whenever an aeroplane was seen above, it was a free-for-all exercise. Every soldier tried to shoot at the machine and a few were indeed shot down. "The troops on the ground found it very difficult to recognise the difference between our aircraft and those of the enemy and had shot down at least one of our own in consequence and, thus, we were forced to adopt national markings as a means of recognition," says Air Vice Marshal Sir Sefton Brancker in his autobiography.

Union Jacks were first painted on pieces of fabric and draped on the underside of the lower wings, but they looked too much like Maltese Crosses and were later replaced by concentric circles with the colours in reverse order of that used by the French. About the same time, General David Henderson, commanding the RFC in the field, issued a standing order that any aeroplane going out on reconnaissance was to carry a rifle and ammunition and one day's ration and water.

The British initially painted the Union Jack on both sides of the fuselage and on the wings. The Germans did likewise, painting the Maltese Crosses on their machines. Unfortunately, the similarity of the Cross of both German and British markings created more confusion. This forced the British to go in for a circular marking. Three concentric circles in red white and blue were painted on all the machines. After that, there was no confusion.

All the aircraft sent to protect the Suez Canal had the new marking painted. After that, the national markings became universal, so that even civilian aircraft had to have national markings to identify themselves in international skies.

Flying Operations in Mesopotamia (Now Iraq)

Egypt was not the only country in which Indian troops were deployed to counter any Turkish attack. In response to the threat posed by either Turkish forces or a German-inspired *jehad* to the Anglo-Persian Oil Company installations at Abadan, on the mouth of the Shatt-al-Arab waterway, it was decided after consultations between the British Government and the Government of India to send a force from India to the head of the Persian Gulf.

The leading elements of the Indian Expeditionary Force 'D' sailed from India in mid-October 1914, and after seizing Fao went on to occupy Basra on November 22, 1914, and Kurna on December 9, 1914.

It was soon clear that any Indian Army operation in Mesopotamia would be dependent on accurate and timely air reconnaissance. The dispatch of aircraft for this purpose had been requested by the commander of the full Indian division in Mesopotamia, Sir Arthur Barrett, as early as January 1915.

When the objectives of the Army's campaign grew more ambitious, the establishment of an aviation detachment became a reality. On March 26, 1915, Captain Philip W L Broke Smith, RE — a former commander of the Indian Army's first experimental balloon section — was appointed Deputy Assistant Director of Aviation, Indian Army, with the acting rank of Major.

On April 1, 1915, the Government of India decided that the Indian Expeditionary Force 'D' should be reorganised as an Army Corps under the command of General Sir John Nixon and his staff when they landed at Basra on April 9, 1915.

Broke Smith's initial tasks were to make arrangements for the establishment of a base aerodrome and depot at Basra and to acquire knowledge of the climatic and geographical conditions. Also, he was supposed to determine the work which would be required of the aeroplanes, and effecting the necessary organisation and establishment of the flying service with the Indian Expeditionary Force 'D'.

Broke Smith returned to Bombay (where a depot had been established to support the aeroplane detachment) on April 17, 1915, in order to begin preparations for the dispatch of the flight.

He embarked for Basra on April 30, accompanied by Captain Reilly — who had been transferred from Egypt to command the new flight with the temporary rank of Major — and by the flight's Engineering Officer, 2nd Lieutenant W R Willis, formerly an Engineer in the

Public Works Department. They were later joined in Mesopotamia by Lieutenant Parr and four mechanics from the Egyptian Detachment, and two of the Maurice Farmans that had arrived in Egypt from India in December 1914, were also sent to Mesopotamia.

The aircraft park was established in Basra in April 1915, and after a false start at Mekina Malsus (which had to be abandoned due to flooding), a site for the aerodrome was selected at Tanouma, opposite Basra.

It was clear from the outset that India lacked the personnel and aircraft to maintain both the Egyptian and Mesopotamian detachments. During early 1915, the RFC's attention was focussed primarily upon the Western Front and India was, therefore, obliged to call upon the rest of the Empire for support. On February 8, 1915, the Australian Government received the Government of India's message asking whether Australia could provide any trained airmen, flying machines and motor transport for service in Mesopotamia. Two days later, the Australian government replied that the Commonwealth could furnish some airmen and the necessary machines and transport but no aeroplanes.

A single Flying Officer from New Zealand was also posted to join the detachment. In addition, both Australia and New Zealand offered to bear all expenses connected with their part of the detachment. The establishment for 'A' Flight and for an aircraft park was completed by volunteers from territorial battalions from India.

When the Mesopotamian Half Flight arrived in the theatre on May 26, 1915, the Australian contingent found at Basra the two Indian Army airmen (Captains P W L Broke Smith and H L Reilly) and a few mechanics. One member of the Mesopotamian Half Flight recalled:

"These two officers with about four British and five Indian mechanics, formed the Indian Flying Corps, which was supplemented by an Indian Army Reserve Lieutenant as engineer officer and six

British motor transport drivers. They possessed two motor-lorries and a few spare aeroplane parts. With the assistance of a few Indian pioneers, a road of date-palm logs had been made from Shatt-al-Arab (the canal on which Basra is situated) across a swamp to an Arab cemetery, where tents had been pitched and a small aerodrome was in the making.

"On the following day, the detachment made its first flight over Mesopotamia when Reilly and Broke Smith carried out an air test in one of the detachment's Maurice Farmans. Although handicapped by inadequate aircraft and chronic shortages of essential spares and equipment, the detachment in Mesopotamia went on to play an important role in the ensuing campaign, culminating with the capture of Nasiriya on July 24-25, 1915."

In his dispatch describing the operation, General Sir John Nixon paid tribute to the excellence of the work performed by the officers and men of the RFC, whose valuable reconnaissance materially assisted in clearing up the situation before the battle of July 24. Although the dispatches sent by Sir Alexander Wilson and Sir John Nixon identified the aviation detachments belonging to the Indian Expeditionary Forces in Egypt and Mesopotamia as belonging to the RFC, this would not appear to have been the case.

Both detachments were established and funded (in large part) by the Government of India and the majority of their personnel would be from the Indian, Australian and New Zealand Armies rather than from the RFC. Although the attention of the War Office was at this time focussed firmly on the air fighting on the Western Front, it nevertheless acquiesced with the Government of India's urgent request to reinforce the Indian Army air unit in Mesopotamia and assist in the creation of a squadron for operations in India itself.

This agreement was not without conditions for, in return, the War Office wished to ensure that all of these units and their personnel came under its control. In a telegram to the India Office on August 22, 1915, the Viceroy referred to a letter from the Directorate of Military Aeronautics, dated July 21, 1915, in which the latter required that air units operating over Mesopotamia and North-West Frontier of India shall form an integral branch of the RFC.

Noting that the Government of India was prepared to assist the War Office in every way and cordially accepted this principle, the Viceroy went on to emphasise that the early establishment of an efficient and adequate flying service in Mesopotamia and on the North-West Frontier was so essential as to press for promptitude in the matter.

Measures to bring both the Egyptian and Mesopotamian detachments into the RFC predated the Viceroy's telegram. On July 31, 1915, Major S Macswaney of the Directorate of Military Aeronautics wrote to Major Massey in Egypt, "To inform you that the detachment of RFC under your command became No. 30 Squadron, RFC, on March 24, 1915."

All of those officers belonging to the Mesopotamian Flight who were not on the establishment of the RFC (including those of the Australian and New Zealand Armies) were gazetted formally into the RFC with effect from August 5, 1915.

It had also been decided that No. 30 Squadron should be concentrated in Mesopotamia and in August, the Mesopotamian Flight was informed that the provision of flying units in Mesopotamia would be taken over by the War Office and that the flight would now become part of No. 30 Squadron.

However, the integration of the Egyptian and the Mesopotamian Detachments as No. 30 Squadron did not take place in practice until November 1915. On November 7, the Mesopotamian Detachment, now reinforced by the arrival of personnel and aircraft from the UK, and joined by a Royal Navy Air Service Flight from East Africa, was reorganised into No. 30 Squadron, consisting of Headquarters 'A' and 'B' Flights and No. 4 Aircraft Park.

Subsequently, the No. 30 Squadron party in Egypt was relieved by the 'A' Flight of the No. 14 Squadron on November 26 and, on December 9, those members of No. 30 Squadron who had not been transferred to No. 14 Squadron, left for Barsa.

During this period, Major Reilly assumed command of No. 30 Squadron in Mesopotamia, pending the arrival of Major Massey from Egypt. However, Major Reilly was shot down during a reconnaissance flight and captured. Major Gordon, Royal Marine's Light Infantry, acted as Commanding Officer (CO) of No. 30 Squadron prior to Massey's arrival at Kut-al-Amara on November 28, 1915.

Although, No. 30 Squadron would continue to operate over Mesopotamia for the rest of the war, it would do so as a part of the RFC, and later RAF, rather than the Indian Army. While the Government of India may have accepted that its flying units in the field should come under the mantle of the RFC, it, nevertheless, sought to maintain some control over Indian Army officers volunteering to serve as pilots or observers.

It, therefore, suggested that every Indian Army officer sent to the UK for flying training should either return to India on completion of his training or be replaced by a suitably experienced officer from the UK. To facilitate this exchange, it once again argued for the establishment of an aviation school in India in which Indian Army officers could be trained.

The War Office rejected this proposal, informing the Under Secretary of State for India on October 2, 1915, "It will not be possible for the War Office to supply instructors or aeroplanes to establish a flying school in India, as every available instructor is already fully occupied in the training establishments in the UK. Moreover, in view of the serious difficulty that exists in obtaining a supply of spare parts adequate to replace the constant breakages that occur in a training establishment, it would be impossible to maintain the equipment of a flying school situated at so great a distance from the source of supply.

"The Army Council is, therefore, of the opinion that the question of the formation of an elementary flying school in India should be dropped. Should there be any officers on the Indian establishment who are desirous of, and recommended for, employment in the RFC, they could be sent to the UK for training.

"As soon as the total number of trained pilots of the Indian Army exceeds the number required for service in India, with Force 'D' and with the Indian troops on service elsewhere, it would be necessary to ascertain in each case, whether having regard to the exigencies of the service, it would be possible to provide a relief.

"Until then, however, the council lays stress on the principle that every officer who graduates as a pilot must be entirely at their disposal, irrespective of the establishment from which they are drawn."

The refusal of the RFC/RAF to acquiesce with the Government of India's wishes to establish a flying school for the Indian Army in effect, to resurrect the now defunct Indian Central Flying School, can, therefore, be seen to have marked the *de facto* demise of the Indian Army's attempt to form its own air arm.

It, therefore, fell to the RFC to form the first air units intended to conduct air operations in Indian skies. In a letter to the Military Secretary at the India Office, General Sir Edmund Barrow, on August 17, 1915, General Sir Percy Lake (the then Indian Army's Chief of General Staff) expressed his concern that the War Office had not yet grasped the peculiar conditions and difficulties to be overcome when operating aircraft over Mesopotomia and the North-West Frontier areas of India.

Lake stressed that the Frontier conditions were as yet unknown and would require careful study. He further urged, "Politically, it will be most important that the first flights undertaken over tribal territory should be successful and we take this to be an additional reason for the provision of none but the very latest and the best obtainable machines, piloted by exceptional men, from the very outset."

A Role of Honour — 1918

The following is the list of aviators' certificates granted by the Royal Aero Club of the United Kingdom to the Indian Army officers, who qualified as pilots at their own expense, during leave period, before the outbreak of World War I, in August 1914, as contained in the 1916 edition of Jane's *All the World's Aircraft*:

- Captain Seaton Dunham Massey of 29th Punjabis (on May 9, 1912).
- Captain Duncan Le Geyt Pitcher of 39th Central India Horse.
- Captain Cuthbert Gurney Hoare of 39th Central India Horse.
- Lieutenant Hugh Lambert Reilly of 82nd Punjabis (he was an instructor at the Flying School, Sitapur, United Provinces, India).
- Latham Valentine Stewart Blacker of the Queen's Own Corps of Guides.
- Lieutenant Cyril Louis Norton Newall of 2nd Gurkha Rifles.
- Major R L Benwell (Certificate No. 165, Brooklands, December 6, 1911).
- Captain H C Fielding of 38th Dogras (Certificate No. 212, Brooklands, April 30, 1912).
- Lieutenant A C H A Eales (Certificate No. 569, Hendon, July 21, 1913).
- Captain G Henderson (Certificate No. 644, Broklands, July 7, 1913).
- Captain G C B Buckland of 8th Gurkha Rifles (Certificate No. 657, Salisbury Plain, October 22, 1913).
- Captain M G Lee of 40th Pathans (Certificate No. 700, Brooklands, December 8, 1913).
- Captain E A H Fell of 12th Bengal Cavalry (Certificate No. 758, Salisbury Plain, March 27, 1914).
- Lieutenant T R Wells of 33rd Punjabis (Certificate No. 851, Brooklands, July 21, 1914).

NOTE: This list is not necessarily exhaustive.

— Clive Richards, Senior Researcher
Air Historical Branch, RAF, UK.

It is a curious fact that in that era *circa* 1910-11, it was thought that good horse riders would make good pilots. One of the famous cavalry regiments of the Indian Army, the Central India Horse (CIH), contributed the following officers to the Military Air Service. Some of their names appear on the earlier given list, but for some, only sketchy information is available.

- Captain C G Hoare, CIH.
- Lieutenant Martin, CIH (his cavalry regiment was sent to France as part of the Indian Corps and saw action there. He was invalidated and was transferred on recovery to the Royal Flying Corps).
- Captain Henderson, CIH.
- Lieutenant Gourlie, CIH.
- Lieutenant P N Leslie, CIH.
- Lieutenant Lucas, CIH.
- Lieutenant Pinney, CIH.

The list includes eight officers from one cavalry regiment of the Indian Army. The Punjab Regiment and the Gurkha Rifles also contributed officers to the RFC, but from the Indian Army, the Central India Horse has the pride of place.

Indian Pilots in the Royal Flying Corps — 1917-18

By 1914, when World War I began, India had progressed considerably in terms of Western education and political awareness. Initial steps had been taken towards local self-government and the educated were being recruited through competitions both as officers in the highly elitist Indian Civil Service and the Provincial Services.

While all this was smoothly progressing, a demand was made that Indians too should be recruited in the armed forces in the officer cadre.

This was, in fact, conceded by the government of the day, when King George V announced at the Delhi Durbar, in 1911, that henceforth, Indians would be offered commissions in the Army.

But the British bureaucracy in India put forth many stumbling blocks in the way of setting into motion steps to achieve this goal. Nothing on the ground was done to initiate the process until the war began in 1914. The initial reverses on the battlefields of France forced the Government to send unprepared, badly equipped Indian Army Corps troops to France to stem the onslaught of the German Army.

Even after this, the British bureaucracy remained unmoved. It was only towards the fag-end of the war that the first batch was commissioned from an Officers' Training School at Daly College, Indore, in 1919, but by then the war was over.

The other concession announced by King George V was that Indian soldiers would henceforth, be eligible for the Victoria Cross. Right from 1858, when the Crown took over the administration from the East India Company, Indian soldiers had been deliberately excluded from being eligible for the award of Victoria Cross. To further introduce a new caste system, the British Government of India instituted a medal — the Indian Distinguished Service Medal (IDSM) — for the Indian servicemen and NCOs. This was given a sarcastic appellation: the Indian VC. Along with that came the distinction between the King's Commission and a newly introduced Viceroy's Commission meant for those below the commission rank.

One overriding reason for denial of commissions to eligible Indians was the deep-rooted distrust of the educated Indian due to the memories of the 1857 mutiny. Along with that was a policy specifically meant to block the advance of the non-white races, especially in India, and of Africans from South Africa. This distinction did not apply to those from Canada, Australia and New Zealand and whites from South Africa.

Senior Aero Researcher of the Air Historical Branch (RAF) Clive Richards has detailed this and discussed this issue:

"All the Indian Army officers who participated in the First World War were of European rather than Indian descent. Nevertheless, a small group of Indian military pilots did take part in the air war, as officers of the Royal Flying Corps and later the RAF rather than the Indian Army.

"The prevailing policy of the War Office prior to First World War was to deny commissions to applicants not of 'pure European descent' on the grounds that 'a British private will never follow a half-caste or native officer'. A similar stance was also adopted by the Admiralty.

"However, the pressure of war led to a gradual loosening of this policy on the part of the War Office and the first Anglo-Indian candidate (W O C Evans) was admitted to the Royal Military Academy at Woolwich, during November 1916. Similar cases were to come as the war progressed."

Lieutenant J P B Jeejeebhoy

In November 1916, Jeejeebhoy Piroshaw Bomanjee Jeejeebhoy became the first Indian to enter the Royal Flying Corps (RFC), being commissioned in the General List for duty with the RFC, with rank of Temporary Honorary 2nd Lieutenant, on November 6, 1916.

Lieutenant Jeejeebhoy's active career with the RFC would appear to have been brief. Papers preserved in the National Archives show that Jeejeebhoy fell ill in January 1917, whilst training at the RFC's Oxford School of Instruction, and was suspended from training to convalesce. A Medical Board concluded in May 1917 that he was permanently unfit for further service and an entry in the London Gazette of May 29, 1917, duly announced that Temporary Honorary 2nd Lieutenant Jeejeebhoy relinquishes his commission on account of ill health.

Jeejeebhoy was to be the first of at least five Indians known to have served in the RFC and the RAF. Although the factors that lay behind their recruitment are unclear, surviving papers suggest that the driving force behind the acceptance of four of the candidates is likely to have been Major General (Air Vice Marshal) Sir Sefton Brancker.

On his return from India, Brancker served as the RFC's senior representative in Whitehall for much of World War I, holding the post of Director of Air Organisation in the War Office between March 1916 and February 1917 and Deputy Director General of Military Aeronautics between February and October 1917.

As such, one of the then Brigadier General Brancker's responsibilities was the selection and commissioning of RFC officers and in a paper presented to the Air Council in September 1918, he referred to the four Indians whom he had trained about two years earlier in the RFC.

Lieutenant Srikrishna C Welinkar

A second Indian applicant, Srikrishna Chunder Welinkar, applied for a temporary commission in the RFC on November 22, 1916. At the time of his application, Welinkar was a student at the Jesus College, Cambridge. According to a hand written note on his application on February 6, 1917, Welinkar had been recommended by Brigadier General Brancker and approved for the Officers Cadet Wing, RFC. Unlike Jeejeebhoy, Welinkar did not receive an Honorary Commission, rather, he enlisted formally in the Oxfordshire and Buckinghamshire Light Infantry on February 13, 1917, and he was posted to No. 6 Officer Cadet Battalion, RFC, on the same day.

Welinkar was appointed a Temporary 2nd Lieutenant (on probation) on the General List (RFC) on May 24, 1917, and confirmed on this rank on June 22. Although his progress to the front line was impeded by injuries that occurred in two flying accidents in the UK, he was passed fit for general service by a Medical Board in February 1918, and was subsequently posted to the Western Front.

Whilst serving with No. 23 Squadron at Bertangles, France, he took off at 9.45 am on June 27, 1918, to participate in an offensive patrol. He failed to return from this sortie, his Sopwith Dolphin last being seen heading east while engaged in combat with a German two-seater near Peronne. Lieutenant Welinkar was shot down behind enemy lines and fatally wounded, dying some three days later.

Lieutenant Eroll Suvo Chunder Sen

Erroll Suvo Chunder Sen, a former member of the Rossall School Officers Training Corps, applied for a commission in November 1916, only to be rejected as being under the minimum age. In April 1917, he reapplied, and on April 24, he was also awarded a commission as a Temporary Honorary 2nd Lieutenant in the RFC, being requested to report to the School of Military Aeronautics, Reading, on the same day.

On completing his training, he too was posted to No. 70 Squadron, a fighter squadron equipped with Sopwith Camels and based at Poperinghe. He took part in an offensive patrol on the morning of September 14, 1917. During the patrol, the engine of his Camel failed and he landed behind German lines, being captured and held as a prisoner of war until the Armistice. 2nd Lieutenant Sen was repatriated to the UK on December 14, 1918.

Lieutenant Indra Lal Roy, DFC

Perhaps the best known of these early Indian aviators is Indra Lal (Laddie) Roy, DFC. In February 1917, a friend of the Roy family approached Brancker directly in order to enquire whether Roy, then a pupil at St. Paul's School and a member of the latter's Officers' Training Corps contingent, could enter the RFC.

Brancker referred this letter to the staff officer then responsible for recruitment, who in February 1917 invited Roy for an interview on the subject of his admission to the Officers Cadet Wing, RFC. Roy submitted a completed application form in the following month, and this was approved on March 26, 1917.

Roy's career as a fighter pilot began in October 1917, when he was posted from the School of Gunnery at Turnberry, to No. 56 Squadron, then at Estree Blanche, in October 1917. He met with little success, and after being injured in a crash on December 6, 1917, Roy was posted back to the UK.

There, he retrained as an Armament Officer and it was in this role that he was posted to No. 40 Squadron at Bruay in April 1918. He was cleared by a Medical Board to resume flying on May 13, 1918, and after a brief period in the UK, Roy returned to No. 40 Squadron on June 19, 1918.

Roy flew his first patrol with the commander of the squadron's 'C' Flight, Captain George McElroy and under the latter's tutelage he was to undergo a remarkable transformation, being credited with nine enemy aircraft destroyed during the next month. Sadly, Lieutenant Roy's career was cut short when he failed to return from a sortie on July 22, 1918. A report from the squadron suggests that his Royal Aircraft Factory SE5a may have been shot down in flames at 8.50 am in combat with Fokkers near Carvin.

The award of a Distinguished Flying Cross (DFC) to Lieutenant Indra Lal Roy, a very gallant and determined officer, was announced in the London Gazette on September 21, 1918.

Lieutenant Hardit Singh Malik

The commissioning of the fifth Indian pilot to serve with the RFC, Hardit Singh Malik, would appear to have been due to the intervention of Director General of Military Aeronautics, Major General Sir David Henderson. A student at Balliol College, Oxford, at the beginning of the war, Malik sought immediately to join the British Army but once again fell foul of the latter's pure European descent criteria. After graduating in 1915, he was rejected once again, but was accepted by the French Red Cross as an ambulance driver.

Whilst in France, he applied, and was accepted, for the French Air Service. On learning this, his former tutor at Oxford wrote to Major General Henderson saying that it was disgraceful for an Indian to be denied the opportunity of joining the RFC, while the French were willing to offer him a commission.

Henderson would appear to have intervened on Malik's behalf, for a notice in the London Gazette of April 26, 1917, records that III-class Air Mechanic Hardit Singh Malik was commissioned as a Temporary Honorary 2nd Lieutenant for duty with the RFC on April 6, 1917.

After training, Lieutenant Malik went on to fly as fighter pilot with Nos. 28 and 11 Squadrons on the Western Front and No. 141 Squadron in the UK.

Honorary Lieutenant Dattatraya Laxman Patwardhan

He was born in Ratnagiri district on the west coast of India. From a young age, his spirit was restless for adventure. He left home and worked at various professions — clerk, fireman, engine driver. He sailed for Europe and became a sailor in German and British shipping.

At 30 years of age, he was commissioned to captain the ship SS *Tukaram*, purchased by the Indian Cooperative Navigation Company of Bombay, on her maiden voyage to India.

Soon after, he left for England. The war had by then started. His coloured skin was a bar but not enough to hold him back. Having been rejected by the Army in the UK, he opted for ambulance work in France, where the battles were raging fiercely. His work won him recognition and he soon enrolled in the Sussex Yeomanry Regiment on March 15, 1915, for a four-year term, as a Private.

As a sailor, he had already specialised in mechanical engineering. Now, he made his mark in gunnery. During the later part of the war, he was transferred to the Royal Flying Corps and was working as a technician. When the Armistice came, he was sent on reserve as AC2. Due recognition came soon after, with the award of the honorary rank of Lieutenant on March 15, 1919, the only one of its kind given to any Indian. He held this rank until 1937. He died in 1943.

The Frontier Experience

The North-West Passage

India is, geographically, a peninsula surrounded on three sides, south, east and west, by the sea. While in the north are the mighty Himalayas, the highest mountain range in the world, the Hindu Kush range in the west straddles the approaches into India.

Since pre-historic times, all traffic from the Middle East and Europe was only through the land passage which crossed the Persian Empire, came through 'Ariana' — the ancient name for Afghanistan — and onto the Indian subcontinent, into the land of five rivers – Punjab.

Thus, it was during recorded times that Alexander of Macedon crossed the Hindu Kush and resolved to recover the Indian satrapies that had once acknowledged the sway of his Persian predecessors whom he had soundly defeated in 327 BC.

To secure his communications, he garrisoned a number of strongholds near modern Kabul and passed the winter of 327-26 BC in warfare with the fierce hill tribes of Kunar and Swat Valleys. The local chiefs submitted and after crossing the mountains, Alexander prepared to enter Hindustan. Among the Kingdoms that lay in his path was Taxila whose King permitted him to pass through his Kingdom to that of the neighbouring King Paurava.

It is believed by one school of historians that Alexander crossed the river Indus by boat in 326 BC and marched to Hydaspes (also known as Vitasta or Jhelum, a tributary of the Indus). He took the route over which the modern Grand Trunk Road runs to the town of Jhelum. Here, he met fierce opposition from King Paurava. Though

Alexander's troops won the battle, they were weary and eventually Alexander was forced to return through the same way that he had come to India.

Though, by modern standards, transport and communications were primitive and slow in that age, the news of Alexander coming through the north-west passage into Hindustan was not lost upon either the Persians or the Turks — that one could just walk in and conquer parts of Hindustan through this route and appropriate all the fabled wealth of this far off glittering land.

Centuries later, around the 10th and 11th centuries, trade between India and the Arab countries flourished and Arab *dhows* continued this until the Portuguese sent out explorers like Bartholomew Diaz and Vasco da Gama to explore the sea passage to India and the Far East in the 15th and 16th centuries. After the Portuguese, came the French and the British, led by the explorer and mariner Sir Francis Drake.

The 17th century saw the beginning of British expansion move eastward with the setting up of the East India Company and its European and locally recruited Indian troops vanquishing the native rulers one by one by using their policy of dividing the enemy by guile and force and annexing their Kingdoms to what was later called British India. After they defeated Tipu Sultan of Mysore, and later the Marathas, came the turn of Oudh and Punjab. By the end of the century, the British had already consolidated their control over Bengal and were ruling the conquered territories from Fort William, Calcutta.

Oudh was easily annexed by force of arms coupled with duplicity, while in the case of Punjab, they had to wait for Maharaja Ranjit to pass away from the scene. Eventually, Ranjit Singh's sucessors put up a fight, although they were betrayed by their own people, and they lost to the British. Lord Dalhousie was the Governor General at that time and being an imperialist to the core, who believed that Britain had the divine right to conquer and rule over India, he annexed Punjab.

On March 30, 1849, Lord Dalhousie, on his own responsibility, annexed Punjab by a proclamation against the wishes of the British Cabinet.

He declared, "However, contrary it may be to our past views and to our present views, annexation of Punjab is the most advantageous policy to pursue. I firmly believe we shall not succeed in establishing a friendly Sikh power." There is no doubt that this move was seen as a bold move which had secured a valuable advantage to the British Empire in India, by extending its frontiers to the natural limits of India, the base of the mountains of Afghanistan.

After the victory over the Sikhs, the British set up a proper administrative system in Punjab which included reforms in tune with the rest of their dominions, under the able guidance of an experienced administrator, Sir John Lawrence. The British now faced a problem which was to dog them over the next 100 years and that was to effectively control Afghan tribal incursions and raids from the tribal territories which lay between Punjab proper and Afghanistan, the next door neighbour to the west.

It needs to be remembered that this area stretched from Gilgit in the Kingdom of Jammu and Kashmir in the north, down to the Makran coast of Baluchistan through the NWFP. Initially, Baluchistan was a part of NWFP but was detached from it to form a separate administrative unit. As the border was not formally demarcated under an agreement with the King of Afghanistan, the people on either side of the border being ethnically of the same stock, namely Pathans, and speaking the same language, indulged in violence against British India or among themselves.

But, violence against British interests was more profitable in terms of loot, weapons, ammunition and sometimes taking a non-Muslim British subject as hostage. A special target were the womenfolk of the Hindu families living in the settled areas and their forcible conversion and marriage. On the other side, the King of Afghanistan, whom the tribesmen, both on the Afghan side and the British Indian side, were ethnically linked to, used them as a weapon against the British, utilising this asset to his advantage. As did successive rulers of Afghanistan, in many of the confrontations, conflicts and wars against what they believed was an attack on them by the infidels.

Two such wars were fought — one, spanning the years 1839-42 and the second in 1878 — which led the British to pursue a 'forward policy' to advance into tribal territory with a large force, set up forts and camps and consolidate their position. This was described as a containment policy, to retain British control by securing lines of communication through such garrisons. However, this was strongly resented by the various tribal leaders who are known even today to be fiercely independent.

Here geography and history decided the moves. There are two mountain passes in this range of the Hindu Kush mountains, namely, the Khyber Pass in the north and the Bolan Pass in the south in Baluchistan. Historically, it was through these two passes that foreign invaders came into the plains of India. This being a strategic area, the British advanced on the two flanks of the tribal territory upto Quetta in Baluchistan on the left and the Khyber Pass on the right.

After the 1878 War, the British put on the throne at Kabul, Amir Abdur Rehman. Ruling his country with British help, he also wanted some kind of control over his tribal territory bordering British India. Thus, both sides needed a demarcated border and so in 1893, a boundary commission was appointed under the famous explorer and diplomat Sir Mortimer Durand to draw and demarcate the border with Afghanistan, which stands today as the Durand Line.

Now that their strategic interests were protected and remained under their control, the British Administration thought that would be the end of it. But, they did not reckon with the tribals in whose areas they had these interests. This was to plague the British Indian Government in faraway Calcutta (and after 1912, in New Delhi) and the British Government in London for decades that followed and even after they left India, the Pakistan government inherited the problem and even as this is being written (2011), the Pakistan Government is facing revolt after revolt in these very tribal areas of NWFP and Baluchistan, with no end in sight. The only difference is that today the Pathans are well equipped and much more determined to fight the *jehad* (holy war) against the Pakistan Government.

Fact File: Physical Features

"The north-west boundary of India (before 1947), from the Arabian Sea to the Hindu Kush is a belt of territory, outside of India proper, which the Indian Government has occupied, to ward off invasion."

— Cameron Morrison,
The Indian Empire and Ceylon, 1926.

In the southern part of the belt, we have Baluchistan (the new spelling is Balochistan – 2010). Native Baluchistan lies west of British Baluchistan, Sulaimans. Between these two ranges is the Kachhi desert, leading from the Indus Valley into the heart of British Baluchistan. Up this valley runs the railway to Quetta, the forts of which command the Bolan Pass from the north.

The second part of the belt between the north of Baluchistan and the Hindu Kush consists of a broad strip of tribal territory, now known as the North-West Frontier Province (NWFP), which consists of four parts:

- The Derajat Frontier: from the Gomal river to the Kurram Valley, including the Tochi and Wana agencies, inhabited by the Waziri tribes.
- The Kurram Valley: a British territory since 1892.
- The Peshawar Frontier: extending from Kurram Valley northwards, across the Kabul, right up to Kashmir, and including the Tirah country, south of Safed Koh, the Mohamand country

farther north, and the Bajaur, Dir, Swat and Buner districts, which lie in the valleys of Panjkora, Swat and Upper Indus.
- Chitral: lying further north, this comprises the Chitral Valley on the southern slopes of the Hindu Kush, a native state feudatory to Kashmir, but under the control of the Chief Commissioner of the NWFP.

Another way to describe the above would be to fix valleys and rivers as:
- The Kachhi Valley leading through British Baluchistan from the Indus.
- The Gomal with its tributary, the Zhob.
- The Kurram and its feeder, the Toch.
- The Kabul flowing into the Indus at Attock.
- The Kabul tributaries, the Chitral or Kunar, the Panjkora and the Swat.

Chief Mountain Passes
- The Bolan and the Harnai Passes guarded by Quetta.
- The Gomal Pass.
- The Tochi Pass.
- The Kurram Pass, called the Peiwar Kotal, over the Safed Koh.
- The Khyber Pass, commanded by Peshawar.
- The Malakand Pass, commanded by the new railway line from Naushera to Dargai.
- The Barogil and Dorah Passes on the Hindu Kush.

The Untamed Country

Even before Mughal rule had established itself firmly in India, every central Government of India based in Delhi had to tackle the problem of invasions from across the north-west passage from Afghanistan into the plains of India, initially Punjab and the rest of the interior of the country. After the British annexed Punjab, the border was demarcated. Even then, the problem continued to plague the administration. This region to the west, north and south of Punjab, occupied and, does so even now, a position of strategic and economic importance and, therefore, it was highly necessary for a ruler of India to maintain effective control over it. The Hindu Kush range, separating Central Asia from Southern Afghanistan, Baluchistan and India, becomes much less forbidding in the north of Herat and through this vulnerable point, an external invader from Persia or Central Asia may easily enter the Kabul Valley and India.

By the middle of the 19th century, the British were in the thick of it, trying to devise a method by which they could retain effective control over the NWFP by building forts at strategic points, garrisoning troops, building roads and improving transport and communications. Added to this 'stick policy', the 'carrot' was dangled by organising local forces to protect the British lines of communication through the length and breadth of the Frontier which was and is dotted by fiercely independent tribes. While the rest of their Indian Empire was stable and peace reigned, the only problem that successive Governor Generals and later Viceroys faced was the constant fear of an enemy knocking at the door and effecting a forcible entrance.

This dilemma was expressed by Sir Alfred Lyall, a far-seeing expert, when he said, "As the expansion of our dominions carried us so much nearer to foreign Asiatic countries, our rapid approach to the geographical limits of India proper, discovered for us fresh complications and we are now on the brink of collision with new races." Expressed simply, Britain did not need extra problems, for this would entail recurring expenditure of men and materials just for keeping a tenuous control over such a volatile area in the hope of deterring a would-be aggressor.

At this point (in the mid-19th century), the ruling East India Company's external policy was French-centric, since the British had been fighting the French on Indian soil for many years, defeating them eventually, which ended with the French getting a toe-hold at Pondicherry, Mahe and Karaikal. What had alarmed the British was Napoleon's expedition to Egypt in 1799 and his open declaration that capture and control of Egypt would cripple and break the British line of communication between England and India.

However, by 1815, after the downfall of Napoleon, a new threat loomed large over Central Asia. Czarist Russia now replaced France as the threat as it expanded its reach in Central Asia, bordering Afghanistan and Persia. The threat, real or imaginary, was with the usual British penchant for understatement, delivered with 'a stiff upper lip' and described by their diplomats, Generals and leaders as "The Great Game."

During the early part of the 19th century, Russian influence increased in Persia and Afghanistan whose rulers tried to remain equidistant from both Britain and Russia. But this did not suit Britain which tried hard to retain Afghanistan as its sphere of influence to prevent a possible invasion of British India through Afghanistan. In a telling comment of such a physical possibility, Sir T H Holdich, an experienced India hand and a Frontier expert wrote, "Near Herat, there exists the only break in the otherwise continuous and formidable wall of mountains which traverse Asia from the Bering Strait to the Caspian Sea. Near Herat, it is possible to pass from the Russian outposts to India without encountering any formidable altitude and this is possible nowhere else."

So the threat was seen as real, despite dubbing it as the Great Game — shadow boxing with an enemy in areas of Central Asia, while dealing with Czarist Russia as part of European politics. Whatever events took place in Europe, its repercussions were felt in India as well. When war broke out in Europe, hostilities were resumed in India and when peace prevailed, in India too hostilities ceased and truce prevailed.

To protect their interests, the British set up and maintained garrisons in almost every district of Punjab. Romantic names of military cantonments and individual units, made immortal by the likes of Rudyard Kipling, have dotted the pages of military history in India. Lahore Brigade, Multan Brigade, Ludhiana Sikhs, Sirhind Brigade, Hodson's Horse and Skinner's Horse are some of the names given to military formations which were kept ready and close to the border of Punjab with the NWFP.

Basing their moves on the perception that the Durand Line was a sacrosanct border, the British divided the entire Frontier area into two broad categories. To the west and north of Peshawar, Risalpur and Naushera, and west of Chitral, lay the northern part of what was termed as the "unadministered tribal area", and just south of it lay Aravalli amidst a small corridor. In the north, lay the tribal territory inhabited by Afridis, and further north, the Mohamands. It is in this part that the Khyber Pass, the gateway to India is located.

In the southern half of the unadministered tribal area, lived the other tribes such as the Datta Khel, Bhittani, Mahsuds and Waziris. It was in this area that the British set up forts, camps, built roads for better transport and communication for the troops. Places which no one knew about became famous through the writings of Victorian writers. Names like Wana, Razmak, Jandola, Sargodha, Miranshah and Dardoni Fort began appearing in the English language press in India and in England too.

This area was under international law — British India — but the population was hostile and not amenable to discipline, with frequent skirmishes breaking the peace. It was then decided that 50 miles east of the Durand Line, an administrative border be demarcated. This was the line that separated the untamed, wild tribal area from the settled areas where the British writ and administration ran.

In the settled areas of this Frontier was and is Peshawar, which eventually became the capital of the NWFP in 1901 during the tenure of Lord Curzon as Viceroy of India. In the north, facing the tribal areas to the west are Risalpur and Naushera and south of the Khajori Plain are Mianwali and Dera Ismael Khan. To the north-east are Rawalpindi and Murree.

All these were and are even today, military cantonments garrisoned by seasoned troops, close enough to the tribal area and yet relatively safe from tribal attacks. However, to control the tribes, and have a certain level of stability and peace, the British divided the entire tribal belt from the north to the south near the Makran coast into five political agencies: Malakand, Khyber, Kurram, North and South Waziristan.

Each of these agencies had a Political Agent, generally drawn from the Indian Army or the political service, fluent in the local language, Pushtu, and generally conversant with the inner state of the tribes they dealt with. They maintained contact with the tribal leaders and elders and would always try to sniff out conspiracies or plans for attacks either in their own area or sneak attacks into the settled area for looting, kidnapping and killing.

It is relevant to recall that when the British initially set up their factories, that is, trading posts at Madras and named it Fort St George, they realised that for the protection of their newly acquired assets, they would need an armed protection force, not just comprising European Company troops, but also local men. Accordingly, they set up a force they named the Madras Pioneers, officered at the middle and lower levels by locals, with ultimate control over the force in the hands of British officers. This move, in fact, laid the foundation of what we know today as the Indian Army.

Keeping the experience of this example in mind, which paid the rulers handsome dividends, the East India Company and later the British Indian Government decided that local knowledge of the tribes, their locations, their leaders and their character and even past record was essential if the British were to gain effective control over the unadministered areas and, of course, the administered areas. The latter was easily done with Peshawar being designated as the capital of the province and seat of administration.

But for the unadministered areas, they devised a system of recruiting local tribals and paying them nominal amounts as retainers. They had no uniforms and in appearance they looked no different from other tribal Pathans except for an arm band with 'K' printed on it. This letter when expanded meant 'Khasadars'.

The task assigned to Khasadars was to ensure that the lines of communication remained free and were kept open without any danger of ambushes by the hostile tribesmen, especially in the unadministered areas. However, the British knew that they could not completely depend on the Khasadars' loyalty. After all, they had to live with their untamed cousins and would not wholeheartedly do their job. With this realisation in mind, the British added one more tier to their defence machinery for ensuring peace in the region.

They created local paramilitary forces with good professional training, each in its ethnic and tribal area, as a buffer behind which came the Army if all else like bribery, cajoling and threats failed. At this stage, the civilian authority represented by the Political Agent was handed over to the Army with one clear instruction: fight as hard as you must, but get the situation back to normal fast, for a prolonged war with the wily tribals who were experts in the art of guerrilla fighting, would cost the exchequer a lot of money.

By 1900, the entire Frontier was divided into five parts which were now backed by properly recruited and trained militias whose names reflect the ethnic identities and geographical locations of the Frontier. They were known as Scout Formations. Gilgit Scouts (which was located in Gilgit that was part of Jammu & Kashmir State, but was formed and controlled by the Government of India), Swat Levies, Khyber Rifles, Kurram Militia, North and South Waziristan Scouts with headquarters at Wana, and Tochi Scouts based at Miranshah. All political agencies and militias worked under the direct control of the Governor of the NWFP, with headquarters at Peshawar.

The Great Game — 1838-1947

"India is like a fortress, with the sea as a moat on two sides, and the mountains (the Himalayas and their offshoots) on the third. Beyond the wall is a glasis (Frontier India) of varying breadth and dimensions. We do not want to occupy it, but we cannot afford to see it occupied by a foe. We are quite content that it should remain in the hands of allies and friends but if unfriendly influences creep up and lodge under our walls, we are compelled to intervene, because danger would thereby grow and menace our security."

— Lord Curzon, Viceroy of India, 1904.

The Russian Bogey

"Why didn't we meet before?"

The speaker was Czar Alexander I, the Czar of all the Russias, and the listener was Napoleon Bonaparte, the French Emperor, who had just then (June 7, 1807) won another victory at the Battle of Friedland.

The victory was so decisive that Czar Alexander made attempts at friendship with Napoleon whose star was at its zenith. The result was the signing of the Peace of Tilsit. After much discussion, it was mutually decided that the two sovereigns meet without any advisers. That resulted in a meeting on board a raft in the middle of the river Nieman.

Napoleon impressed the Czar, charmed him and not only signed the treaty but offered to sign a new comprehensive treaty of alliance, both offensive and defensive. He gained a diplomatic victory after a series of victories on the battlefield and changed the face of the diplomatic balance of Europe.

"Exercising upon Alexander all his powers of fascination, flattery, imagination, he completely won him over, thereby, provoking the

Czar to ask and answer the question of why they should have met earlier," comments eminent historian Charles Downer Hazen. Now, after the event, he basked in the newfound friendship with Napoleon and both of them studied the map of Europe and decided to divide it.

Alexander was conditionally offered Finland, which he wanted to take away from Sweden. Added to this, Napoleon dangled the carrot of vast areas of the Ottoman Empire in Eastern Europe. No concrete assurance, but something that Napoleon shrewdly held before the Czar to make him more amenable to what in the future would be more demands for territory and concessions.

However, Napoleon had other plans, among which was the longstanding one of controlling the whole of Europe. While he had subdued most of Europe, he could not do so with England which stood defiant as it did more than a century later when history repeated itself and Adolf Hitler tried to bring England down to its knees, but failed.

Both Czar Alexander and Napoleon were envious of England, not for itself, but for the Empire she had carved out in the far corners of the globe, with India being the brightest jewel in the Crown. This desire of both, to deprive England of her Indian Empire, turned into an obsession which both shared and bequeathed to another dictator of the 20th century — Adolf Hitler.

Napoleon's ambition to rule Europe and through that the rest of the world, had been thwarted at every stage by the British. Belatedly, he realised that England's naval power was the key to her success. He dreamt of ways to crush England, including invading the island, for which thousands of barges were built, just as Hitler planned more than a century later, but gave up the idea since he realised that England's strength came from her Indian Empire.

This thought remained with him when he saw on the map the distance England had to traverse to reach India and hold it secure for herself. He looked at Egypt and decided that this region would ideally suit him as a staging post, since its loss to England would cut off the very lifeline on which she depended. This thought was in tune with his grand vision of seeing himself as master of the world.

"This little Europe has not enough to offer. The Orient is the place to go to. All great reputations have been made there," he told a friend. "I do not know what would have happened to me if I had not had the happy idea of going to Egypt," he exulted.

He went to Egypt but it turned out to be a disaster and during his stay there, he realised that while he was away from France, things could go out of control at home. In 1798, he left for Egypt and had successful campaigns to his credit in Egypt and Syria, but lurking around the sea was the British Royal Navy which soon enough totally annihilated the French fleet in the Battle of Nile.

Meanwhile, the ebb and flow of developments in Europe had their repercussions in the Orient. The Seven Years War and the Peninsular War would start the conflict between the British and the French and as soon as peace would prevail in Europe after new treaties were signed, so too in India would peace reign.

The watershed turned out to be 1815, when England, Prussia and Russia joined and together defeated Napoleon at the Battle of Waterloo. Czar Alexander was pleased at this victory as Napoleon had not shared anything substantial with him after their famous meeting and alliance. Instead, he had attacked Russia as Hitler did a century later, but both returned empty-handed.

In India, the East India Company heaved a sigh of relief at the fall of Napoleon but did not forget the partnership that Russia had tried to foster with Napoleon. Earlier, Russia would have had a share of any spoils from the partnership, but now, after Napoleon fell, the way was clear for it to take the place of France and press forward with her plan to extend her sway over Central Asia and target countries like Persia and Afghanistan. The corridor would provide and fulfil the long felt need of a warm water port for the Russian Navy and maritime trade.

Fear and Reality

From 1757, the defence of Oudh (modern Uttar Pradesh) on the north-west border of Bihar was a matter of deep concern to the East India Company. Till the close of the 18th century, the fear of an invasion from the north-west by Ahmed Shah Durrani, the Afghan adventurer was uppermost in the minds of Warren Hastings and his successors at Fort William, Calcutta.

This led to the steps beginning with the annexation of Punjab and Sind to buttress the defence of the plains of India against possible attacks from Afghanistan. The entire British policy was a series of moves by trial and error, failures, corrections, backing the wrong Amir or Sultan or skirmishes with hostile tribals, but not gaining permanent peace as they did in the plains of India.

However, behind this was the overpowering fear of Russia making inroads into Persia and Afghanistan. Though it was not openly acknowledged, the Russian bogey was ever present and with their penchant for understatement, the British dubbed it the "Great Game".

This was especially so as the British considered Afghanistan their sphere of influence as the Company's ships used to carry pilgrims to Jeddah for Haj, skirting the Makran coast to the south. Even before Sind was annexed, by virtue of their naval superiority, the British controlled the sea around and along the Makran coast.

Before the opening of the Suez Canal in 1869 and the advent of steam ships, communication between India and England took months. This resulted in decisions being taken by the authorities in India, without approval by Whitehall, which proved disastrous.

One of these was the forward policy of establishing military control in the tribal areas but it did not subdue the tribes, though all kinds of efforts at cajoling, bribing and threats were employed.

From 1838 to 1947, there was not a single year when some tribe or the other did not rise in revolt, screaming *jehad.* And Pakistan, which inherited the area, thought at first that due to the affinity of religion against the hated infidel *firangi*, and now with him out of the way, they would be able to control them. But it was not to be.

The British wanted Afghanistan as a buffer between their Indian Empire and the Afghan border in the north bordering Russian territory. Though the Russians did not attack through Afghanistan, the threat was always there. And when they did in recent times, their objective was not India but Afghanistan itself. However, they too had to withdraw in view of the changed geo-political environment encased in an expression coined by the Americans as part of the Cold War. The Russians realised early the futility of this venture, much before the Americans did in Vietnam, and withdrew with heavy loss of life and equipment.

The US spearheaded the war against the Russian presence in Afghanistan through a surrogate state, namely Pakistan, which benefitted from the huge influx of armaments generously contributed by the Americans. But, Pakistan, ever since it was created as a nation, has always regarded India as its enemy number one. Pakistan's military think-tanks, facing the reality of its smaller size compared to India, decided that Afghanistan should become a vassal state.

Even when the Taliban took over the country, Pakistan, in order to retain some kind of control and influence over Afghanistan, recognised this rogue regime. Saudi Arabia was the other country to do so. Thus, the Pakistani Generals decided that Afghanistan would provide the space they would need in any conflict with India and called it their "strategic depth." The Pakistani General Staff has clung to this dream for the past sixty years, with no end in sight. Even today, the urging of the US to wipe out Taliban terrorism from Pakistan's border with Afghanistan, have brought no enthusiastic response from the Pakistan Army which is the deciding authority in that country, no matter which political party is in power.

Since the 9/11 bombing of New York's World Trade Centre, American and North Atlantic Treaty Organisation (NATO) troops have been battling it out with the Taliban in Afghanistan, with Pakistan as an unwilling partner. The people of Afghanistan are medieval in their thoughts and actions and tribal-centric, and no amount of persuasion or force has been able to bend them.

History's Verdict

Lord Roberts, who was serving during the Second Afghan War and carried out the famous march from Kabul to Kandahar in 1880, was a great supporter of the "forward policy" of his Government. He believed that "to stop at the foot of the hills was weakness."

In a concise survey of British military history, Colonels D H Cole and E C Priestly, in 1945, held that, in spite of nearly a century of effort, the Afghan problem remained a military problem. Afghanistan was the only (in the annals of British military history) country in the world, which the British Armies had twice invaded, twice largely occupied and twice evacuated.

This is a telling comment but long before this was written, some of the foremost military experts from Britain had expressed vehement disapproval of British moves both in Afghanistan and the Frontier province adjacent to it.

Sir Arthur Wellesly, later Duke of Wellington, wrote: "The consequence of crossing the Indus once to settle a government in Afghanistan will be a perennial march into that country." And so it has been, even as this is being written.

His remark was prophetic. He was the military leader who defeated Tipu Sultan, fought in the Peninsular War and defeated Napoleon at Waterloo in 1815.

Russophobia

"When the Amir of Afghanistan, annoyed with the English for their refusal of help against the Sikhs, had begun negotiations with Persia and Russia, it ('Russophobia') also deeply stirred the Whig Cabinet of Lord Melbourne in England. The then enterprising Foreign Secretary Lord Palmerston, saw in Russian designs imminent peril to the security and tranquillity of the Indian Empire and goaded the Government of India to take effective steps to checkmate them.

"The Select Committee of the Court of Directors wrote to the Governor General on June 25, 1836, to judge as to what steps may be proper and desirable to take to watch more closely, than has hitherto been attempted, the progress of events in Afghanistan and to counteract the progress of Russian influence in a quarter which, from its proximity to our Indian possessions, could not fail, if it were once established, to act injuriously on the system of our alliances and possibly to interfere with the tranquillity of our own territory."

— Dr R C Majumdar, Eminent Historian
Advanced History of India.

Shadow Moves

Russia's dream of conquering Central Asia went back a long way, fired by terrifying memories of Chengiz Khan's invading hordes who had swept down on them in the 13th century and kept Russia under Tartar domination for 200 years. Now, the Russians wanted vengeance and more — India, the glittering jewel in the British Crown, which lay just beyond this inhospitable terrain (Afghanistan).

"Russian designs on India had so far remained merely speculative, but as the 19th century dawned, the British learned that Czar Alexander and Napoleon had made a pact to join hands in their march through Central Asia, after which their combined Armies would drive the British out of India.

"Seriously alarmed, they now decided to keep a close watch on Russian activities in Central Asia and, at the same time, to win the allegiance of the powerful independent Khans and other tribal leaders of the region.

"Thus, began the Great Game, a shadowy war of moves and counter moves, intrigue and deception, fuelled by rumours and suspicions, many of them unfounded. At the start of the play, the two Empires were 2,000 miles apart; by the time it ended, nearly a century later, Russian outposts were less than 200 miles from India."

— Peter Hopkirk, *The Great Game*
Reviewed by Nandini Mehta,
The Indian Express, April 12, 1992.

Russian Invasion Plans

The chief of *Vanity Fair*, a reputed British journal, recorded the following about "The Great Game":

"I was talking the other day to a very distinguished man who has a complete acquaintance with the East, from not only having lived in India, Central Asia and Persia, but also having made a special study of Eastern politics on which he has written with great ability.

"Russian General Skobeleff, who is a frank soldierly man, said to me: 'We, of course, tell the world that we have no ulterior intentions in our annexations in Central Asia, but you know too much about the matter to be taken in. The fact is that Russian policy and English policy are antagonistic. I am sorry for it, because I like the English, but so it is. And as it is, so we have to deal with it. Now, in Europe, you have all the advantages. You can shut our ports and ruin us and we cannot get you at all, since you are stronger on the sea than we are.

'But in India, you have a soft and vital spot. We have never yet supposed we could invade India, or proposed to do so; but what we can do is to press on your Indian Frontier and to send agents among the Indians, who being a conquered race, are ready to be worked upon and whatever you may do in Europe or elsewhere, we can then answer in India by stirring up troubles there, and by making it impossible for you to hold the country. As you advance, so shall we advance and when our frontiers touch, we shall hold over you India in reply to anything you may attempt elsewhere'."

— *The Times of India*, November 13, 1879.

An Expert's View

Napoleon Ney, a French officer, who travelled widely in the East on military missions, published an interesting article on Central Asia, in which he recounts a conversation with General Skobeleff, a short time before his death, on whether Russia would, if she could, invade British India.

"It is not for me to give any opinion on the political aspect of the question. My personal belief is that there is no Central Asian question, but only a regrettable misunderstanding between England and Russia which I confidently hope will one day cease. I can never believe that a few European Powers will fight about a few Asiatics.

"From a merely military point of view, the enterprise seems to me more difficult than is generally supposed. When I took Akhal, having with me only 5,000 men, I had more than 20,000 camels brought from Crembourg, Khiva, Bokhara and Mangashlat at great expense and with great difficulty.

"To invade India, would require 150,000 men — 60,000 to enter the country and 90,000 to guard the lines of communication and who shall calculate the number of camels that would be wanted and where could they be found. Afghanistan is a poor country and could she maintain an Army of 60,000? No, Russia has completed her task in Asia. She has settled her frontier with Persia, where she enjoys an influence analogous to that of England in Afghanistan. Our relations with Tehran are excellent. It is a good thing that Afghanistan separates England and Russia, just as Kashmir is a barrier between us and China."

— *The Statesman*, September 24, 1884.

Impetus of the War

Meanwhile, in England, the impetus that the war, which was soon to come in 1914 gave, is revealed in the way the air services expanded. By the end of the war, the RAF, on the Western Front consisted of 99 squadrons and the total number of aeroplanes and seaplanes in service were 22,647. In 1918, the RAF, could claim to be "the largest and the strongest of the air forces in the world."

In his autobiography, RFC, HQ, 1914-18, Cyril Falls recorded that on February 5, 1915, he spent a night with No.2 Squadron and mentioned one of the songs that was sung in which there was a line: "It is a long way to 8000." This0 was an oblique reference to the indifferent climbing power of British planes.

Enemy anti-aircraft were called, derisively, "Archie". In World War II, it was "Flak" or "ack ack", No account of the RFC is complete without Maurice Baring. He had become a distinguished writer and journalist long before the war broke out; and in the most casual way, he found himself in uniform as a staff officer and ADC to General Sir David Henderson, who first commanded the RFC in France. A plumpish, bald-headed, middle-aged intellectual, he had an endearing manner, which made him one of the greatest characters in the RFC.

Cyril Falls had said of the airman of the first war: "The young men of the air forces, national and racial characteristics apart, resembled each other closely."

It was the end of an era, though at that time the average Englishman did not realise it. The Empire, the stability and the advancement taking place in the British Isles, was something every citizen took for granted.

England was insulated from Europe – just the way she wanted. It was to the Continent that the middle classes went to spend their summer vacations, and students interested in history and art went for visits.

A new toy called the aeroplane had made its appearance, but it was just a curiosity at country fairs and the newspapers were offering rewards for crossing the Channel in one of these contraptions.

A Frenchman shattered the insularity of England by flying from France to England. What Louis Bleriot did by that one flight, the war formalised by developing the air arm. Not until the guns started booming on the Continent, did the average Englishman understand that his island home was no longer a fortress.

But the mood during that glorious summer of 1914 was unforgettable. The Labour movement had started. Fabian pamphlets were being distributed. Oxford undergraduates had not yet got full freedom to entertain young ladies in their rooms. Shaw's "Pygmalion" was playing and H G Wells wrote an imaginative book entitled *World Set Free*. In it, he configured the vision of what the world later would call an atom bomb in 1945.

There were faint stirrings of the earthquake beneath the outwardly placid surface in Europe. On June 28, the heir to the Astro-Hungarian throne and his wife were brutally assassinated in a Bosnia town named Sarajevo.

Someone said it might lead to war, but John Bull said stuff and nonsense. But the war did come. And with it a new form of war —the air war.

Maurice Baring, in *Per Adua, 1914-18*, describing the opening scenes of the war said, "Their RFC squadrons which went to war, flew across the Channel as gaily as to a dance. To the troops departing for France, the cheering crowd shouted: 'Bring back some German sausage.' The British Expeditionary Force that went to France, never came back, But most thought that it would be over by Christmas."

War, to the generation bred on Empire building, meant a great adventure. They were occupied with other things. The topic most discussed was Home rule for Ireland. More than this, the world heavy weight title bout between Gunboat Smith and Frenchman George Carpenter had thousands betting on the winner.

When the war broke out, only four squadrons were available to the British, with 60 planes. Added to this pitiful number, were 39 planes with the Royal Naval Air Service and 52 other aeroplanes. Across the Channel, the Germans had visualised (as it turned out correctly) that war from the air was definitely coming.

But the British had contempt for this frail bird that could never become a war bird. They did not know that the armed Pegasus of the 20th century would transform the very concept of war. Britain depended on the Royal Navy to defend the isles, but this was shattered by the roar of guns from above heralding the air age.

The Victorian British were a race apart, they had a sense of destiny about them and yet they were conservative in their lifestyle. Coastal England was crowded over the August bank holiday. Mixed bathing was still not in style. Men and women bathed in separate preserves and splashed each other over dividing ropes.

Their most virulent epithet was "bally…you bally idiot, you". The word "damn" was taboo in polite company, "Bloody" was never used. "Rotter" was the word for a bounder. "Decent" was the most common adjective.

Among cricket heroes were Fry and Ranjitsinjhi (an Indian, but then he was a Prince) in county cricket, S. F. Edge on the car racetrack, Grahme White in the air, Max Linder on the film screen, Sherlock Holmes in fiction.

Their greatest thrill had been on seeing the first men to fly. They had witnessed the advent of the railways with the steam engine, the motorcar, they had seen the first moving picture. They had heard the first wireless signals.

What, since 1898, had been building up as the "German menace" was hardly seriously taken note of. Alsace-Lorraine, the war of 1870, the Pan-Slav agitation and German naval expansion came to notice but occasionally.

Lord Roseberry talked in 1909 about "the dress that patriotism will have to wear in days not far distant and perhaps, imminent, will be greater than has yet been known in the history of this country." And with the Agadir crisis, Winston Churchill, could think of nothing but "the perils of war."

Lord Roberts toured the country trying to rouse the people, but did not make any impact. Journals like the *United Service Institution Journal* carried prophetic articles. The works of Bernhardi, Treitschke and Von der Glotz were studied at Sandhurst and Woolwich.

An invasion play, "The Englishman's Home," thrilled the people. Robert Blatchford, a socialist Editor, wrote for the *Daily Mail* a series of articles about Germany's dreams of conquest, which the *Liberal Daily News* dismissed as ravings.

In 1913, the future Chief of the Imperial General Staff, Sir William Robertson, told the OTC camp in Salisbury Plain that war could come soon. At Oxford, military history was recognised and given a professional chair.

Every German town had a memorial to its dead of 1871. The French bowed their head before Napoleon's tomb. In England, they lived a sheltered life, secure in its island fortress.

"The Position in Europe", *The Times* reported on Tuesday, August 4, 1914, striking an unexpectedly dramatic pose, "is one of breathless anticipation of the beginning of hostilities on a large scale." Canterbury cricket week opened with the season's return match in the ancient rivalry between Kent and Sussex.

Not for 100 years had England fought a war in continental Europe. Moltke, who in a moment of weakness, had said that if an English Army landed in Germany, it would be arrested, gave a more sober assessment when asked about the English. The English were not a military race, he agreed, "but very war-like."

Later, on August 4 evening, Army depot commanders in England received a telegram kept ready in advance: "Mobilise. Stop. Acknowledge". The Expeditionary Force was planned for 160,000 but millions more would be needed. But they didn't know it then.

On August 14, five years after Bleriot's epic flight, people at Dover and Folkestone saw the exciting spectacle of 37 aircraft, mostly BEs and BE2s flying to France. The RNAS also had 20 machines standing by.

Alfred Leete, one of the Savage Club members and an artist was commissioned to redesign the front cover of the *London Opinion*, a popular weekly. Recruiting was the topic. Leete drew a cartoon of Kitchener, whose pointing of his forefinger stressed the message: "Your country needs you." The War Office secured the right to reproduce it in poster form. Soon it was displayed in every recruiting office.

And so, the Great War began.

The Great War (1914–18)

The first decade of the 20th century saw many radical changes brought about by new ideas, innovations and inventions. Four of them stand out among others — the wireless, the automobile, the aeroplane and the telephone. After 1903, constant attempts were made to make the aeroplane more safe and reliable in flight by giving it more engine power and incorporating control and safety devices in it.

In Britain, the efforts were on only due to individual initiative and enterprise — the Government, the War Office and the Admiralty did not have much faith in this new invention. But individual officers of the Army and Navy were excited at the prospect of being able to fly and many learnt to fly at their own expense.

After the opening of the Suez Canal in 1869, communication between India and England became faster and easier and developments in England made their impact on young officers of the Indian Army. Within the English press in India, news and views began to appear in the newspapers. British officers serving in India would learn to fly at their own expense while on furlough in England. This group of officers became an important component when the new Royal Flying Corps (RFC) came into existence on April 1, 1912, despite opposition from the Army and Navy.

Meanwhile, in India, exactly seven years after the Wright Brothers' epic flight, several crates containing three Bristol Boxkites were unloaded from a ship at Karachi port in December 1910, and were sent by train across India to Calcutta, where the crates were opened and the aeroplanes were assembled and flown. One of these aeroplanes was also flown at the Army manoeuvres in Aurangabad and Jalna in western India in January 1911, which proved the usefulness of an aeroplane as a means of reconnaissance to the Army.

This was followed by the demand for opening a flying school for British officers of the Indian Army which was conceded and a school opened but before the first course could commence in September 1914, World War I had broken out in August.

While the war formally began in 1914, it was already being fought in the Balkans between 1911 and 1913, when the Ottoman Empire subject races in Eastern Europe rose in rebellion and further cut to size the Turkish Sultan's already diminishing hold over these territories. Added to this was the ambition of the Austro-Hungarian Empire which tried to add to its territory by trying to forcibly occupy territories which were once part of the Ottoman Empire.

This was perhaps the main reason why, when Germany and Austria declared war against England and France, Turkey saw an opportunity to take revenge. In the event of a victory for the Central Powers (Germany and Austria), it would get a share of the war spoils and recover some of its colonies in Eastern Europe. Turkey entered the war on the German side in 1915 but it had its repercussions in India's North-West Frontier.

When the war began on August 4, 1914, it was just a war. As it continued and more and more nations got involved, it became "the Great War." After it was over, four bloody years later, historians gave it a new name and that was World War I, a war that ended on November 11, 1918.

The reasons for the outbreak of World War I are many, but two of them stand out. One was the steady loss of control by the Ottoman Empire over its colonies in Eastern Europe and the various revolts by its subject races against Turkish rule. The other reason was colonialism practised by Portugal, Spain, Britain, France, the Netherlands, and Belgium. They had colonies to exploit but Germany had none.

The West European countries had carved out colonies in South and North America, Africa, Middle East, South Asia and the Far East. The only country that had largely been left out was Germany because she was busy with her internal affairs and after 1870, became united and took the name Germany instead of the names of its various Kingdoms. A spirit of nationhood swept the country and nationalism as a binding force made itself felt. What Germany lacked in colonies, she tried to make up by building up her military strength to become the most powerful country in Europe. However, she too had ambitions of carving out colonies in Africa and succeeded to some extent by controlling an area in East Africa which was named Tanganyka. Even this colony was lost after the World War I under the Treaty of Versailles.

When Turkey joined the Central Powers, it sought to take advantage of the situation by helping her German ally by attacking the Suez Canal which was England's lifeline to India and Australia. The attack was beaten back but back in India, especially the North-West, the various tribes grew restless and murmuring of *jehad* began to be heard. As the Turks were defeated in battles, the *jehad* cry became more shrill.

After subduing the tribes and installing a friendly King in Kabul, the British hoped that peace could be maintained within the British territory east of the Durand Line in what they called the unadministered territory. But it was not to be. Turkey's entry into the war gave the disaffected tribesmen an excuse to rise in revolt.

Meanwhile, with the closure of the flying school at Sitapur in UP, there were no aeroplanes left in India as all the pilots and machines had been sent to England and some to Iraq. Since the efficacy of the aeroplane as an instrument for aerial reconnaissance had already been proved at Aurangabad and Jalna in 1911, the Viceroy of India approached the British government to provide a unit of aeroplanes of the Royal Flying Corps to police the entire region of the NWFP and the long border along the Durand Line.

Arms and Equipment

In order to determine whether the proposal to use aircraft on India's North-West Frontier was a viable one, the War Office turned to one of the Indian Army aviators in the UK — the former Captain Pitcher, now serving as Assistant Commandant at the Central Flying School (Upavon, UK) with the rank of Lieutenant Colonel.

On August 28, 1915, Pitcher completed a report detailing "Flying Conditions on the North-West Frontier of India and Suitable Types of Machines for the Same," and this report was forwarded to the India Office. In it, Pitcher outlined many of the difficulties inherent to operations over the Frontier. These included the need to be able to climb to altitudes of between 8,000 and 15,000 ft above sea level; the winds and extremes of temperature typically encountered in the Frontier region; the paucity of suitable landing grounds and the difficulties in supporting aircraft when deployed into the hills.

Aircraft suitable for Frontier operations would need to be capable of a speed of at least 80 miles per hour and should be able to fly from Dargai to Chitral, a round trip of approximately 200 miles, which (together with the time taken to climb and descend) would require the aircraft to be in the air for up to four and a half hours.

For offensive purposes, "the bombs for use against *sangars* and villages and some form of incendiary bomb for the purposes of firing crops would be used." Given the absence of hostile aircraft or anti-aircraft guns, defensive armaments were unnecessary, but rifle fire from the ground would pose a threat and aircraft would, therefore, need to be armoured to some degree.

The limited performance of the aircraft then available led Pitcher to recommend, "Dead weight will have to be kept to a minimum. With an inherently stable machine, there is no real need for an observer. Pilots would need to be provided with a revolver or carbine, iron rations and water in order to give them a chance of finding their way back on foot in case of a forced landing." Pitcher added a grim warning with regard to the possible fate of a downed pilot. Pitcher's report concluded that both the Royal Aircraft Factory BE2C and the RE7 aircraft would, after modification, be suitable for operations over the Frontier. The BE2C was duly selected and in November 1915, 'A' Flight of No. 31 Squadron departed from the UK to India.

First in the Indian Skies (1916-41)

Accordingly, No. 31 Squadron of the RFC was earmarked to be sent to India and that began a new chapter in utilisation of the Air Force to help the Army and to undertake missions for the Army for keeping the tribals under control and ensuring peace, albeit an 'uneasy peace', for the duration of the war and thereafter.

Initially, to meet this request, 'A' Flight of No. 31 Squadron was formed from the nucleus of four officers, 44 other ranks and five BE2C aircraft — all from No. 1 Reserve Squadron, South Farnborough, on October 11, 1915. The first Commanding Officer (CO) of this new squadron was Captain C R McDonald. An aircraft park to support the squadron was also planned, comprising one officer and 35 other ranks.

Both the groups moved to Liverpool and sailed by the SS *Elysia* for India via the Cape of Good Hope for India, arriving at Bombay on December 26, 1915.

They moved to Naushera and shortly thereafter, three BE2Cs were assembled in January 1916, and the first flight was made by Captain McDonald on January 20, flying a BE2C No. 445.

This was a Red Letter Day for India because Captain McDonald's BE2C was the very first military aeroplane to be seen in the Indian skies and his squadron, No. 31, was the first military aviation unit to serve in support of the Army in Frontier operations in north-west India.

Five days later, Lieutenant Hughes tested the BE's ability to climb in the rarefied atmosphere of the Indian skies and reached a height of 7,000 ft. On February 8, 1916, two of the squadron's pilots performed the first loops ever witnessed on the Frontier and in the Indian skies.

At a Durbar held in Peshawar during the same month, two BEs were demonstrated before a gathering of all the assembled tribal chiefs. At first, the tribesmen were inclined to disbelieve that these iron birds could be controlled by any human, but on being shown the cockpits and watching the two pilots in action, many of the chiefs were openly dismayed that their future raiding sorties across the Afghan border into India were obviously going to be clearly observed from the air.

Flying Operations

Meanwhile, in England, six BE2Cs were withdrawn from No. 22 Squadron at Gosport and, with a nucleus of airmen from this unit's 'A' Flight, were designated 'B' Flight, No. 31 Squadron, and earmarked for immediate embarkation to India on January 18, 1916. The aircraft were embarked on February 4, followed by the personnel on February 9. Reaching India, 'B' Flight joined up with 'A' Flight, which on March 1, had moved from Naushera to Risalpur, an established Army cavalry depot. By the end of April 1916, lack of accommodation at Risalpur had meant another move of base and, 'A' Flight flew to Murree with aircraft strength of 10 BE2Cs. On March 27, 1916, Major C R Bradley was appointed in command of No. 31 Squadron and was responsible for the aircraft park nominally, says air historian Chaz Bowyer in the *Cross and Cockade Journal*.

To bring the squadron up to full strength, 'C' Flight of No. 31 Squadron was formed by VI Brigade and embarked on May 10, 1916, arriving in Bombay on June 17, from where they moved upcountry to join 'A' Flight at Murree on July 4. On July 29, 'B' Flight arrived from Risalpur and No. 31 Squadron became complete. Now that necessary personnel and aircraft were being made available by October 5, the entire squadron of three flights returned to Risalpur along with the aircraft park.

The early days of operations proved frustrating in that local temperatures of the order of 112°F in the shade tended to restrict all flying to a few hours after dawn. Any attempt to fly later in the day merely resulted in overheated engines and consequent loss of power. It was necessary to place rush mats over the aircraft wings when parked in the open if violent warping of wing structures was to be avoided. Actual flying was a laborious business, e.g. one BE with the usual two-man crew took some 15 minutes to climb its first 1,000 ft of height, though thereafter, performance slowly improved. Dust storms made maintenance a thankless chore.

Mohamand Operations

The first operation commenced in October 1916. The Mohamand tribes carried out trans-border raids into the Peshawar area. A blockade line comprising a series of block houses connected by a wire fence was constructed and manned. During this construction, four BEs of 'A' Flight carried out air cover patrols along the whole Frontier from Michni to Abazai, commencing October 27, 1916. The 'B' Flight aircraft repeated this procedure on the following day.

On November 13 and 14, air reconnaissance revealed a strong *lashkar* of 6,000 tribesmen concentrated near Hafiz Kor, threatening Shabqadar. From Jalal Kor to Hafiz Kor, these hostile tribes had piqueted every worthwhile high piece of ground with some 50 to 100 men on each vantage point. The 1st and 2nd Infantry Brigades of the 1st Peshawar Division under the command of Major General Sir F Campbell, plus a proportion of Frontier Militia and Constabulary, were concentrated on the blockade line and orders were issued for an attack on November 15. This ground attack was carried into the foothills near Hafiz and by 4 pm, the *lashkar* had been scattered and broken up.

Twelve aircraft from Risalpur, using Shabqadar as their forward landing ground, cooperated with ground troops throughout the day. Operations commenced with wireless equipped BEs searching for tribesmen and then ranging artillery guns onto their targets. The 74th Howitzer Battery engaged nine such targets during the day, immediately dispersing each group of tribal hostiles. Similar cooperation was given by the BEs to the 16th Royal Field Artillery.

During the afternoon of November 15, three BEs armed with Lewis guns attacked a variety of tribal targets from some 800 ft, whilst four other BEs loaded with 20 lb bombs harassed enemy formations and encampments in the hills. All aircraft returned safely, although many were riddled with rifle fire damage — the hill tribesman being no mean exponent with his rifle, having been taught since childhood that marksmanship was a fighting man's first necessary accomplishment.

An early reconnaissance next morning reported a significant decrease in tribal strength and the 74th Howitzer Battery was called up to disperse the remaining few groups. During the afternoon, three aircraft bombed the village of Martin Kale, dropping 19x20 lb bombs, 15 of which were seen to fall on the village.

Throughout the two days of operations, some 440 small arms and ammunition were fired and 59x20 bombs dropped. Further reconnaissance on November 17, 18 and 19, revealed no enemy presence and all aircraft were permitted to return to Risalpur. Their work was specially commended by the General Officer Commanding (GOC) General Campbell.

For the remainder of 1916, an uneasy 'peace' prevailed along the Frontier, and No. 31 Squadron continued the routine of training, with particular attention being paid to wireless cooperation with artillery guns at Naushera and the Akora Artillery Camp. By the end of 1916, No. 31Squadron's strength stood at 28 officers and 84 other ranks.

The year 1917 opened quietly on the Frontier. No. 31 Squadron began extending its activities by utilising forward landing strips at a variety of locations, including Bannu, Tank, Dera Ismael Khan and Khost. 'A' Flight, under the command of Captain Cooper was detached for duty with the Bannu and Derajat Brigades. Their arrival in the area created an immense impression among the local tribes of North Waziristan and Khost who had previously doubted the rumours of these 'iron birds'.

A *lashkar* of Mahsuds, estimated at some 2,000 had been reported as approaching Tank, from where a reconnaissance was made of the Frontier line forts, both visually and photographically. 'A' Flight moved to Dera Ismael Khan on February 5, and from there continued to reconnoitre the surrounding territory. Eventually, on February 11, this flight returned to Risalpur.

Destruction from the Skies

When aircraft first appeared on the Frontier in early 1916, no one among the tribals would believe that the *firangi* could fly. In January 1917, when 'A' Flight of No. 31 Squadron took to the air to disperse a *lashkar* of 2,000 Mahsuds in Bannu, the Political Agent of the district reported that the arrival of aircraft caused a 'stupendous' effect on the beliefs commonly held among the Frontier tribes, among them being:

- That the aeroplanes did not exist at all.
- That if they did, they were exclusively manned by Germans.
- That the preparation of forced landing grounds was a bluff.
- That no one but an expert could even sit in a machine.

These beliefs were soon dispelled and several thousand tribesmen saw machines land and take-off with the Political Agent whom they all knew and recognised, as a passenger.

Comments from tribesmen were to this effect: "The day of judgment has arrived — the Afghan Government is now nothing better than a pack of cards — the day of the robbers and outlaws is over."

— History of No.31 Squadron, RFC/RAF, 1917.

Iron Birds Perching

After several raids by tribals for looting weapons and kidnapping in the cantonment areas of Risalpur and other places, the authorities made arrangements for several tribal chiefs to visit Risalpur and see the aeroplanes, which were their chief antagonists, presumably in order to impress the tribesmen with the "awful" power of the white "Raj" (rule).

"One chief enquired, particularly in one of the hangars, where he was genuinely astounded to find that there were no facilities for the 'iron birds' to 'perch' at night (in the manner of feathered varieties). When it was explained to him that the 'birds' never perched, he remarked that in an earlier raid, his men had been told specifically to fire at upper parts of the hangars in order to destroy these birds on their 'perches', but went on in good humour to say that next time they would shoot low."

— Chaz Bowyer, *The Flying Elephants*, 1972.

Contrast this with today (2010). Today, they (actually their fifth or sixth generation descendants) are armed with Stinger missiles, howitzers, rocket launchers and AK47s and the deadly RDX and state-of-the-art communication equipment.

News was received that a large *lashkar* was on the move towards Sarawakai, a garrison post manned by the South Waziristan Militia. At the request of the Chief Commissioner, two aircraft were detached to Tank on March 2, a third aircraft joining them four days later. After the usual cooperation with the ground forces, all three aircraft returned to Risalpur on March 15. During April, in connection with the continued construction of the border blockade line, reconnaissance flights were carried out daily along the Mohamand tribal borders.

On May 5, 1917, three BE2Cs were detached from 'B' Flight to Tank to cooperate with the forces of Derajat Command. Daily recces were flown and on May 12, a large encampment was discovered close to the source of Tor Masnda Nala. One BE dived and fired five drums of Lewis ammunition among some 1,000 Mahsuds who scattered into the hills. One pilot, having exhausted his Lewis ammunition, dived to tree top level and dispersed a group of about 100 tribesmen by firing his service revolver. On the following day, 8x20 lb bombs were dropped on this encampment, four direct hits being observed. A reconnaissance on May 14 revealed no sign of the enemy. Three more aircraft were sent on May 19 to Tank and on May 21 and 22, five of these aircraft cooperated with a column of infantry in escorting a convoy from Murtala via Nili Kach to Kanukri Kach. A wireless ground set strapped on the back of a camel kept them in communication with the GOC. May 23 saw the command of the No. 31 Squadron pass into the hands of Major Hutcheson.

The 'B' Flight at Tank was relieved by 'C' Flight on May 31, in time for imminent operations in the Khaisara area. As a preliminary, the whole area west of Jandola was photographed, some 200 plates being exposed in all and a map was drawn and delivered by air to the GOC, Waziristan South Field Force, at Jandola. The actual operations started on June 20 when 'C' Flight harassed tribesmen with bombs and machine gun fire, bombing Lalrazai and destroying several crop fields. On June 24, four aircraft with high explosives and incendiary bombs flew up the Khaisara Valley in advance of an infantry column and set several villages ablaze. Among others, Shinghai village in Takhi Zam, and Baddar Toi, near Kaniguram, were bombed.

A particularly successful raid was flown on June 26, when nine direct hits were observed on Makin and six more on Marobi, home of Mullah Fazel Din, titular chief of the Mahsuds. At Kaniguram, one bomb killed 12 men and wounded many others and destroyed cattle. These bombing attacks were a major factor in bringing the tribesmen to terms and on June 27, orders were issued to cease such operations, while peace terms were discussed.

On August 1, 1917, a fully representative *jirgah* of 3,000 Mahsuds ratified the Government's terms of peace settlement and two days later, 'peace' became official. Dispersal of ground troops to their normal stations began at Jandola on August 12, but 'C' Flight of No. 31 Squadron remained at Tank until August 18, before finally flying to Risalpur. While their influence on these operations had been decisive, it had been at the expense of many of the flight personnel falling sick with sandfly fever and sunstroke and thereby, reducing the maintenance teams.

Baluchistan Erupts

On July 22, a new commander for the squadron, Major R G H Murray, MC, took over and the remainder of 1917 was taken up by an intensive training programme, which included wireless practice, photographic reconnaissance, message carrying, camera obscura, cross-country and formation flying and more artillery observation practice.

In addition, many recces were flown seeking out fresh possible landing strips for future use. In September 1917, several BE2Cs, 2Es and Henri Farmans were hived off No. 31 Squadron to form a new unit, No. 114 Squadron at Lahore. The parent unit could certainly afford the losses, having at the time an aircraft strength of 34 Henri Farmans, 26 BE2Cs and 2Es, one Maurice Farman on 'trials' and some

FE2Bs. On December 31, 1917, the squadron suffered its first fatal casualty when a pilot completed a loop in a BE and then attempted a second loop. The starboard wings folded back alongside the fuselage and the BE spun into the ground, killing its pilot and mechanic.

At the start of 1918, the Frontier was relatively quiet apart from the normal trans-border raiding skirmishes which constituted almost a way of life for the tribal inhabitants. Throughout January, No. 31 Squadron spent most of its time in photographing all the airfields and possible forward landing grounds, while in the following months various methods of artillery cooperation were tried. One experiment utilised the klaxon horn signalling and on February 26, one aircraft ranged two batteries simultaneously by this method.

The training routine was soon to be interrupted, however, due to general unrest in Baluchistan among the Marri tribes, culminating in an abortive attack on Gumbaz Fort on February 19 and 20. On March 7, the Khetran tribes, assisted and encouraged by the Marris, burned Government buildings at Barkhan and looted the local treasury. To cooperate with the local ground forces, one BE2C and one BE2E were detached to Sibi, one 2C and 2E to Duki and five BE2Cs were posted to Dera Ghazi Khan.

Towards the end of February, daily reconnaissances revealed no sign of the hostiles. On March 1, however, an urgent message was received at Sibi airfield that some 3,000 Marris were approaching Sibi from some 155 miles away at Chandia. A BE was hastily loaded with four 20 lb bombs, a Lewis gun and six drums of ammunition and immediately flown to Chandia — only to discover that the 'uprising' was no more than a tribal sports and horse race meeting.

The potential danger from the Marri tribe continued to threaten the peace of the Frontier and on March 13, two aircraft were called to bomb the village of Rakhni and a gathering of rebel tribesmen around Bawatta Post. The main offensive for the RFC opened on March 15 when Vitakri was successfully bombed. Daily bombings of Kahan, capital of the Marri district, was ordered by the General Headquarters (GHQ) staff on March 22, 1918.

High winds and frequent dust storms prevented any air action until March 24 when a 112 lb and two 20 lb bombs were dropped. As the first 20 lb bomb was dropped, some 200 Marris were seen to rapidly evacuate the village and the 112 lb bomb was dropped amongst them, killing at least 14 and seriously wounding many others. Kahan was once again bombed on March 29 when ten 20 lb bombs were dropped on the village, causing considerable building damage.

By the end of the month, most sections of the Khetrans had surrendered, leaving only the 'hard core Marris' still in dispute. An advance on Kahan by ground forces was, therefore, ordered. One BE bombed Kahan on April 3 and then, no further air support being required, three detachments returned to Risalpur on April 17. Kahan was occupied without opposition on April 19 and by May 7, the Marris had surrendered unconditionally. It was virtually the last uprising during 1918 and the RAF support had been of extreme value in bringing it to a satisfactory conclusion.

By September 1918, the headquarters and two flights of No. 31 Squadron were still stationed at Risalpur, the third flight being detached to Khampurk. The temporary commander was Captain O. Hughes who eventually handed over the reins to Major E L Miller on December 1, 1918. November 11, 1918, brought the Armistice in Europe, but this event held little significance to the RAF on India's North-West Frontier.

In the same month, two awards of DFCs were announced for No. 31 Squadron's pilots, and at the end of November, a total of 34 officers was shown as on the strength of the squadron, before the toll of demobilisation reduced its numbers. No. 114 Squadron was still at Lahore by Christmas 1918, although this was its nominal location, its three flights being all on detachment, one flight going to Aden.

No. 31 Squadron had been the nucleus of air power on the Indian continent, being the first in the Indian skies. This honour of being a pioneer was reflected in the badge and motto "First in the Indian Skies" of the squadron.

"Its task throughout World War I was to become virtually a microcosm of the RAF's later tasks from 1918 to 1947 — attempting to keep the peace along the wild and constantly turbulent North-West border of India."

— Chaz Bowyer, "Wings Over India,"
Cross and Cockade Journal, United Kingdom.

The Chequered Years Ahead

The Native Syndrome

Within the British establishment, Whitehall, the War Office and the Air Council, one common thread was predominant and that was that in the order of precedence, the British Army was superior and the Army of India was one step lower. This was evident from the practice which began at Sandhurst where cadets at the admission stage were earmarked for the Indian Army. These cadets were quite often English and white sons of retired Indian Army officers.

Looking back at this distance in time now (2010), reference to the British Army and Indian Army needs an explanation, for the difference between the two was a fundamental factor in the social and military life of imperial India.

There were two distinct bodies of armed soldiers in India at that time: first, large detachments of the British Army and, second, the whole of the Indian Army. Of the British Army, there were some 48 battalions of infantry, four regiments of cavalry and a host of artillery. They were British throughout.

The Indian Army was about three times the size of the British forces in the country. Its soldiers and NCOs were Indians, while the officer corps was mainly British and was gradually being nationalised by commissioning Indians. The whole establishment, British and Indian together, was known as the Army in India and was ruled by a Commander-in-Chief (C-in-C), selected alternatively from the British and Indian Armies.

Even those cadets who were meant for the Indian Army were English and the reference to the selection of C-in-C alternatively from the two parts meant in effect that either of the two filling up the top slot would be an English officer. But here, too, was a sophisticated kind of 'caste system'. British officers from the Indian establishment were considered one step lower on the military's social scale.

This was abundantly clear in the system, whereby, everyone commissioned from Sandhurst had to spend one year as a subaltern attached to a British regiment. Thus, John Masters who passed out of Sandhurst in 1934 and was earmarked for the Indian Army, had to spend one year with the 1st Battalion of the Duke of Cornwall's Light Infantry, before he was absorbed as an officer in the 2nd Battalion of the IV Gurkha Rifles of the Indian Army.

Recalling his days in the Indian Army, John Masters says, "Some British regiments treated their attached Indian Army subalterns like dirt. One even made them sit at a separate table in the mess.

"These poor fellows spent a miserable year, but obtained revenge the night the regiment had a local General as a guest of honour.

"The General, seated at the Colonel's right at the main table, asked in a whisper who the young men (at a separate table) in exile were.

"The Colonel said: 'Oh, those are Indian Army people'.

"The General said: 'What a coincidence! So am I!' and joined them."

This gulf can further be explained by another episode during the tenure of Lord Kitchener as the Commander-in-Chief of the Indian Army. It was his fond hope that more facilities would be opened up in India to professionalise the officer corps which at that time was entirely English.

So it was argued that instead of sending officers all the way from India to the Staff College in England, why not set up a Staff College in India. His proposal was approved by the Government, but he was in such a hurry that he ordered the setting up of the college in 1905 at Deolali in Western India.

The Staff College shifted to Quetta, once all the buildings had been constructed in 1907. Here, Major General (Air Vice Marshal) Sir Sefton Brancker takes up the narrative:

"Our Commandant, (at Deolali in 1906) was Colonel Thomson Capper who was later killed leading his division in France in 1915. He was one of the most gallant, devoted and able men I have ever met. Lord Kitchener was the Commander-in-Chief in India at the time and the Indian Staff College was one of his 'ewe-lambs'.

"A discussion arose with the Home Authorities as to whether a certificate given at the new Indian Staff College should rank equally with that obtained in the old and well-established institution at Home.

"Red-tape at the War Office said that equality was impossible; India asked why; the War Office indicated that students at the Indian college could not have the advantage of visiting the modern battlefields of Europe — the fields of 1870 — to wit.

"'Oh!' said Lord Kitchener, 'really! But my students are going to see the battlefields of 1904-05 in Manchuria" and it was my good fortune to go with Colonel Capper as one of the party of 20 Staff College students on a tour round the Manchurian battlefields in 1907.'

"Though the officers in question were all English or of European descent, as they had the 'Indian' label attached to them, they were treated as second class citizens."

— John Masters, *Bugles and the Tiger*, 1956.

— Norman Macmillan, *Sir Sefton Brancker*, 1935.

Which Staff College is Better

In 1926, Captain J W Slim* was selected for the Staff College course at Quetta. Commenting on this, Major General G C Evans says in his book, *Slim As A Military Commander*, "The annual intake of students at Quetta was about half that of the Staff College, Camberley (UK), and for that reason, they were of the opinion that they benefitted more from the course, whilst the Directing Staff, because of the smaller numbers, came to know individuals well and were able to form a better judgment of their ability."

But in the period between the wars, at both establishments, more was expected of the students than mere military capability. There was a diehard fetish for hunting, polo and hard ball games, and it was felt that unless one took active part in these sports, one's chances of becoming an efficient staff officer were remote. Such statements as 'good rider to hounds' or 'always found in the van' appeared in officers' confidential reports, accomplishments which were presumably considered to be some of the finer characteristics of a good staff officer.

Here Slim was at a disadvantage. He was an indifferent horseman and hunting did not appeal to him; nor did he show an aptitude for games. In fact, he did not do the things that were expected of a Staff College student and it is said, the Commandant was in some doubt when he came to writing Slim's report.

But in the end, the Commandant decided that on sheer merit alone, Slim deserved the highest grading and this he was given.

The blemish of 'Indian' attached to British officers of the Indian Army can be seen in the following comment: "Although he represented the Indian Army, nobody regarded him merely in that capacity and I know that his standing as an instructor (now at the Staff College, Camberely) was very high indeed among his contemporaries." This comment came from a fellow instructor General Sir Archibald Nye, Vice Chief of the Imperial General Staff.

*General Sir William Slim, General Officer Commanding-in-Chief, XIV Army in Burma.

White Indians in RAF

Those Englishmen whose families served in India through generations felt a certain kind of kinship with India as a badge of honour. The moment they heard of a new invention or an innovation in England, or even a facility granted in the UK, they also wanted it in India.

From India's point of view (the native point of view), no one thought about the aspirations of the people, and even the various demands put up by Indian political leaders on Indianisation of the officer corps, although promised by King George V at the Delhi Durbar in 1911, were carried out at a snail's pace with a bit of a spurt due to the exigencies of the Great War.

However, as soon as the war was over, even though one batch of Indians was commissioned as officers, further advance came practically to a halt as the bureaucrats and policy-makers in Whitehall decided that there was now no need to hurry. After repeated reminders by Indian leaders in and out of the Viceroy's Council and in the Central Legislative Assembly, a half-hearted scheme was presented to ostensibly satisfy Indian aspirations.

This was the eight-unit scheme, whereby Indians holding the King's Commission could only command troops in the battalions of the eight regiments of the Indian Army and nowhere else. For instance, from the beginning, no Indian officer could be posted to a battalion of the ten Gurkha regiments of the Indian Army. That was exclusively reserved for British officers.

This was carried to such an extent that when World War II broke out and the 2/4 Battalion of the Gurkha Rifles was posted to the war zone in Iraq in 1941, Major John Masters, then Adjutant of the battalion, was surprised to receive an Indian Medical Officer posted to his battalion by the Army Headquarters in India. Until then, even Medical Officers in Gurkha regiments had to be British.

This was also the case with the Indian Central Flying School which the Indian Government had paid for and had instructors for it from the Indian Army, who had learnt to fly at their own expense. By 1918, the Government of India did not attempt to resurrect its pre-war proposal for the formation of an Indian Flying Corps although, the RFC (later the RAF) had absolutely no objection to the formation of an Australian Flying Corps and recruiting Canadians and New Zealanders directly into the RFC/RAF during the war and even after. The only exception was India.

Once, during the course of the 1914-18 War, it was clear to the aviators belonging to the Indian Army (five of them, all British) that the War Office had supported the flat refusal of the RAF for the Indian Army to have its own air arm, these five who performed exceptionally well, went their separate ways.

Perhaps, the seniors must have been disappointed. They were still held onto the strength of their respective regiments. Massey returned to the 29th Punjabis in 1917; Hoare, though he served in the RFC/RAF for the duration of the war, opted to return to the Indian Army and retired in 1923 as a Brigadier General.

The remaining three former Indian Army officers pursued careers in the post-war peace-time RAF. Pitcher retired as an Air Commodore in 1929 and Reilly in 1934. However, the most significant post-war career was that of Cyril Newall. After holding a series of senior appointments at home, Sir Cyril Newall served as the Chief of the Air Staff of the RAF between 1937 and 1940.

He had been an officer of the 2nd Gurkha Rifles and a Flying Instructor at the Indian Central Flying School, Sitapur, in 1913-14.

Colour Bar Issues

All Indian Army officers who participated as pilots in World War I were of European rather than Indian descent. Nevertheless, due to the exigencies of war, the RFC did recruit five ethnic Indian military pilots out of whom four took part in the air war as officers of the RFC/RAF rather than the Indian Army.

The prevailing policy of the War Office prior to World War I was to deny commissions to applicants not of 'pure European descent' on the grounds that "a British private will never follow a half-caste or a native officer." A similar stance was also adopted by the Admiralty.

However, the pressure of war led to a gradual loosening of this policy on the part of the War Office, and the first Anglo-Indian candidate (W O'C Evans) was admitted to the Royal Military Academy, Woolwich, in November 1916. In the same month, on November 6, 1916, Jeejeebhoy Piroshaw Bomanjee Jeejeebhoy became the first Indian commissioned in the General List for duty with the RFC with the rank of temporary honorary 2nd Lieutenant. He was followed by four other Indians into the RFC.

On September 23, 1918, the Secretary of the Air Council, W A Robinson circulated a minute prepared by Major General Sir Sefton Brancker — now Master General of Personnel — with regard to the "proposed recruitment of pilots from India."

In this minute, Brancker drew the attention of the Air Council to an increasing shortfall in the number of candidates for flying training and the emerging overcapacity in the RAF's training facilities — particularly those in Egypt and Canada.

While the Australian government had already been approached with regard to the training of Australian applicants in Egypt, Brancker now suggested, "We should now start training carefully selected Indians from the fighting forces of India. I am convinced that they would make excellent pilots and would be quite trustworthy except, perhaps, in their own country."

This memorandum was considered by the Air Council on September 26, 1918. Brancker opened the discussion by referring to correspondence he had already received from General Cox of the India Office, in which the latter had suggested that "Indians would make excellent pilots in view of their keen sight and their abstinence and general temperament." He thought that if the conditions of service were favourable, the India Office would agree, and suggested that an official letter on the subject should be sent. "Brancker went on to emphasise that a previous experiment in this direction had proved very successful, and that really good material was available to be drawn upon."

Despite his enthusiasm, Brancker's minute got only a grudging approval from the Air Council. Major General Sir Hugh Trenchard "deprecated the proposal but noted that in view of the present day conditions in India, the proposal was one which might have to be accepted — if so, it would be wise to take the lead and get the scheme on the right lines."

Major General Sir Geoffrey Paine, the Inspector General, called for the recruiting of Indian observers and pilots, as it would be impossible to have an English observer with an Indian pilot.

In conclusion, the Secretary of State, Lord Weir, thought the proposal followed the lines of the policy for India. There would be no need to bring it before the War Cabinet, but the outlines of the scheme should be very carefully laid down in a letter to the India Office.

On October 2, 1918, a letter informing the Secretary of State for India that the question of employing Indians as pilots and observers in the RAF, had lately been considered, was sent to the Secretary of the India Office on behalf of the Air Council. It went on to propose:

"If the Secretary of State for India is agreeable to select 100 Indians of good family and high physical qualifications for training as pilots or observers in Egypt, these gentlemen would be enlisted into the Air Force on the same terms in all respects which British personnel obtained for the same purpose.

"Whilst under instruction, they should be graded as cadets, and after successful completion of their course, they would be granted temporary commissions in the RAF, either as pilots or observers and it is proposed that they be considered as available for service in any part of the world. If at any point in their training they prove unsatisfactory, they would be returned to India."

Indianisation: Objections

The Air Council's proposal was forwarded to the Viceroy of India, Lord Chelmsford, and his Government by the India Office in a telegram sent on October 7, 1918.

It was rejected in a telegram sent by the Government of India on November 1, 1918. In a second telegram dated November 9, 1918, "Lord Chelmsford's Government explained at length their objection to the employment of Indians in the RAF and other technical services of the Army."

To secure the maintenance of British supremacy in the event of internal disturbance (with the 1857 events in mind), the Government of India had pursued for many years past, a policy, the cardinal points of which had been the retention of artillery in British hands, the maintenance of a fixed ratio of British to Indian troops, and the permanent occupation by British garrisons of strategic points and that in their opinion, *post bellum* conditions would not permit any relaxation of these precautions, at any rate in the near future.

They pointed out that the number of Indians in the country with a military training would be largely increased on demobilisation, and that the danger of the revolutionary spirit, which had lately swept over Russia, spreading to some extent among Indians, could not be overlooked.

Ordinary prudence, they observed, demanded the continuance of the policy hitherto followed, and its application as a natural corollary to the RAF and other scientific and technical services which had attained a high degree of development in the course of the war.

They, therefore, recommended that all positions assigned to officers and those allotted to skilled NCOs and men, other than workshop ratings, should be filled entirely by Europeans in the following services:

- Royal Air Force.
- Royal Artillery other than Frontier Garrison Artillery and Indian Mountain Artillery.

- Royal Engineers other than Indian Sapper and Miner units
- Trench Howitzer units.
- Machine Gun Corps including Armoured Motor Batteries other than Frontier Brigades.
- Wireless telegraphs whether in the Indian Telegraph Department or in the Signal service.

The objections raised by the Indian Government were relayed by the India Office to the Air Ministry in a letter dated December 24, 1918. By this stage, support within the Air Ministry itself for the recruitment of Indian officers had waned.

With the end of hostilities, the RAF's requirements for pilots and observers had eased markedly; moreover, in January 1919, the primary advocate of Indian recruitment in the Air Ministry, Sir Sefton Brancker, retired from the RAF. As a result, the Air Council accepted the Government of India's objections without protest and chose not to press further the case for recruitment of Indians.

However, the prevailing conditions in India alluded to by Trenchard in September 1918, would result in a dramatic change with regard to the question of the admission of Indians to the RAF.

The immediate post-war period was marked by growing demands within India for democratic reform. Some very limited steps towards broadening the franchise and increasing Indian representation in the country's provincial and central legislative councils had been taken prior to the outbreak of war.

However, the "invaluable loyalty" shown by India during the war itself — combined with "a commitment to gradual political devolution" — led the British Government to acknowledge what they saw as India's "maturing status" and value within the Empire. One sign of this acknowledgement was an "announcement of the goal of British policy in India" made on August 20, 1917, by Edwin Montagu, Secretary of State for India. The 'Montagu Declaration' committed the British Government to achieving "the increasing association of Indians in every branch of administration, and the gradual development of self-governing institutions with a view to the progressive realisation of responsible government in India as part of the British Empire."

The internal unrest that erupted in India in 1919 (due to the Jallianwala massacre), did not result in the armed insurrection feared by the Government of India.

Nevertheless, the end of World War I did mark a watershed in the struggle for Indian independence as Indian nationalists sought to move beyond the largely cosmetic changes wrought by the Government of India Act and make real the promise of democratic self-government advanced by the Montagu Declaration.

The first tangible change occurred as a result of a decision by the War Council in 1917 to allow ten places each year at Sandhurst to the natives of India, as well as the granting of permanent King's Commission to twenty deserving Indian officers on Viceroy Commissions, and temporary commissions to a further 200 Indians.

However, the War Office did not envisage that those Indians granted King's Commissions would serve as King's Commission Officers (KCOs) in the fullest sense.

In response to an enquiry from the Permanent Secretary at the Admiralty, the War Office's Director of Staff Duties wrote in December 1918, "We are taking Indians into the Royal Military College for training for commissions in the Indian Army only. It is not correct to say that 'there is no position in His Majesty's Army for which the Indian will in future be debarred' by reason of his race, for we are not going to let Indians command white men in British Regiments."

Army in India Committee

In 1919, an "Army in India Committee" led by Lord Esher was appointed by the Secretary of State for India "to enquire into and report upon the administration and, where necessary, the organisation of the Army in India, including its relations with the War Office and the India Office and the relations of the two offices to each other."

On this committee's report, American military strategist and writer Stephen Cohen says that while paying lip-service to the 1917 declaration on the future status of India, the committee proposed little which would have actually led to an Indian officer corps.

The question of Indianisation was, in fact, evaded except in the minutes by the two Indian members — Sir Krishna G Gupta and Sir Umar Hayat Khan. In his minute, the former called for a series of reforms to the structure and administration of India's armed forces, the first of which was that "the superior ranks of every branch of the Army, including the Artillery, Air Force, Engineers, Transport and Supplies, etc should be freely open to qualified Indians, and for this purpose, the number of King's Commissions to be given to the Indians should be materially increased every year."

This minute was of significance to the RAF in two respects. First, it would mark the first formal call for commissioning of Indians into the RAF; as such, it can be regarded as the point at which the RAF entered the Indianisation debate. Second, it is indicative of the failure on the part of Indian politicians and nationalist leaders, both within and outside the Legislative Assembly, to recognise the existence of the RAF as a separate service, rather than a specialist arm of the British and Indian Armies.

The reason for this confusion was that unlike in the rest of the British Empire, in India, the RAF was not an independent service even as the Royal Indian Marine was not, though the British Government, in its wisdom, had placed the RAF and the RIN in India under the control of the Commander-in-Chief of the Indian Army.

The Esher Committee report was presented to the British Parliament and was also considered by the Indian Legislative Assembly. On

March 7, 1921, a resolution was moved in the Assembly that called for the appointment of a Select Committee to consider the Esher Report and submit its findings before March 21. This resolution was accepted by the Government of India and a 15-member committee led by Sir Tej Bahadur Sapru was duly formed.

The Select Committee reported its conclusions in the form of fifteen draft resolutions for the Legislative Assembly. These were subsequently introduced in the Assembly by one of the members of the Select Committee, Sir P S Shivaswamy Aiyer. These resolutions, therefore, "present a clear picture of what sophisticated Indian moderates and liberals wanted on defence matters."

The debate in the Legislative Assembly took place but due to the absence of several members, the Government lost its majority in the House. After attempting to modify the resolutions by amendment, it gave up and accepted them almost *in toto*.

As a consequence, on March 28, 1921, the Shivaswamy Aiyer resolutions were passed by the Assembly. One of the most controversial of the resolutions introduced was Resolution No.7. Part A of this resolution required:

- That the King Emperor's Indian subjects should be freely admitted to all arms of His Majesty's military, naval and air forces in India and the auxiliary services and the auxiliary forces.
- That every encouragement should be given to Indians, including the educated middle classes, subject to the prescribed standard of fitness, to enter the commissioned ranks of the Army, and that in nominating candidates for the entrance examination, unofficial Indians should be associated with the nominating authority, and in granting King's Commissions, after giving full regard to the claims in promotion of officers of the Indian Army who already hold the commission of His Excellency, the Viceroy, the rest of the commissions granted should be given to cadets trained at Sandhurst.

- The general rule in selecting candidates for this training should be that a large majority of selections should be from the communities which furnish recruits and as far as possible in proportion to the numbers in which they furnish such recruits.

Although Resolution No.7 was concerned primarily with removing the obstacles that prevented Indians from gaining King's Commissions in the Indian Army, it also called for RAF recruiting conditions to be lifted for units in India. On accepting this resolution, the Government of India also gave an undertaking that "we would endeavour to secure for Indian subjects the privilege which was demanded on their behalf by the Legislative Assembly."

Accordingly, in a dispatch to the Secretary of State for India on September 1, 1921, the Government of India raised three questions, which are inter-allied: the admission of Indians into commissioned ranks of the RAF for service in India; granting of commissions to Indians as artillery and engineering officers; and the possibility of increasing the number of cadetships reserved for Indian cadets.

Indian Government's Arguments

The Government of India argued in support of all these proposals. With regard to the commissioning of Indians in the RAF, it began by citing the Air Ministry's own suggestion of three years earlier that 100 Indians should be selected for pilot training and go on to serve as RAF officers.

While acknowledging that this had been rebuffed by the then Viceroy and his administration, it pointed out that "great changes have taken place, consequent upon the passing of the Government of India Act, in the form of the government of this country. Public opinion has been directed more and more towards securing for Indians equal rights, with other citizens of the Empire, in the matter of their admission to all arms of His Majesty's services."

It went on, "It is true that our acceptance of this proposal is diametrically opposed to the views stated in November 1918. We have, however, examined the question afresh, and are satisfied that the time has come for making a distinct step forward and for recognising the rights of Indians to serve in all branches of the naval, military and air forces of their own country, subject only to their attainment of the requisite standard of efficiency.

"Moreover, we do not endorse the views put forward by Lord Chelmsford's Government in 1918 regarding the danger to British supremacy which would result from the admission of Indians into the Royal Air Force. We do not, of course, contemplate that the RAF in India should be officered entirely, or even mainly, by Indians, and it would be easy to guard against this possibility by imposing definite limitations on the numbers of those commissioned.

"We cannot, however, see that any danger is likely to result from the admission of a limited number of duly qualified Indian gentlemen as officers in the RAF for service in India."

Drawing a parallel with the Indian candidates for King's Commissions in the Indian Army, the Government of India stipulated that "Indians desiring commissions in the RAF should undergo the same training and receive education as British candidates for similar commissions."

Should these recommendations prove acceptable, the Secretary of State was requested to move the RAF authorities to permit a limited number of suitable Indian lads being sent Home for training in the RAF.

RAF's Recruitment Policy

This volte-face on the part of the Government of India was forwarded by the India Office to the Air Ministry for comment in 1921. However, the Air Ministry's own policy towards recruitment of non-European personnel had also shifted since 1919.

The commissioning of Indians in the RFC had not represented a change to the rules governing British military recruitment policy, but was rather a war-time 'expedient' adopted for a handful of Indian volunteers then resident in the UK. While the demands of war had obliged Britain's armed forces to relax their peace-time recruiting policies, the post-war period saw a return to earlier practices.

For the RAF which had not existed prior to 1918, this meant the adoption of the 'pure European descent' criteria used by the other two services. Although, the first RAF recruiting instructions issued in 1919 made no reference to the ethnicity of the candidates, an Air Ministry weekly order promulgated in July 1921 required that with the exception of boys, recruits must be of pure European descent and the sons of natural-born or naturalised British subjects.

Subsequently, even the exception granted to boys was abandoned; the first recruiting regulations to be issued in codified form as an Air Publication (AP 948) stated that "recruits, including boys, must be of pure European descent and the sons of natural born or naturalised British subjects.

"In no case will a recruit who does not fulfill the above conditions be sent forward for attestation."

Similarly, the membership of the Auxiliary Air Force and the RAF Special Reserve was also opened only to those of pure European descent. In an article published to mark the release of regulations relating to the Auxiliary Air Force and RAF Special Reserve, the *Flight Magazine* observed that "it would not be astonishing if the colour bar regulations aroused protests from India at the next Imperial Conference, seeing that during the war, at least three Indians (actually five) were commissioned as pilots in the RFC and RAF."

Commissioning of Indians into the RAF

The attention of the Indian Military Requirements Committee focussed primarily on the Indianisation of the Indian Army; no reference was made to the RAF in its final report. Nevertheless, the issue of 'commissions to Indians', including the grant of commissions in the RAF was raised by the Secretary of State for India, Edwin Montagu, during the committee's eighth meeting on January 12, 1922. In this meeting, he reiterated the request of the Government of India that "Indians should be allowed to take commissions in the Air Force." And stated that "he considered that in respect to the Air Force, disabilities on Indians, as such, should also be removed."

Both Chamberlain and General Sir Claude Jacob (the Chief of the General Staff, Indian Army) supported this proposal.

The commissioning of Indians in specialist branches was opposed by the Chief of the Imperial General Staff (CIGS) Sir Henry Wilson, while the Secretary of State for Air, Sir Freddie Guest was of the opinion that "it would be most dangerous to entrust to Indians the secrets of the most technical arm — the Air Service."

The committee requested that "the Secretary of State for Air and the Chief of the Imperial General Staff ascertain the views of their respective Councils as regards the removing of the disability on the Indians obtaining commissions in the Air Force and the Artillery, Engineers and other branches of the Army." A memorandum on the "admission of Indians into the commissioned ranks of the RAF" was submitted by Trenchard to Guest on January 23, 1922, and circulated to the committee on the same day. In this, the members of the Air Council restated their inability to accept "the Indian Government's present proposal to grant a limited number of permanent commissions in the RAF to Indian candidates for service in India." The latter, they noted, rested upon "a fundamental misapprehension as to the character of the RAF units in India, which are units of a British, not an Indian service.

"The Government of India does not recommend that Indian gentlemen should be given commissions in units of the British Royal Artillery or Royal Engineers serving in India, but only in Indian

Artillery and Indian Engineers; the recommendation that they should be granted commissions in the RAF is, thus, inconsistent with the remainder of their proposals." Additional factors cited as precluding the commissioning of Indians included the impossibility of British airmen being subordinated to Indian officers, and the administrative problems caused by creating "a limited category of officers in the RAF who would only be available for service in India."

It also alluded, somewhat coyly, to other arguments which had been adduced from time to time against the grant to Indians of commissions in technical services which applied with still greater cogency to the RAF. But the Air Council did not feel it necessary to recapitulate them.

Significantly, however, although it was "impossible" to "Indianise" the RAF in India as "presently constituted", the Air Council pointed for the first time to an alternative.

"If it is considered that the air service in India should comprise Indian elements, it will be necessary to build up a distinctly Indian Air Force to supplement (and, may be, some day, to replace) the units of the British RAF at present stationed in that country."

This is precisely what happened in 1942 when RAF squadrons deployed in the North-West Frontier were withdrawn for coastal patrolling on the west and east coast of India in view of the Japanese onslaught. The RAF squadrons were replaced by the lone No.1 Squadron, to be joined later and replaced by other newly raised squadrons of the Indian Air Force.

While conceding that the desirability or otherwise of instituting such a 'force' was primarily a political question, the Air Council went on the advice that if an Indian air arm was created, it should be built up as a "Dominion Force" and that should this come to pass, then it would be willing to undertake the training of a few Indian cadets at the RAF College at Cranwell, provided that the requirements of the British service permitted.

On February 6, 1922, Trenchard forwarded to Montagu a draft copy of a second paper examining the question of commissioning of Indian candidates. This took a rather more conciliatory line, acknowledging the desirability, on political grounds, of acceding as far as practicable to legitimate Indian aspirations and opening the possibility that in two years time, the RAF might be prepared to take one or two cadets at the RAF Cadet College at Cranwell with a view to testing their aptitude for flying and other duties, side by side with British cadets.

The time qualification was significant in so far as Trenchard made clear in his covering letter the real purpose of the draft as "to try to postpone this discussion by a couple of years or so." He concludes, "I rather feel myself, privately, that you should look into the question of forming an Indian Air Service one day."

It took them ten years. During this period, the question of Indians being commissioned in the Indian Army was settled as the plan to set up separately as distinct from Sandhurst, an Indian Military Academy at Dehra Dun which began in 1933.

Although, the Air Ministry was not called upon to admit Indians to Cranwell on the basis described by Trenchard, the exchanges with the Indian Military Requirements Committee at this time are, nevertheless, the first manifestation of the arguments that would later lead to the creation of an Indian air arm.

Indian Sandhurst Committee and the Formation of IAF

Although the question of the creation of an 'Indian Sandhurst' was raised by the Indian members of the Esher Committee, the committee's report concluded that the time was not then right for the establishment of such a college.

One of the resolutions submitted by Sir P S Shivaswamy Aiyer to the Legislative Assembly in March 1921, called for "the establishment in India of a Military College such as Sandhurst and during the 1920s pressure continued to mount for the creation of an Indian equivalent to the Royal Military College."

In February 1925, Shri B Venkatapatraju moved a resolution on this issue in the Legislative Assembly. In response, the establishment of a committee under the chairmanship of the Chief of the General Staff of the Indian Army, General Sir Andrew Skeen, "to examine measures to improve the quality and number of Indian candidates for the King's Commission and to discuss whether an Indian Sandhurst could or should be created" was announced by the Finance Member during discussions on the budget in March 1925.

The committee's terms of reference required it to report on the following:

(a) By what means it might be possible to improve upon the present supply of Indian candidates for the King's Commission both in regard to number and quality.

(b) Whether it was desirable and practicable to establish a Military College in India to train Indians for the commissioned ranks of the Indian Army.

If the answer to (b) was in the affirmative, how soon should the scheme be initiated and what steps should be taken to carry it out?

Whether, if a Military College was established in India, it should supersede or be supplemented by Sandhurst and Woolwich so far as the training of Indians for the commissioned ranks of the Indian Army was concerned.

The composition of the Indian Sandhurst Committee (or Skeen Committee) was announced in June 1925. In addition to Sir Andrew, it was made up of five members of the Legislative Assembly (including Pandit Moti Lal Nehru and M A Jinnah), two members of the Council of State, three representatives of the Indian states and three additional members.

The committee convened at Simla in August 1925. Following a wide-ranging enquiry — including visits by a subcommittee to establishments in the UK, including Cranwell, France, Canada and the USA — its report was completed by November 1926 and was published in April 1927.

The conclusions of the Skeen Committee were wide-ranging. While "the Government of India was taken aback by the liberality of its own officers," the Legislative Assembly was not and it welcomed the committee's report and pressed for its implementation. Although, most of the committee's report related to the Indian Army, a specific reference was made to the failure of the RAF to accept Indian candidates for commissioning.

The refusal of commissions in the Air Force was singularly indefensible because a number of Indians were actually employed as officers in the RFC during the Great War. They rendered efficient service. One was awarded the DFC and he and another of the officers were killed in action.

In order to address this, the committee recommended that an initial two places be made available at Cranwell for Indian cadets in 1928, and that this number be progressively increased.

The comments of the Skeen Committee would appear to have both surprised and irritated senior RAF officers in India and London. In a letter to Trenchard dated April 21, 1927, the Air Officer Commanding the RAF in India, Air Vice Marshal Geoffrey Salmond, the brother of Sir John Salmond, noted that "until it was published, I had no idea that they had touched on the RAF, as it seems to me entirely outside their terms of reference. However, under the curious circumstances that exist out there, it was quite inevitable that the report should have made some mention of the possibility of Indians getting into air services."

The inclusion of the RAF in the deliberations of the Skeen Committee would appear to have resulted from the continued perception of the RAF in India as a specialist arm of the Army. The committee's report had said, "It was recommended that they (Indians) be admitted in the commissioned ranks in the artillery, engineers, signals, tank corps and air arms of the Army and for this purpose, be admitted to the Royal Military Academy, Woolwich, and the RAF College at Cranwell."

Salmond's first formal response to the Skeen Committee Report took the form of a lengthy memorandum dated May 10, 1927. In this, he reiterated the objection to the commissioning of Indians into the RAF first employed by Trenchard in 1922: the RAF in India was on the same basis as the British Army in India; if Indians were commissioned in the RAF in India, they would be liable to serve in the RAF in all parts of the world where units of this service were stationed. It would be impracticable to guarantee that they would always remain as officers or in RAF units in India; to do so would be creating a precedent never before established. This principle, without question, would be unacceptable to the Air Council.

The alternative he advanced was that "Indians should be commissioned in order that ultimately they should form part of an Indian Air Force unit in India."

Salmond went on to detail the manner in which "the first Indian Air Force squadron might be formed by creating an Indian air unit with a cadre of British personnel to train and develop the unit; as the Indian officers and airmen gain the necessary experience, the British personnel should be gradually withdrawn until the unit becomes entirely Indian."

Cadets were to be trained at Cranwell at the rate of two per year and the squadron was to commence forming five years after the first cadets proceeded to Cranwell, being fully up to strength, fourteen years from the date of formation.

Salmond's memorandum was approved generally by Trenchard, although the latter was concerned that the mixed unit advocated by Salmond might be found more efficient than those consisting purely of Indian personnel and that "they might place Indians in command of British personnel, which I must strongly oppose."

However, neither would appear to have felt any enthusiasm for such a unit. In a letter dated August 18, 1927, Salmond attempted to reassure Trenchard, "You may think that I am advocating an Indian Air Force whereas, of course, it is the last thing which anyone, including myself, really wants. I put up this scheme as a result of the Skeen Report (which was a surprise and a shock) because I was called upon as AOC to make remarks. I ascertained the lines that the Army was taking and I informed by cable of the general lines I wished to go on; this you approved of but, no doubt, I went further in forming a constructive proposal which appeared more or less inevitable in any case."

Salmond's prediction was to prove correct, although political realities in both India and the UK drove forward the creation of the Indian Air Force at a rather faster rate than anticipated by the AOC in his memorandum. On December 3, 1927, the Government of India sent a telegram to the India Office urging, "I think that we must all agree that it is very desirable that an Indian Air Force should be encouraged and started as soon as may be."

The Secretary of State for India gave his approval in principle to the creation of an Indian Air Force in his military dispatch No. 6 dated April 5, 1928.

Considerable discussion ensued on the legislation required to establish an independent Indian air arm, and in an attempt to circumvent the many legal problems encountered, the Secretary of State for India proposed in October 1928 that an Indian Flying Corps analogous to the RFC [and indeed the original Indian Flying Corps that served in Egypt, Mesopotamia (Iraq) and Persia (Iran)] should instead be created as an integral part of the Indian Army — a proposal that was roundly rejected by both the Air Ministry and the Government of India.

Eventually, steps were taken by the Central Legislative Assembly to pass the Indian Air Force Act which received the assent of the

Governor General of India on April 8, 1932. The Act came into force on October 8, 1932, and the first Indian Air Force unit, No. 1 Squadron, was formed on April 1, 1933.

Keeping Peace on the Frontier

Expansion and Consolidation

From early 1916 when No. 31 Squadron, RFC, arrived on the Frontier and undertook operations in cooperation with the Army, the RFC and after April 1, 1918, the RAF, proved to the sceptics that military aviation was not a toy but an essential and useful partner for the Army in such difficult terrain and treacherous locations.

This one squadron proved that it was indeed a useful partner where information and intelligence about the enemy observed from the air was indeed helpful to the Army in deciding on battlefield tactics. Even artillery directing fire from an aeroplane had already been successfully tried in the war that was raging in Europe and was being carried out on the Frontier in cooperation with artillery batteries.

The RFC/RAF in India at that time had no big organisation, nor did it have any ground assets such as buildings, control towers, or a meteorological organisation or even a ground organisation for communication, or barracks to house the staff. Even its ground transport was confined to a limited number of Leyland lorries and Crossley tenders. For that, they depended on the Army. So glowing was the appreciation expressed by the Army commanders in the field, that it was decided to add one more squadron to the existing one. Meanwhile, efforts were made to make the lives of the pilots, mechanics and the rest of the staff a bit more bearable, if not comfortable.

The gaps in the bare minimum facilities soon made themselves starkly visible. By the very nature of its activities, the Air Force was a highly technically oriented service, the needs of which, while seemingly similar to the Army as a service, were in reality totally different. The planes were of no use to the service unless they were airworthy which meant serviceability and that meant maintenance.

A look at the way No. 31 Squadron had to operate considering the conditions on the ground, gives one an idea of the difficulties that the airmen, the pilots and other staff faced. When it was decided to send one squadron for 'watch and ward' duties to India, all that the authorities could muster was one flight. 'A' Flight of the squadron arrived in Bombay on December 26, 1915. 'B' and 'C' Flights joined them soon after and the entire squadron was based at Risalpur on March 1, 1916.

During the various Army expeditions of 1916, No. 31's machines (BE2C) flew on reconnaissance in support, and on November 15 and 16, in particular, proved their worth many times over. In support of a pitched battle in the Hafiz Kor district, 12 of the squadron's two BEs provided wireless ranging for the artillery, while the remaining ten dropped a total of 49x20 lbs bombs and fired 500 rounds of Lewis gun ammunition among the hostile tribesmen. This air action proved to be the turning point of the battle and the tribes quickly dispersed.

Throughout 1917, the squadron continued to provide valuable assistance to the Army and its work was considered so successful that a second squadron, No. 114, was formed at Walton in Lahore in September 1917, from a nucleus provided by No. 31. The parent squadron could certainly spare the men and the machines as it had on strength 34 Henry Farmans, one Maurice Farman, 26 BE2Cs and 2Es.

Within six months, both units were engaged in active operations, bombing and strafing the Mari tribal area. Their sterling contribution, undoubtedly, helped in bringing hostilities to an end.

The Awesome Power of the War Birds — 1919

Soon after the November 1918 Armistice, Major General W H Salmond, Air Officer Commanding (AOC) Middle East, RAF, commenced an aerial inspection tour of his command and then extended his journey to India, where he arrived in Delhi on December 12. Following his entourage was a Handley Page V/1500 bomber, then a most modern and technically superior machine in the British inventory. The machine was piloted by Captain Robert 'Jock' Halley.

After the Great War, India was greatly troubled by internal political problems, with public protests increasing. In 1919, the Jallianwala Bagh tragedy took place and resentment against British rule was becoming pronounced.

Afghanistan, where long lasting peace has been, and is even today, a distant dream, found at this point in time an opportune moment to attack. In February 1919, Amir Habibullah was assassinated and was succeeded by his son Amir Amanullah. Prior to this, the Peace Conference of 1919 had granted independence to Afghanistan. During the Great War, Amir Habibullah had been friendly and of great service to the British Government. It was expected that his successor would continue the same policy towards British India. But that was not to be.

Amanullah was at once besieged by court intrigues and numerous pretenders to the throne, with the result that general unrest spread throughout the country. Since Afghanistan was technically now an independent country, Amanullah, in a bid to rally the country to his side, declared 'holy war' on the British on May 8, 1919, although he knew very well that he could not win. It was just a plot to save his throne.

To encourage his Army to fight the British, he made many lavish promises to the former. Among them was the promise of getting Karachi as an Afghan port. He launched his troops across the Indian frontier in the Khyber, Khost and Baluchistan regions in the hope of scoring quick victories.

Luckily, there were plenty of troops in India and the general revolt that Amanullah had hoped for did not take place. His troops, who were on a semi-regular footing, had forfeited the advantage of irregulars without gaining the efficiency of the regulars. The northern Afghan invaders were defeated at the Khyber and the British forces advancing through the Khyber Pass occupied Dakka in the Afghan territory on May 13, 1919, establishing permanent piquets on the route. Jalalabad was frequently bombed from the air by planes from Nos. 31 and 114 (which later became No. 28 Squadron).

In the south, Spin Baldak in Baluchistan, opposite New Chaman, was captured on May 28. Kabul, Amanullah's capital, and Kandahar were threatened and, the Frontier tribesmen, who had been watching the events, now displayed a disconcerting tendency to go in for plunder in Afghanistan rather than in India.

To bring hostilities to a quick end, the British utilised the huge V/1500 Handley Page bomber as a force multiplier to overawe the Afghans. Accordingly, the bomber, piloted by Captain Halley, appeared over Kabul and dropped a few bombs on the Amir's palace. The giant bomber impressed the rebel tribes, while the delivery of its bombs on the palace convinced Amanullah of his folly and he promptly sued for peace and signed a peace treaty on August 8.

"There is little doubt," runs the official dispatch, "that this raid was an important factor in producing a desire for peace at the headquarters of the Afghan Government."

This event amply demonstrated to the sceptics in the Army hierarchy that the Air Force could be easily utilised in furtherance of the policies of the Empire and at a fraction of the cost that would accrue for sending a complete Army task force, with its attendant costs. The helping hand provided by the Air Force along with the Army operations on the ground was perhaps one of the earliest examples of combined arms operations.

In retrospect, one must record that this rebellion of Amanullah did turn out profitable for him. Though he forfeited an annual subsidy, he obtained the cancellation of the clause in previous treaties to the effect that the foreign affairs of Afghanistan were to be under British control. This clause, the British never enforced, as there were no means of doing so, short of occupation of the country, but Amanullah made most of the concession and set up a "Monument of Victory" in Kabul in which the British lion was shown heavily chained. He also adopted the title of "King" of Afghanistan instead of Amir.

"During my service in India as a pilot of the 'Old Carthusian' (the Handley Page V/1500), I was a freelance and only took orders from the AOC in India either at Delhi or Simla. However, coming from the north of the Tweed, and as an officer personnel, I received an extra Rs 100 a month for serving west of the river Indus. I wangled to be put on the strength of No. 31 Squadron!" recalled Captain Robert 'Jock' Halley.

A distinguished bomber pilot in World War I, Halley had won the DFC and Bar and, at the end of 1918, was chosen to co-pilot a Handley Page V/1500 to India. With Major Stuart MacLaren, they took off from Martlesham Heath, UK, on December 13, arriving in Karachi on January 15, 1919. It was the first flight made from England to India and Halley received the Air Force Cross (AFC) for his part in the historic flight. The V/1500 was named "Old Carthusian."

A short time afterwards, Halley was ordered to bomb Kabul in a Handley Page 0/400 bomber. He flew this to Risalpur on May 13, 1919, only to have it wrecked in a storm. It was, therefore, decided that his V/1500, which was at Lahore, would be used. Since its flight from England, it had been left in the open (there were no hangars large enough to house it), but it was made ready after some difficulties, and was fitted with 112 lb bomb racks taken from No. 31 Squadron's BEs.

Halley continues: "These racks were attached to the lower wing spars and operated in conjunction with a bomb sight fitted in the front cockpit. Further 16x20 lb bombs were stacked in the mid-cockpit, to be dropped through the bottom doorway by two of the crew when they saw the 112 lb bombs dropped.

"The machine was ready by May 23, and Jock Halley took off at 3 am the next morning, Ted Villiers flying as a 'volunteer' bomb aimer.

"The route lay, towards the Khyber Pass and the clearing height was about 3,000 ft. This meant flying around for about an hour to gain height before going over the ridge of hills. The Khyber was only dimly visible, as were a few lights at Jamrud Fort. We flew over the Kabul river and as daybreak came, we reached Jalalabad, and to my horror I saw water leaking from the base of the second cylinder. I called Flight Sergeant Smith up to me and with engines throttled back, we hurriedly conferred on the course of action.

"The leak came from a defective rubber connection running along the base of the six cylinders of the starboard engine but it was not possible to judge the extent of the water loss. Kabul was still 90 miles away and we had to get back. Finally, with Villiers and Smith, we decided to carry on, me keeping a watchful eye on the leak as we passed through precipitous mountains. Then we came to Jagdalak Pass which I could see high above me. Chancing all, I hauled back on the stick and just cleared the top and then dropped down the other side. Even now, I can see the look on Villiers' face. Below Villiers could see dozens of camels of a long caravan scattering in all directions, several falling over the edge of the mountain side.

"On the other side, I saw our target spread over a vast fertile plateau. With a population of 300,000, I was not surprised at the extent of the area covered by the city. Still nursing our leaking engine, we made the bomb run and our missiles achieved good results, and if that did not frighten the inhabitants many of whom could never have seen an aeroplane before, the sound of 'Old Carthusian' just a few hundred feet up, with four engines roaring, certainly did.

"On the return flight, we again scraped over the Jagdalak Pass, helped by a lightened aircraft and a following wind (tail wind). Finally, the leaking engine's temperature rose so I had to close it down but we landed safely at Risalpur after six hours in the air, being all greatly relieved," recalls Halley.

Jock Halley received a second bar to his DFC for his part in the raid.

— Norman L R Franks, *First in the Indian Skies*

Organisation of RAF India

It is a fact of history that in matters military, as in other matters, whatever was decided by Whitehall in London, was implemented by the War Office. To get an idea of the extent of post-war demobilisation, one needs to look at the size of the Air Force as on November 11, 1918, the Armistice Day.

From four squadrons that went to war as part of the British Expeditionary Force (BEF) in August 1914, the RFC, till April 1, 1918, and thereafter, the RAF, grew to a staggering 95 squadrons and seven flights, "battle-scarred but unwearied, the winged might of a country and an Empire which had won a resounding victory over a remorseless but by no means an invincible foe."

Further in a field bordering the Mediterranean, in Mesopotamia and in distant India, 34 more squadrons with 8 flights were resting from battle, while at Home, 55 operational and 199 training squadrons completed the formidable array. The Air Force consisted of 30,000 officers and 300,000 airmen. A total of 6,166 were killed in action, 7,245 were wounded, 3,128 were missing and prisoners and 84 were interned, thus, making a total of 16,623. Over the entire period of nearly four years, 50,000 machines (aeroplanes) were manufactured and deployed, of which 36,000 were destroyed in combat.

The estimate of personnel and machines given by air historians C G Grey and Hilary St George Saunders, stresses that after the war, the Government was keen to reduce the size of the Air Force as soon as possible, even as a furious debate was on about its very future.

A historic example best illustrates how decisions taken by far-sighted individuals have helped their nations when in dire straits. A hundred years prior to this, after the Battle of Waterloo in 1815, the Duke of Wellington had hidden a part of his Army overseas to avoid losing such valuable, experienced servicemen due to demobilisation. In post-war Britain, with Lord Trenchard at the head of the service and Winston Churchill as Secretary of State for Air, they practically did the same by 'hiding' the overseas squadrons in Egypt, Iraq and, to some extent, India (eight in India and seven in the Middle East) — thus, the nucleus of an effective Air Force survived.

Meanwhile, the first peace-time establishment for the now greatly reduced, almost an infant, RAF was being implemented with special emphasis on the overseas posts of the Empire.

As part of the Empire commitment, three squadrons were allocated to India, in addition to the two which were already in India, namely, Nos. 31 and 114. All the three new squadrons (Nos. 20, 48 and 99) arrived in India by June 1919. They were based respectively at Risalpur, Quetta and Ambala. Their aircraft were the Bristol F2s (20, 48) and DH9A (99) bombers.

No. 31 (the first in the Indian skies) remained at Risalpur, but No. 114 was split into three detached flights at various bases, including one at Aden. A sixth squadron, No. 97, equipped with 12 DH10 bombers, arrived on August 12, 1919, and in September was based at Lahore.

All the six squadrons were organised as an Indian "Group" under the overall command of the C-in-C, Indian Army, based at Delhi, although, during the hot season, the C-in-C moved to cooler Simla.

By September 1919, Air Commodore T I Webb Bowen took over as Air Officer Commanding (AOC) "India Group".

A history of the Air Ministry details all the military aviation commands within the United Kingdom and, for the first time, details of the overseas Air Force Commands were given in 1920. Until then, the Middle East and India did not figure in the list, but thereafter, till March 1939, the India Command was mentioned every year with an AOC initially and later AOC-in-C, as the air establishment expanded. However, there is an entry in the history of No. 31 Squadron that reads as follows: "Brigadier General M D K MacEwen, CMG, DSO, commanding the Royal Air Force in India, inspected the squadron on March 2, 1919, and left by air for Lahore the next day." One presumes that he was an Army Brigadier, for until then there was no India Group for the RAF. The Air Ministry started mentioning the India Group, and later Command, from 1920 in its lists of overseas commands of the RAF.

To back up the squadrons spread over the NWFP, Punjab and other parts of North India, an aircraft 'factory' and aircraft park were set up at Walton, Lahore, the park having a port depot at Bombay and a detachment at Drigh Road, Karachi.

Initially, being directly under Army control, the headquarters of the RAF India was located at Peshawar, the big sprawling cantonment of the Army from 1916 to 1922, when it was shifted to Ambala. In 1923, Air Vice Marshal Sir Philip Game took over as AOC-in-C, RAF India, when the post was upgraded as a result of Sir John Salmond's recommendation. At about this time, it was realised that the controlling authority of the Air Force should also be in the capital where the Army C-in-C had his office. Consequently, the headquarters of the RAF moved to New Delhi (earlier called Raisina).

The sixth squadron, No. 97, after it arrived from England, was immediately involved in air operations in support of the Army fighting the Mahsuds in Waziristan. Though fighting against the Afghans ceased on June 3, 1919, the effect of the "Afghan incursions from Khost was serious in the central portion of the frontier."

Meanwhile, the names, numbers and identity of the squadrons underwent a change as given below:

- No. 31, the first squadron, remained unchanged.
- No. 114 Squadron was renumbered as No. 28 Squadron.
- No. 48 Squadron was renumbered as No. 5 Squadron.
- No. 97 Squadron was renumbered as No. 60 Squadron.
- No. 99 Squadron was renumbered as No. 27 Squadron.
- No. 20 Squadron remained unchanged.

Although the immediate situation was relatively quiet and manageable, the task facing this tiny group of RAF squadrons was formidable. In their role of aerial policemen, they were collectively responsible for supporting land operations in an area covering over 27,000 square miles of unadministered territory alone, apart from even larger administered territories. Within the whole, lived the world's largest tribal population numbering perhaps some 10 million (over 25 million in 2010) and including such tribes as Mahsuds, Afridis, Wazirs, Bhittanis — some of the world's finest (and most merciless) fighting men. Each of these and the lesser tribes were in turn divided and sub-divided into sub-tribes, each fiercely independent and in constant feud with each other. These feuds had their origins in centuries of bitter dispute over three things basic to any tribesman — gold, land and women.

Overwhelmingly Muslim in faith, these fanatical tribesmen lived in the most inaccessible hills and mountains on the northern border of India and Afghanistan. With their own language (Pushtu) and known collectively as Pathans, the tribes were (are) a law unto themselves, albeit tenuously allied by race and creed to the rulers in Kabul.

Bred from childhood to regard a rifle as the badge of manhood and expert marksmanship as a perfectly normal accomplishment of early adolescence, the Pathans' logic of life and peculiar brand of callous humour was not restricted to the males of the tribes. Their women were equally cruel to any captured enemy, of whatever race, and Rudyard Kipling's verse of the 19th century might easily have applied to the 1920s (and even 2010) when he wrote:

"When you are wounded and left on Afghanistan's plains
And the women come out to cut up what remains
Just roll up your rifle and blow out your brains
And go to your death like a soldier."

The Pathans' logic can be illustrated by the perfectly serious applications they made through their Political Agents for the India General Service Medal at the cessation of every specific uprising.

When refused, they could not understand this denial, for had they not provided most excellent training for the King Emperor's soldiers and airmen. Indeed, without their efforts, the British fighting men would have had no training at all!

Ghooley Chits

From 1838 to 1916, the British Indian Army was deployed almost constantly in the NWFP against the various Pashtun tribes, none of whom was willing to live by the White Man's rules. However, over a period of time, certain conventions developed which, by and large, were observed by both sides. The Army had many facilities and weapons at its disposal while the 'wily' Pathans had an innate ability to judge ground and a superb tactical skill to inflict as much damage as possible upon the enemy in as short a time as possible.

After they saw the flying iron birds in action from 1916, they were annoyed. This was not 'cricket'. It was unfair — they could shoot and be shot at, but on the ground. Now the enemy could see them from the sky. They thought that aeroplanes were unsporting and pilots had to be protected in a special way against the fearful savagery waiting for them on the ground if they were shot down or had to jump.

By the 1930s, the tribesmen had become adept at shooting down aircraft and no longer thought the use of aeroplanes unfair. Sometimes, they welcomed their arrival because there was a lot of loot in a crashed warplane and by Pathan standards, the chance of getting it was well worth the price of a few bombs and machine-gun bullets.

Another instance of the 'ghooley chit' saving two airmen comes from the pen of Sydney Chapman of No. 60 Squadron. It concerned the rescue of the civilians in the British Legation at Kabul in December-January 1928-29. They set out from Risalpur to fly into Afghanistan. When passing over the mountains, Flight Lieutenant Chapman and Flying Officer Davies had a shock — the petrol pipeline had become frozen and the engine suddenly stopped.

However, they were fortunate in quickly finding a flat piece of ground and although the machine was damaged (DH9A), only Davies sustained an injury — a bruised knee. Around the little plain on which they landed were steep precipices, but as soon as they touched the ground, a crowd of armed Afghans came swarming around.

It looked as though the plane would be smashed and the pilots massacred. One of the airmen produced a 'ghooley chit', a document stating that a reward would be paid for producing the bearers unharmed, but none of them could read.

Matters were getting a bit too exciting when a man in authority restored order. The pilots were taken to a house, when the Afghans, on learning that the airmen were not Russians, became more friendly. A hard and tedious journey to the camp of the Afghan Army followed and after further delay of some days, the pair was sent under armed escort to the British frontier.

Their troubles, however, were not at an end. Gangs of hostile tribesmen stopped the party and one lot tried to turn them back. At last, they reached Jalalabad, a fortified town near the border of India, only to find that the British Consulate had been forced to clear out months earlier.

What a fix to be in. Doggedly, they set out again, eventually reaching Charbagh. Here a friendly chief conveyed the news that owing to there being a hostile tribe nearby, they could go no further. A native runner got through with a message to Peshawar and a plane was sent with the ransom money and the two pilots returned to Risalpur safely.

Do We Need a Separate Air Force?

War of Words

"An independent Air Force, coming from God knows where, going God knows where, and doing God knows what!"

Tradition is a mighty word in England. It is held aloft as a banner of the eight centuries of the country's slow but steady progress towards becoming a pure democracy, which is even today held as a model for the rest of the world. As the institutions of the state matured and became its pillars, two of them, the War Office controlling the British Army, and the Admiralty, controlling the Royal Navy, stood like the Rock of Gibralter, resisting any change that might affect their tradition-bound status and working.

And so it was with military aviation. At first, it was dismissed as a mere toy, of no use in military or naval operations, but when other nations began building up their air strength and the pioneer airmen showed its usefulness, the Generals and the Admirals wanted the new service to be part of their own service. And from this emerged the rivalry and the desire to build their own subordinate Air Force.

Initially, there was ignorance followed by confusion. Where could this third dimension be fitted in the existing framework of defence/ military infrastructure? For fear of being left behind other European nations and the USA, the Government created an Air Battalion within the Royal Engineers in 1911. Within a year, it was clear that it was not enough, so to take the next step was logical. In 1912, the Royal Flying Corps (RFC) was created as part of the Army. At this point, the senior service, the Royal Navy, rebelled and set up its own air arm, the Royal Naval Air Service (RNAS) with its own in-house training schools. Both served in the war separately and the rudiments of inter-service cooperation began under war-time conditions.

Once war broke out, military aviation showed how important aerial reconnaissance had become. During the four years of war, each success of the RFC was followed by frantic expansion, keeping in mind the exigencies of the war, which had to be won at all costs. Throughout the duration of the war, Lord Trenchard became an ardent votary of air power as a separate, but essential component of the war machine. The Government was enthusiastic to the extent that even as the war was on, it created an independent Air Force in the field and put Lord Trenchard in command.

Earlier, even as the war was progressing, opinion back Home had crystallised: it favoured making the aviation element into a separate service. While the civilian leadership wanted the amalgamation of both the RFC and the RNAS into a single combined entity, the Admiralty remained adamant. However, the Government decided to create the new service and the Royal Air Force (RAF) came into being officially on April 1, 1918, while the war was still on.

At the Armistice, on November 11, 1918, the RAF, with nearly 99 squadrons, was the most powerful Air Force in the world. However, as soon as the war was over, the old animosities surfaced again and both the Army and the Navy began to question the very existence of the RAF. Sarcasm and criticism were rife in the corridors of Whitehall as Air Chief Marshal Sir Philip Joubert de la Ferte discovered to his dismay. He writes in his autobiography, *The Fated Sky*, "In 1919-20, some of our more elderly military men seemed incapable of envisaging a combined operation directed to a national or international end. Each had to consider war as carried out in watertight compartments labelled

Army and Navy. Besides, it never seemed to occur to them that civilians might have a say in the conduct of operations in the future."

Once the war was over, the old animosities returned and a sustained campaign was carried out in the corridors of power against granting legitimacy to a new service that had already come into existence. This campaign intensified further as the Government was trying to economise on overseas defence expenditure in its turbulent colonies. It reached such a pitch that Lord Trenchard, the Chief of the Air Staff, wrote on February 10, 1922, to AVM Sir Sefton Brancker, "Thank you for your effort at the Air Conference, on the service side. I am being attacked by many quarters just now. The attack, however, will not come to much, owing to efforts which I fancy you, among others, made."

It seems hard to realise today (2010) that there could have been a campaign to destroy the separate Air Force, but such was the position which existed in 1922.

In a letter to the *Daily Telegraph* on February 13, 1922, Brancker wrote: "The attacks on the Royal Air Force have been far more bitter and jealous than the public have imagined; and even today the War Office is deliberately obstructing the transfer of Palestine to Air Force administration and, for a time, refused all assistance in the way of a small land garrison in Iraq."

However, clearer minded individuals began to think of both the experience of the war in Europe and the contribution of the Air Force. It was the experience of the battles in Egypt, Jordan and Palestine, buttressed by the experience of the few squadrons in the North-West Frontier of India, that proved that the idea of using the Air Force as a watch and ward element would achieve the objective of command and control in the far flung inhospitable, often mountainous and sometimes desert areas of the British Empire.

C G Grey, the celebrated air historian, describes the first military operations directed, controlled and conducted solely by the Air Force.

He quotes the *London Gazette* of February 8, 1920: "A mixed force of all arms under Group Captain Robert Gordon, RAF and Wing Commander Frederick Bowhill had defeated and utterly broken the Army of the so-called Mad Mullah of Somaliland late in 1919. This Mad Mullah had defied detachments of the regular Army and the Anglo-Egyptian Sudanese Army and the various police forces for 15 years.

"He was completely cleaned up by the use of air power in a few weeks and the tribes, which had suffered from his depredations for so many years were, henceforth, able to live peaceably with no more disturbance than is provided by normal inter-tribal raids."

This was the first triumph of the RAF in the various campaigns which were conducted entirely under Air Ministry control. One might say that it was the Air Ministry's first private war.

Countering Criticism

Sir Sefton Brancker, whose India connection has been described earlier, fought the battle for the retention of a separate air service responsible to a separate Air Minister independent of the older services. As a senior serving officer (Air Vice Marshal), he stressed that "punitive expeditions in the far corners of the Empire must always be necessary on our turbulent frontiers such as India, Africa and Iraq and by virtue of the terrain and the size, they are usually expensive for the actual results achieved, particularly in India.

"In 1896-97, some 35,000 fighting men and 20,000 followers were employed for six months to deal with a stretch of country, the whole of which lay within 90 miles of Peshawar, the headquarters. Now, aviation is beginning to provide new punitive weapons which promise to be in every respect vastly cheaper than existing methods. The power of aircraft against troops on the ground was first vividly demonstrated in Palestine, and in the last months of the war in France. In 1919, one squadron in Somaliland satisfactorily concluded a most successful punitive campaign practically unaided by troops.

"In the Tirah campaign (in the North-West Frontier of India) one squadron of quite mediocre aeroplanes of 1918 could have dropped 200 tons of high explosive bombs and fired thousands of rounds on selective objectives in that 90 mile radius from Peshawar in one month. Granted that the tribesmen would have taken cover and hidden, even if a tenth of the money expended on the occupation of hostile territory in 1896-97 could have been devoted to aviation, it seems most certain that just as satisfactory results could have been attained in two months, without any advance of punitive columns, as in six months with 55,000 men."

As for the opposition from the War Office to an independent service, Brancker hit back vehemently: "I never quite understood why the War Office did agree (to an independent Air Force) and curiously enough, one of the leaders of the party anxious to destroy the RAF today is Sir William Robertson, the particular Chief of Imperial General Staff (CIGS) who agreed to the creation of the new service in 1917."

Response to the Navy

Regarding the vehement opposition to the RAF and the Air Ministry from the Admiralty, Sir Sefton Brancker writing to *The Times* on December 22, 1920, on the value of capital ships in a future war, said: "Let us consider torpedo attacks from the air with torpedo attacks from destroyers. I would claim for it at least equal accuracy; it will probably prove superior, its speed will be at least three times as great. The difficulty of hitting aircraft must always be considerably greater than hitting surface craft on account of the unknown and variable factor of height and of the higher speed of attack. Further, an attack from the air can be delivered against ships lying in harbours and anchorages, where it would be impossible for destroyers to penetrate.

"The problem of the naval experts in dealing with the threat of aerial attack is to decide whether capital ships can be employed efficiently if they are liable to be attacked both at sea and in harbour by a torpedo assault. Some writers have stated that the duty of the Fleet is to destroy the enemy's sea bases, coaling stations, fortifications and commercial harbours, and others have contended that submarines have rendered such enterprises impossible.

"But they are not impossible to aircraft, and I am certain that in the future, the Air Force must become par excellence the arm of offence against hostile territory and commerce. If this is admitted, then that proportion of the money available for armaments allotted to the Air Force, as compared to the other services, must be very high. If this high allotment to the air renders the allotment to the Navy insufficient for the construction of capital ships, then they must go.

"No nation can neglect power in the air in order to preserve a form of defence so expensive in its maintenance and so problematic in its utility."

To the *Daily Telegraph*, he wrote, "Our future lies in the air, just as our past has come from the sea. By virtue of our supremacy on the oceans, our little country has been able to spread our high ideals and standards throughout the world. Aviation will help us to maintain our position and continue to lead the human race in its progress towards the new conditions."

Despite opposition, this idea of conduct of operations by the Air Force independently gained acceptance and in 1920, the thinking was that this idea should be given practical shape and tried out in practice. At that time, the League of Nations had given the mandate for Syria to France and Mesopotamia (Iraq) was handed over to England. However, in Iraq, a general uprising was taking place and there was an urgent need to restore order. The British Government needed Pounds 38.5 million in a single year to employ 92 units of British and Indian troops and four Air Force squadrons. Even after the uprising had been put down, Pounds 20 million a year to support 61 Army units and five squadrons of Air Force was needed. Winston Churchill, who was then the Secretary of State for Air, saw a ray of hope in Lord Trenchard's plan to hand over the entire command of Iraq to the RAF. Trenchard's proposal envisaged reduction of Army units from 61 to 12 and reduction of expenditure from Pounds 20 million to Pounds 7.5 million, provided the Air Force squadrons were raised to eight and command transferred to the Air C-in-C. This was an offer to use mobility of air power in place of the slower and clumsier methods of the past of Army deployment.

At this juncture, Sir Samuel Hoare persuaded the Cabinet that in such a country as Mesopotamia, where neither British nor Indian troops could compete in mobility with the well-mounted Bedouin tribesmen, the best way of keeping the country quiet was to hand over the High Command to the Air Force. He called this method of pacification "control without occupation," a phrase which exactly describes the value of the Air Force in dealing with hostile tribesmen (Ironic! As this is written in 2010, the American and NATO forces in Afghanistan are extensively using the Air Force in the fight against the Taliban).

The honour of being the first Air Force officer to have complete military command of a country fell to Air Vice Marshal Sir John Salmond, who held supreme command in Mesopotamia for several years and brought the country into a state of peace such as it had never known. This experience helped the Air Force to plan for both operations in cooperation with the Army and independent operations on its own. The Iraq experience is unique in the history of military aviation worldwide, as despite being a young service, it was entrusted with such an important assignment. Already, the experts in the Air Ministry were planning to utilise this experience elsewhere. The result was a far flung outpost of the Empire that, keeping in view the yeoman service rendered, was brought fully under Air Force administration and control.

Palestine — 1929

Shortly after the war ended in November 1918, the military control of Palestine and Transjordan was handed over to the Air Force. In 1929, the forces stationed there were two squadrons of the RAF with some armoured cars, together with Palestinian Police, a small force of gendarmerie with British officers and NCOs. There was also the Transjordan Frontier Force, raised in 1926, whose special function was the defence of the desert frontier against Arab attacks.

By 1929, the problems arising out of the Balfour Declaration of the 1917 and the subsequent post-war Jewish immigration from European countries had become acute. The Arabs, who had sold their land to the Zionist organisation, were numerous and dissatisfied. In August 1929, serious anti-Jewish riots took place. The RAF could not deal with street fighting; its armoured cars could not penetrate efficiently into the narrow alleyways of Palestinian towns and villages.

The first necessity was to restore order, and for this purpose, three British battalions were immediately brought in, two from Egypt and one from Malta. From Egypt, two platoons were sent on in advance by air. This was the first example of mobility facilitated by the use of aeroplanes. Soon, order was restored. However, to prevent recurrence of violence, the garrison of Palestine was augmented by two battalions of British infantry that came under the control of the Air Officer Commanding (AOC).

Defence of Aden

In early 1928, the defence of Aden and the surrounding areas was placed under the command of Group Captain W G S Mitchell. This was the second instance — following on Iraq — in which the Air Force took complete command of a foreign country. This new command waged war against the Zaidi Imam Wawa of Sana, an area which lies north-east of Mocha (whence comes the best coffee).

Sana lies high up in the hills and the Air Force pilots had to climb to a height of 8,000 ft. so that they might drop bombs on villages only about 800 ft. below. The Imam of the Zaidi sect instigated his tribes to raid the coffee growers of Mocha and also "our own tribes" in the Aden Protectorate and "at intervals, we had to bomb the Imam's tribes to remind them to leave their neighbours alone," says C G Grey in his book *A History of the Air Ministry*.

Air Power Controversies in the United States

In America, the Naval Air Service did not chafe unduly at its subordination to the Navy, but the Army Air Corps took a different view. Its leaders were thinking along lines that were anathema to the War Department. The success of the RAF (in becoming a separate service) encouraged them to demand a unified Air Force. They had strong faith in the importance of strategic air bombardment (what Lord Trenchard's independent Air Force did in the closing stages of World War I) and there was an insistent demand for a long-range heavy bomber.

The Army authorities were determined to suppress these ideas, and this caused resentment among the able and enthusiastic younger leaders of the Air Corps. Prominent among these was Brigadier General William Mitchell, Assistant Chief of the Army Air Corps from 1919 to 1925. He was a distinguished airman who combined ability and experience with an unusually forceful personality. Realising the traditional importance of sea power in the US defence organisation, Billy Mitchell concentrated his attacks mainly against the Navy.

Mitchell claimed that aeroplanes could sink any warship by means of bombs and torpedoes, but his repeated requests for target ships, in order to test his theories, were ignored. In 1920, the Navy decided to mount some very inadequate trials under its own conditions, but increasing pressure from Congress compelled it to abandon this idea.

In 1921, three former German warships, the battleship *Ostfriesland*, the cruiser *Frankfurt* and a destroyer, were made available for bombing trials in the Cheasapeake Bay. With a hurriedly assembled bomber force, Mitchell sank all three ships. The Navy was furious and much argument raged about the validity of these trials. But no one could deny the fact of the sinkings. Encouraged, Mitchell went on to sink the old US battleships *Virginia* and *New Jersey* in 1923.

These experiments aroused a tremendous amount of interest throughout the world and especially in Britain. Mitchell made full use of it to further his demand for a separate air service and this made the Army and Navy Chiefs determined to clip his wings. He was removed from his post and banished to the Eighth Corps Army Area in San Antonio. Mitchell was too ardent to bear this exile with patience and he published a statement in the press on the occasion of the loss of the naval airship *Shenandoah*, accusing the Army and Navy of neglecting, and even sabotaging, military aviation.

He was recalled to Washington and tried by general court martial on charges of insubordination. Found guilty, he was suspended from duty for five years, and soon afterwards, he resigned his commission. Mitchell's service career was over, but his ideas continued to find expression in his writings. In 1921, he had written a book *Our Air Force: The Keystone of National Defence*, followed in 1925 by one called *Winged Defence*, in which he claimed that air power had brought with it new doctrines of war and that the basis of air power was the bomber aircraft.

"His martyrdom in the cause of air power gave force to his views — which closely resembled those of Lord Trenchard — although it was to be many years before they were translated into action. The American people had to wait until the disaster of Pear Harbour in December 1941 to see his ideas fully vindicated."

— Air Marshal Sir Robert Saundby, RAF (Retd),
Early Aviation, 1971.

Aerial Proscription — Pros and Cons

While the benefits of air action have been described earlier, a new factor emerged in the late Twenties and Thirties against Britain's plea before a League of Nation's Disarmament Conference that it should be allowed to retain and utilise its bomber force to control rebellions in the tribal areas in India and the Middle East. Pacifists and 'peace mongers' were up in arms against what they dubbed as a barbaric method of warfare against civilians. Sir William Barton accused Britain of hypocrisy and double standards and started a campaign against Frontier bombing. His statement which was issued on March 22, 1938, was given wide publicity within the Empire, in Europe and America.

"The defence of the Afghan Frontier is one of major problems of British Imperial strategy. It has not been solved in nearly a century of constant warfare. Tribesmen in their mountain fastness still defy the might of Britain, for some trivial grievances provoke a major campaign in which millions of Indian money is spent and hundreds of lives are lost.

"Twenty years ago, when the aeroplane was first used on the Frontier, military experts thought that at last they would be able to get on equal terms with the tribesmen. The aeroplane would pursue them to their remote haunts, destroy their forts and villages, break up their *lashkar* and finally persuade them to throw in their lot with India. What has been the result? It is true that an aeroplane or two contributed to an unstable peace with the Mahsuds in 1917. A bomb dropped on Kabul by a Handley Page in 1919 induced a desire for peace in the Afghan mind.

"Against this, despite the intense use of the air arm, it took nearly two years to clear up the aftermath of disturbance left by the war with the Afghans among the tribes on the British border. For the next 10 years, there was comparative peace in the tribal hinterland, but it is to be ascribed not so much to the thermal effects of air attack as to the policy of the government of constructing a network of roads in Waziristan and dominating the Mahsud hills from strategic points.

"The lesson was not lost on the Afridis and other tribes in the north. The existence of a strong Air Force in the Peshawar district did not deter the Red Shirts seditionists from establishing a reign of terror in that part of the world; it did not deter the Afridis sweeping down into the Peshawar plain from virtually laying siege to the Frontier capital for the first time since the British flag was hoisted over its battlements.

"The great Mohamand tribe, three or four years later, provoked a major campaign which, despite the Air Force efforts, was a still stronger proof that the aeroplane has not brought a solution to the Frontier problem. In the disturbances of last year, it was necessary to employ 40,000 troops before the resistance of the tribes was broken down. Even so, there has been no settlement.

"An essential element in the pacification of the Frontier is to conciliate the goodwill of the tribesmen. Bombing breeds a feeling of resentment, men whose village has been destroyed often prolong their opposition simply for that reason. In India, the policy of using the aeroplane in this way has had its reaction. Extremist politicians have exaggerated the inhuman aspect of bombing the tribes in order to discredit the British regime. Muslims in India sympathise with their co-religionists on the Frontier; to them bombing is a loathsome aspect of British Imperialism, an attitude all the more regrettable because Muslim friendship is of the greatest importance to the British in these troubled times."

Another writer, keeping in view the then current developments in Europe, especially the rise of Adolf Hitler in Germany, opined that Britain should adopt a more humane policy towards the tribesmen to prevent development of an anti-British revolt in the various parts of the Empire. Quoting the example of the Great War, he said: "When the Kaiser was informed that Britain was going to side with France, he burst out, our Consuls in Turkey and India and our agents and all such must inflame the whole Muslim world to frantic rebellion against this detestable nation of shopkeepers, for if we are to bleed to death, England shall at all events lose India."

Despite all this criticism, the British continued with their policy of aerial proscription. However, in north-west India, they did not go all the way of handing over the control of the whole province to the Air Force as they did in Iraq and Aden. It was a judicious mixture of the carrot and stick — first warning and only then action; dropping leaflets before actually bombing an area. One benefit from this accrued to both the Army and the Air Force. The air element became the spearhead in extreme cases and the Army supported the operation on the ground. The beginning of practical cooperation and the birth of the combined operations was possible only when the two services actually fought together under a single command, towards one objective.

Looking at the world today (2010), one can see that what the British Empire did in north-west India, Iraq, Palestine and Aden and called it aerial proscription, has its modern version in Israel using similar tactics. In terms of numbers, Israel cannot match Hamas, but in terms of quality, it has an edge.

Birth of an Air Force — April 1, 1918

At the beginning of World War I in 1914, the RFC sent 105 officers and 775 other ranks along with 64 aeroplanes (including those travelling in cases with the aircraft park), and 95 mechanical transport vehicles as part of the British Expeditionary Force. They left behind at Home 41 officers and 116 machines of which only 20 were fit for flight.

The RFC had become the RAF on April 1, 1918, and had 30,000 officers and 300,000 other ranks in 99 squadrons. This tremendous expansion due to the exigencies of war produced an organisation that performed magnificently, both independently as also in support of the

Army, and developed expertise which was to stand it in good stead in the years to come in the far flung corners of the Empire.

After the Armistice began the thankless task of dismantling this vast organisation and putting the RAF on a permanent footing with a fixed number of squadrons, stations and staff. By then, after a great struggle, the Air Ministry had been set up, which circulated a memorandum on December 13, 1919, by Air Marshal Sir Hugh Trenchard, Chief of the Air Staff, outlining the permanent organisation of the RAF. What could have been of interest to India was that in the proposed overseas establishment, the RAF was to have eight squadrons and one depot exclusively for India.

In 1917, with the Gotha bomber scare behind them, the British Government took the crucial far-reaching decision of appointing a committee under the chairmanship of Field Marshal Jan Smuts, a South African, which recommended the creation of an Air Ministry "to control and administer all matters in connection with air warfare of every kind and that the new Ministry should proceed to work out the arrangements for the amalgamation of the two air services and for the legal constitution and discipline of the new service."

When the decision to go ahead with the Air Force as a separate independent service was taken, the other two services were totally averse to it, but it was war-time and the emphasis was on winning the war. However, soon after the Armistice, the murmurings became vocal protests. By early 1920 and for quite some years to come, the other two services had not reconciled themselves to the position of having to accept the RAF as a separate and equal service.

All this notwithstanding, the Government went ahead with its plans to organise the Air Force as a separate service with an identity of its very own. The first question to be resolved was that of the uniform that RAF officers and men should wear. During the war, pilots wore a variety of uniforms, often sporting emblems of their previous units such as the artillery, or cavalry or infantry regiments.

However, improvisation was the name of the game during war-time. The most prominent among them was designed by Colonel Sykes and promptly nicknamed the "maternity jacket".

The double-breasted khaki of the Royal Flying Corps and the blue reefer jacket of the Royal Naval Air Service gave place to the slate-blue tunic of the RAF, and stars, crowns and gold rings yielded to rings of plain braid. By April 1, 1918, all formalities were gone through and the new service was inaugurated and became the Royal Air Force (RAF).

Far away, in India, the first RFC squadron, No. 31 (the first military aviation unit to come to India in December 1915) was fighting hostile tribals still wearing the maternity jacket and other items of Army dress as late as 1920 and still using Army ranks until mid-1920. The No. 31 Squadron History records: "The days of many and varied uniforms came to an end about the middle of 1920. The Service dress and Mess uniforms were finally settled and officers were ordered to obtain these by December. The pattern of the Tropical Mess Kit was changed from the open pea-jacket with the light blue cummerbund and dark blue shoulder straps to the 'old cavalry pattern' jacket with white waistcoat and shoulder straps. The shoulder straps were later changed to dark blue with gold batches of rank."

An interesting episode is narrated by Air Chief Marshal Sir Philip Joubert de la Ferte, in his autobiography, *The Fated Sky*, about the reaction to the new uniform of the RAF, when he was himself commanding a wing of the service.

"So, when the RAF was formed, it produced only a ripple on the surface of our daily activities. What did achieve a sensation in the Wing was my return from a trip to London (where I had gone to plead for more aircraft and better-trained pilots), clothed in the new RAF uniform which soon became known as 'Gerti Millar's Own'. In an endeavour to retain a certain amount of the Navy's glamour, and to get away from dark blue and khaki, the new Air Ministry had concocted a uniform that was a cross between the French horizon blue and a Ruritanian Hussar's full dress. During its ephemeral existence, it caused a certain amount of confusion among our allies.

"The question of the uniform stirred other differences too. Some thought blue-grey too fancy for a fighting service, others preferred a short jacket and jodhpurs, almost everyone detested the full dress helmet.

"During these exciting times, the minds of officers and men of the Royal Air Force (RAF) were nearly as much exercised by the question of their uniforms as they were by the perils and adversities which were inflicted on them by the enemy. Even before the formation of the RAF was officially announced, but when its coming was well known, people were beginning to talk on the subject. I have a very distinct recollection of a very distinguished General Officer of the RFC, with whom I was staying in France, addressing another officer who had freshly come from London on a special mission, saying: 'What is all this about the new uniforms they are going to put us into? You were always a dressy sort of chap, you ought to know all about it.' And then he added grimly, 'Lowest form of soldiering, dress; lowest form of soldiering.'

"The uniform of the RAF became a stock joke. Originally, it was light blue, almost the colour of the blue that is so popular on the houses of French villages, and the rank stripes were of gold lace. The cap badge was an elaborate affair of which the most prominent feature was a spray of gold leaves which were disrespectfully likened by their enforced wearers to a bunch of bananas. Nobody attempted to wear it on active service but at Home it did much to brighten the dullness of the war-time streets and places of entertainment. Definitely, the uniform was not one of the Air Ministry's early successes. The design was commonly attributed to a popular star of the light opera of the period.

"Only active service officers and men continued to wear the variegated uniform of their respective services. The people who had been in the Royal Naval Air Service (RNAS) wore naval kit sometimes in blue and sometimes in khaki, with naval rank stripes. Those who had been in the RFC wore either the usual double-breasted jacket commonly known as the 'maternity jacket' which had been invented by Major Frederick Sykes when the RFC was formed, or else the tunics of the regiments to which they had originally belonged. Thus, the naval kit, others in Scottish Glengarries and the short jackets with scallopped edges of the Highland regiments, ordinary infantry kit with the ordinary infantry hat, and full RFC kit with the fore-and-aft cap.

"After much argument, the blue-grey uniform of today (1939) was evolved and it has turned out to be a very useful service dress."

— C G Grey, *A History of the Air Ministry*, 1940.

With the uniform went the badges of rank for both officers and airmen. The names by which the ranks in the new service were to be known proved difficult to choose. Hilary St. George Saunders, the air historian explains in his book *Per Adua*: "The first proposals aroused the opposition alike of the War Office and the Admiralty; the first was quick to note that under them all the senior officers were to be given naval titles and all the juniors, military; the second confined itself to the bland statement that the use of any naval title was objectionable.

"The Air Organisation Committee spent many hours weighing the rival claims of 'Reeve', 'Banneret', and 'Ardian', the last being compounded of two Gaelic words, ard meaning chief and ian or eun a bird. It was considered, however, that the literal translation of the word might impair the dignity of a senior officer, especially if he was elderly, and it was rejected. Military titles were chosen as a temporary measure."

Adds C G Grey, "Quite an important event occurred on August 4, 1919, when new rank titles of the RAF came into force. Even today (1940), the ordinary person, especially anybody who has been brought up among Navy or Army people, has considerable difficulty in placing rightly the ranks of Air Force officers."

While the controversy over rank titles was raging, someone suggested the prefix 'Sky' to the rank of Marshal. This would mean that an Air Marshal, as we know it today, would be Sky Marshal. Winston Churchill added fuel to the fire when he insisted on using the word Marshal. When the proposals were sent to King George V, he was reported to have written on the margin: "Let us not venture into the Kingdom of God — the sky is his domain." The King was persuaded to accept Marshal but he is said to have changed Sky to Air as prefix for senior Air Force officers' ranks.

"Once the names of the ranks and the uniform on which the badges would be worn were finalised and announced, there remained the question of gallantry awards. Until then, Army medals were awarded to RFC pilots for distinguished service or an act of bravery in the face of the enemy. The Air Ministry presented to the nation two new decorations, to correspond with the Distinguished Service Cross (DSC) of the Navy and the Military Cross (MC) of the Army. These were the Distinguished Flying Cross (DFC) and the Air Force Cross (AFC); the former was given for war flying or operational missions and latter for civil flying.

"A humourist remarked: 'The DFC was given for flying in the face of the enemy, whereas the AFC was given for flying in the face of Providence.'

"While the task of introducing new badges of rank on the shoulder and the uniform and gallantry awards was eventually completed, what is interesting is the award of wings to be pinned on the chest at the time of commissioning a pilot. How and when did the order to pin the double wing on the chest of a General Duties Pilot (GDP) get issued?

"The double winged pilot's flying badge was approved in Army Order No. 40 in 1913, for use by officers and airmen whilst they remain efficient pilots."

— British Air Forces, Men at Arms,
Series No. 341 (1914-18).

Wings and Pilots

Man's yearning to fly came when he saw birds flying. Even an icon like Leonardo da Vinci drew sketches of flying machines with two wings on either side of the main plane. It was reasonably asked: if birds could fly with the help of wings, why could a man not fly? Many a scientist after da Vinci, made efforts to somehow strengthen a man's arms so that they could take the place of wings as in birds. History is replete with experiments where initially wings were sought to be transplanted on a man, but much later, it was thought that a pair of artificial arms could be attached to the main body of the contraption.

Once the principle of propulsion by an internal combustion engine was accepted, designs were made to conform to the original idea of the wings of a bird. Years have passed, two World Wars and various conflicts have taken place, we have celebrated the centenary of manned flight but the birds' wings have remained the symbol. One could argue that the helicopter is different but the helicopter is an additional and useful vehicle which certainly cannot replace the aeroplane.

Most of the research in aviation took place in Europe, the US and Russia. And military aviation came into its own by the time World War I broke out. By trial and error, new tactics were tried, terminology developed, ranks became different, helmet and scarf clad pilots became the symbols of the air service. Before the war broke out in August 1914, the Royal Flying Corps was established as a service distinct from the Army and yet a part of it.

But, how to differentiate a pilot from an Army man or officer? While badges of rank would give the status of the man and a shoulder badge his speciality such as infantry, artillery or cavalry, there was nothing available to distinguish a pilot from the others. Before 1914 and right through the war and almost to the end of it, even though the RAF was born on April 1, 1918, the Air Force ranks in Britain were the same as those of the Army.

Almost a year before the war, the Army think-tanks decided what a pilot should wear on his uniform to identify his calling. Thus, was born the concept and shape of the wings, for it was the birds that gave the idea. A pair of double wings with the national insignia in the middle was ordered to be worn by pilots on their uniforms.

This was formalised by the issue of the Army Order No. 40 in 1913, mandating that pilots shall wear the wings as a part of their uniform. Almost all nations have this symbol of wings to denote a pilot. While the British and Commonwealth countries use cloth made wings, Americans use metal ones. After the war was over in 1918, the twenties saw the beginning of commercial aviation. Even there, the pilots wear wings. Both military and civilian pilots all over the world, flying either fixed-wing aircraft or rotary or single-engined or multi-engined machines, wear the pilot's wings.

The Flying Bullet

In 1923, in the RAF 'aerial gunners' were issued a badge to be worn between the shoulder and the elbow. This took the form of a flying bullet.

Subsequently, the air gunner's badge became a half wing brevy.

The Observer Brevet (Badge)

During the early part of World War I, on the Western Front as also later in the Middle East, two-seater aircraft carried a pilot and an observer. Most of the observers were Army officers who volunteered for the job. Initially, they were tried in the field by flying with pilots over the lines and when found suitable, were awarded the observer's wing — a single wing. This was instituted in August 1915, two years after the pilot's wings were formalised by an Army Order.

During autumn 1916, an Observers' Section was formed at the Wireless School, Brooklands (UK), which at that time had an output of 20 observers per month. The great need for the necessary numbers of trained observers culminated in the formation of a School of Aeronautics at Bath (UK) during the spring of 1918, whereon observers were systematically and uniformly trained.

Decades later, when India's first aircraft carrier steamed into Bombay harbour in November 1961 and was welcomed and received by the first Prime Minister, it had a full Indian crew and six Flying Branch officers, one of whom had been trained as an observer. He was Lieutenant M K Roy (later Vice Admiral M K Roy, FOC-in-C, Eastern Naval Command, Vizag, India).

Qualification Tests in Flying — As on March 23, 1916

- The pilot must have at least 15 hours in the air solo.
- He must have flown a service aeroplane satisfactorily.
- He should have carried out a cross-country flight of at least 60 miles successfully.
- During this flight, he must land at two outside landing places under the supervision of an officer of the Royal Flying Corps (RFC).
- He will climb to 6,000 ft. and remain at that height for at least 15 minutes, after which he will land with his engine stopped, the aeroplane first touching the ground within a circular mark of fifty yards diameter.
- He will make two landings in the dark assisted by landing flares.
- He will attain a standard of eight words a minute signalling on the buzzer.

For Further Training

Newly qualified flying officers who may remain with squadrons at Home (UK) are to be given every opportunity of gaining air experience. They should be made to fly in bad weather on all possible occasions; and they should practise landing over a tape 10 ft. from the ground, bomb-dropping over the camera-obscura, fighting in the air, night flying in formation. Wireless work and photography should be practised where possible.

Training in Military Aviation

Delivering a lecture on 'Training in military aviation' under the auspices of the Royal Aeronautical Society in London on January 24, 1917, Air Vice Marshal Sir Sefton Brancker said:

"Before the war (World War I)flying was comparatively difficult and was the chief factor in the pilot's training, military qualifications being considered of secondary importance. Now flying upto a certain standard is extraordinarily easy, but the standard of military qualifications required is getting higher and higher and more difficult to attain, and, at the same time, the quality of flying demanded is growing greater every day. So, our task at Home (UK) grows harder.

"The way in which war has forced a higher standard of training on us is remarkable. There is only one point which has simplified training. The modern designed aeroplane (1917) and the latest engine make flying pure and simple and much easier than it used to be. Aeroplanes are comparatively stable, and engines have a considerable reserve of power than in the old days, and these two factors have helped a good deal in the training of pilots.

"One of the great bones of contention used to be the advisability of training a pupil by means of his instruments as opposed to balance. Instruments of late have become more and more reliable, and personally I am the greatest believer in using them for training (simulator training 70 years later). The most common type of accident follows engine failure. The cure will assuredly come in peace. When we can devote more energy towards real reliability in the engine (progress did come when peace prevailed), I think the day will come when an unstable machine will be looked upon as impossible.

"The most unexpected people make good pilots and very often the most promising ones never attain more than mediocrity in the air. Personally, I think any sound man with sound nerves (and women too for that matter) can make a good, useful pilot, but it is only the exceptional individual who will make the really brilliant fighting pilot."

— AVM Sir Sefton Brancker, RFC.

Behind the Wings

Experts have estimated that to keep one soldier at the firing line, one needs, at least, eight men to support him by providing various services in the peace area as also in the field area.

In the military air service, which is today known as the Air Force, initially planes were unreliable and crashes were frequent. While the pilot bore the brunt of the elements in an open cockpit, he could only rely on the mechanics on the ground to make his aircraft technically serviceable. They were called fitters and were very much in demand because of their technical ability to maintain and repair warplanes.

In India, the very first flying machines appeared in early 1916, on the North-West Frontier. Once the teething troubles were over, fresh pilots from the flying schools in England were posted to India. A certain period was allotted to acclimatise them to the living conditions and to the environment as also to the important job of flying safely on reconnaissance, carrying out ground attacks and bombing and, finally, trying their best to bring themselves and their air gunners back to base.

Initially, fresh pilots found themselves commencing local training as soon as they had settled in domestically. Such training consisted normally of cross-country flights, steering clear of unadministered (tribal) territory, at first, practising formation flying, front and rear machine-gun firing, bombing and photo reconnaissance.

Pilots were mainly required to complete at least ten hours solo flying before being permitted to carry any passengers, especially ground crew such as fitters and riggers, and a total of 40 hours before commencing night flying. The ban on taking air gunners many of whom were volunteers but were by profession ground technicians, was aptly explained by a seasoned contemporary pilot of the RAF who had served many years on the Frontier: "Pilots we can always get, but good fitters are bloody hard to find……" So is it today.

Colonel T E Lawrence as Aircraftsman T E Shaw

Over 75 years have passed since the legendary British archaeologist turned soldier, Colonel T E Lawrence died in a motor cycle accident in England on May 19, 1935. While World War I produced many Generals and Field Marshals, Lawrence alone evoked curiosity, admiration and criticism, long after the war and much more after his death. His book *The Seven Pillars of Wisdom*, a widely acclaimed and read book, throws some light on the man, his mission of helping the Arabs to throw off the Turkish yoke and his disappointment with his own country's promises to the Arabs which were not honoured subsequently.

After the war was over, Lawrence, having left the Army, tried to get back into the common man's obscurity. But that was not to be. So, to lose himself in a sea of uniforms, he joined the RAF in the UK under an assumed name – T E Shaw. His linkage with India begins when he was transferred to the aircraft park and depot which the RAF had built at Drigh Road, near Karachi.

Much as he tried to keep aloof as an anonymous aircraftsman, he could not hide from his past. A first person account given by another aircraftsman, a fitter named Mathew Clarke who served in No. 5

Squadron, RAF in India, in the Twenties and Thirties, throws some light on Lawrence's sojourn with the RAF in India.

"There had been some vague reports in the English papers that T E Lawrence or aircraftsman (AC2) Shaw had been posted overseas from the Home Establishment, but there was no mention as to which overseas command he was supposed to be going to. I think most of us were interested in this mythical character that since World War I had caused so much conjecture after he disappeared into the Tank Corps and the RAF, trying to live down his war-time exploits and subsequent disappointments. For some reason, his arrival at Drigh Road with a few other postings from the UK was completely unheralded – not even a rumour that he was on the camp seemed to have got around.

"I (AC2 Mathew Clarke) went to the barber shop one afternoon and had to wait my turn whilst the chair was occupied, the *nappi* (barber) was busy at the job and I was reading a paper, I heard the barber strapping his razor for the old finishing touches of the hair cut, a light neck shave, and I heard a cultured but irate voice calling out, 'Don't you dare put that razor near my neck'.

"I looked up and saw reflected in the mirror a face which was vaguely familiar. At the same time, this customer jumped from the chair and turned to me and said: 'I cannot stand the touch of a razor on my neck,' and with that, paid the barber and walked out. I sat there having my hair cut and it dawned upon me as to who this chap was. I could not get back to my room quick enough to break the news. Of course, I was accused of seeing things but by dinner time that night, the news had spread of the distinguished visitor in our midst.

"Shaw was posted to ERS and was, for some time, permanent bungalow orderly; he got on well with his room-mates, was unobtrusive, very frugal in his habits, a small eater who never went to the canteen. If he needed toilet articles, he would get one of his room-mates to get them. He only went out of the camp once to my knowledge and that was to buy a super gramophone and records for the billet; his choice was classical music which he would listen to whilst in the billet on his own when doing his few orderly duties. When the lads were back from work, the 'pop' music of the period played and Shaw used to good humouredly listen. I believe that his room-mates used to good naturedly pull his leg, but left him alone to his reading and writing articles for some of the more erudite magazines.

"He was soon a familiar figure, strolling around the camp, never venturing outside the guard room gates; he was shortish and used to walk with his arms folded behind him and his head slightly forward. He was constantly being told off by SPs for going across to the bathhouse in the heat of the day with no topee on."

Phobias and Camp Life

"I remember early on when he came to us, our Sgt SP, a real old-timer and a very rough diamond, bawling out, 'Come here, that airman without a topee, at the double.' I told the Sgt that this airman was Colonel Lawrence and he shot back, 'I don't give a bugger if he is Lord Kitchener, he is not getting a sun tapped on this camp'.

"Lawrence had a phobia for hot baths and some of my mates would remember that our bath at the Depot was unheated showers — although in the summer, the showers were pretty hot as the pipes ran so close to the surface that the sun heated the water. However, Shaw needed a proper bath. One of his buddies from ERS got a fifty gallon oil drum and cut the top out and Shaw got him to buy giant blow lamps to heat the water in the drum. Each afternoon, one could hear the blow lamps roaring away so that Shaw could have his bath at a time when most of us were flat out on our *charpayees*. I do remember seeing him standing in his tub on one occasion and noticing scars on his back. This was, of course, before *The Seven Pillars of Wisdom* had revealed his capture by the Turks and the beating he had had from them.

"The first Christmas Shaw was at the Depot, he did guard duties for those of his room-mates who had been detailed over the holiday period, so that they could enjoy the X'mas festivities in full — I believe he did three consecutive duties in consequence. He was promoted AC1 (he could not get his LAC as, he told me, he had not passed his educational exams for LAC) and lost his job as room orderly and became a sort of Stores Assistant in the ERS Stores (which he soon organised with some system of his own, which took some sorting out, when he was posted to the Frontier).

"Of course, his trade group was ACH Group 5. With this change of status, he left the barrack room and occupied a bunk, primarily, I think, so that he could have privacy to do his reading and writing, perhaps the only instance of his getting any favours. He also assisted the Camp Librarian and some quite valuable books found their way to the library shelves after he had received them from the publishers."

Seven Pillars of Wisdom

"Because of my friendship with the librarian, I read some proofs of *The Seven Pillars of Wisdom* and also some letters Shaw had from Winston Churchill which he had let the librarian borrow. I think that he schooled himself on the bare minimum of food and sleep. He would take two or three slices of bread and a pot of tea and a pat of butter and would take them back to his bunk at tea time and not go for his evening meal. The light would be on in his bunk at all hours of the night when he would be reading or writing.

"He had no intimate friends but was very friendly with a couple of chaps who were far from intellectual types one would associate with a 'Fellow of All Souls' (Oxford) and a noted scholar. In fact, one was a friend of mine with whom Shaw kept up a correspondence after he had left the RAF. Neither of these chaps betrayed a confidence which Shaw may have passed to them. And he was in the know of lots of things because of his many friends in high places and never ever revealed anything to the press about Lawrence's life with us, in spite of tempting offers.

"I know that Shaw was pestered for interviews by the editor of the local paper. Shaw would not even see him. After Shaw's death, I read an article in the press, *The Sind Observer*, written by this editor purporting to be recollections of Shaw at Karachi (which shows that one must not believe all that one reads in the papers).

"Rumour at the Drigh Road Base and Depot had it, and no doubt it was true, that our Commanding Officer (CO) Wingco R J Bone was not happy with Shaw's presence on the station but he had to put up with it as Shaw was a personal friend of the Air Officer Commanding (AOC) G Salmond or was it Sir John. We had a visit from an aircraft of the Royal Yugoslavian Air Force, one of many pioneer flights we had landing at Karachi about this time.

"Shaw was detailed to escort the two Yugoslavian officers around the camp – showing the sights, they came into the MT workshops. I remember asking Shaw if he had been detailed to look after them because, perhaps, they spoke Turkish (remembering that parts of Yugoslavia had been part of the old Turkish Empire). He replied that the reason was that he appeared to be the only chap on the camp who spoke French which was a language the Yugos understood. I knew a couple of chaps who both spoke good French and they said to Shaw that perhaps he was the only erk (airman) who spoke good French and had time to spare. He laughed at this saying, 'Perhaps, you are right.' Both the Yugos had served with our forces in World War I when they were with the Serbian Air Force – one of them wore the DFC ribbon."

Frontier Posting

"Not long after this (1927-28), Shaw got his posting to the North-Western Frontier (Miranshah) and again rumours were rife about him. We had a major scandal at the Depot involving the alleged striking of an airman by the CO. Shaw was apparently blamed for forcing the reluctant airman to make a case against the CO, which incidentally was untrue. Anyway, Shaw was on his way. Wingco Millyard (then a Warrant Officer) told me that he had Shaw as his store's clerk there (Miranshah) and again put the place in one hell of a mess.

"His next visit to Karachi was a very short one, when he was posted to the UK in a great hurry because certain Indian political parties said that Shaw had been sent to the Frontier to stir up trouble and assist the British Government in subduing the tribes. All this was, of course, strenuously denied but the powers that be no doubt thought that he would be best out of the way. Shaw was sent Home as a civilian passenger on a PO boat – I think it was Rawalpindi. I know he borrowed a civvy suit from an acquaintance to travel in. Thus, ended the story of Lawrence in India.

"I next met him after I got my ticket in Plymouth. At that time, he was stationed at the RAF base at Mount Batten. I was window shopping at a ship's chandlers, and happened to notice an ordinary looking airman gazing in the window as well, it was Aircraftsman Shaw. I passed some banal remark about the weather or something, he nodded and said hullo and we both went our ways.

"At Mount Batten, Shaw was helping to develop high speed launches which later became our Air Sea Rescue Boats. A friend wrote to me about the same time that he and Shaw had a motorbike dust up on Salisbury Plain. As you may know, Shaw was a speed fanatic, partly because George Brough (a contemporary speed champion on motor bikes) gave him a new bike every year. And so was my pal. They both had long talks about bikes at Karachi and it was quite by chance that they encountered each other on the road.

"I know that my friend was full of glee that he had left Shaw miles behind in the course of their encounter. The strange thing about Shaw was the fact that a discussion about him, even at that time, would start an argument — was he genuinely hiding or was it all a gimmick to get further publicity. These sorts of arguments have been going on ever since and the man is still a mystery."

Miranshah

In their attempt to control the various tribes in the unadministered areas between the Durand Line and the administered and settled areas further east, the British Government of the day devised various methods of ensuring peace. The plans centred round transport, communication and intelligence.

Roads were built where there had been none and forts were built where troops and auxiliary forces were quartered, telegraph lines were strung across so that any outbreak of violence could be dealt with speedily. Political Agents who could speak Pushtu, the Pathan's language, and glean the intentions and plans of the hostile tribes so that the trouble could be nipped in the bud, were appointed.

One of the forts built was at Miranshah in the area on a stony plain, immortalised by Rudyard Kipling's poetry. It was a Beau Geste type, with an airfield within its perimeter. The fort housed a unit of the Tochi Scouts one of the local paramilitary units which had knowledge of the terrain and the identities of the tribal leaders. Also, the Political Agent was operating from the fort. Apart from that, the RAF used the flat ground in front of the fort as an airfield and at any time at least a flight of aeroplanes would be by rotation stationed there for watch and ward duties and to help the Army during operations.

And it was to this fort that Lawrence alias Aircraftsman T E Shaw was next posted. Lawrence's stay in India began in 1927 when he was posted to Drigh Road, Karachi, and from there to the Miranshah Fort on the Frontier. In an account of Lawrence's presence there, famous aero historian, Chaz Boywer, who served the RAF for 26 years, mentions in his book *The Flying Elephants*, which is the history of No. 27 Squadron, RAF, that served in India, the arrival of Shaw at Miranshah in June 1928.

"It was during this period that an almost legendary figure made his appearance on the North-West Frontier – AC1 Shaw, T E, known to millions of people as 'Lawrence of Arabia', posted to Miranshah in June 1928 as a clerk on the strength of No. 60 Squadron.

"Shaw performed all the duties of his rank and trade, and despite many stories to the contrary, never once left the confines of Miranshah Fort during his short service there. He was a popular figure with the airmen (although something of a nuisance to some officers when he occasionally became stubborn about wearing a spine pad or sun helmet).

"His rare collection of books, many of them prized first editions, was eventually presented to the Fort Library and one off-duty project with which he was concerned was the construction of a hard court for tennis. Eventually, due to ill-founded political pressures, it was considered expedient to remove Shaw from India and, on January 12, 1929, he sailed from Bombay in the SS *Rajputana*, bound for Plymouth."

— M Clarke

Legacy of Lawrence and the Aftermath

Just three years after his death, publishers Jonathan Cape published a book *Letters of T E Lawrence*, edited by David Garnett, which discussed the thoughts expressed in the letters that Lawrence wrote.

A write-up in the *Times of India*, dated December 10, 1938, entitled "Lawrence of Arabia," said:

"In this big book, 896 pages containing 583 letters, the reader can study 'Lawrence of Arabia' from his boyhood in 1906 to his death in 1935. Whether the study will result in a clear idea of the sort of man that Lawrence was, is more than doubtful. He was an abnormal man, possessed, as the editor of these letters notes, by a desire to suffer. It was that desire, 'an irrational urge to submit to and to subject himself to most obviously his inferiors,' which led him to enlist and this trait constantly recurrent through his life.

"His attitude to money, physical suffering, to his own ability shows that abnormality. At times, he seemed fully conscious of it. At others, he scoffed at it. 'Please do not let the public feeling that I am different from the crowd… I am a very natural sort of Anglo-Irish', he said in 1929. He was, of course, nothing of the sort. But even his beloved Bernard Shaw could not tease him out of his 'maddening masquerade' in the RAF.

"In Lawrence's letters then, one sees the growth of a very strange character and no matter what pre-conceived views of his exploits in Arabia one may bring to the reading of the letters, one cannot help repeatedly lamenting the way in which his talents were thrown away in mechanical drudgery. He would not have wished to be judged in that way. His testimony is to be found in *The Seven Pillars of Wisdom* (especially in a part omitted from the subscribers' edition) but here reprinted and it is on that, presumably, he meant judgment to be based.

"'If I have restored to the East some self-respect, a goal, ideals, if I have made the standard of rule of White over Red more exigent, I have fitted those people in a degree for the new Commonwealth in which the dominant races will forget their brute achievements, and white and red and yellow and brown and black will stand up together without side glances in the service of the world.'

"How many of his impetuous assertions, one wonders, would he have wished to be published? For instance, in 1928, he wrote 'The nearest approach to an Arab Empire at present is Ibn Saud's. It is a figment, built on sand. Nothing static will rise in the desert, it will pass.' Two years later, he was writing, 'Ibn Saud has my respects as a King.' One could find many similar contradictions in this volume. Lawrence's political views were anything but static.

"To many readers it may appear that these letters are most worth reading for their literary criticism. Lawrence read widely and liked to record his judgments, some of them obviously of little value, but many of them thoughtful and of great interest. Thomas Hardy, to whose house he often went as a visitor, was one of his chief heroes.

"'They used to call this man a pessimist,' he wrote of Hardy, 'while really he is full of fancy expectations.' In the same letter, he wrote that 'he had not found in Hardy, any bowing down, moral or material or spiritual.' The criticism, one feels, is of the man rather than of his writing."

Fifty Years Later: Still an Enduring Mystery

By 1985, Lawrence had been dead fifty years, but the mystery surrounding his life still lingers at his graveside. The church in the village where he sought obscurity after his world famous exploits in the Middle East during World War I, was to hold a service in his memory on Sunday, says an Associated Press report, dated May 21, 1985.

Rev Dennis Ackroyd said a mysterious note appeared on Lawrence's grave saying: "I have kept the secret still," and added, "People do leave many notes here — why, I have not worked out yet. It is obviously someone who knew him."

Another mystery was a bunch of roses delivered annually to his church on Lawrence's birthday – August 15, with one less bloom each year. In 1984, there were 36 roses, meaning that by 2020 there will be none. Rev. Ackroyd tried to contact the sender through the international flower company that delivers the roses but without success. He believed they came from a woman in America.

Lawrence, a Welsh-born archaeologist, was recruited by the British intelligence at the outbreak of World War I, to organise an Arab revolt against the Turks who were siding with Germany in the war. His exploits made famous in his autobiographical account, *The Seven Pillars of Wisdom*, included numerous battles in what are now Iraq, Jordan and Syria and acts of sabotage that crippled the Turkish war effort.

The image of Lawrence, adopting the Arab garb and the ascetic desert life of a Bedouin, captured the imagination of his countrymen. But Arab scholars have questioned the part that Lawrence played in the Arab uprisings and some see him as an agent of Western imperialism. A new biography says that not only are there questions about Lawrence's life among the Bedouins, there are doubts about the official version of his death in a motorcycle crash on May 19, 1935.

Backing into the Limelight, by British journalist Michael Yardley, questions several of Lawrence's accounts, including one in which he botched the execution of an Arab and another in which he was beaten and homosexually assaulted at the hands of a Turkish Governor.

"Part of the problem," Yardley says, "is that Lawrence often was unaccompanied by any other British soldier who could have substantiated his stories." Further, "the media had much to do with building up Lawrence's mysterious and heroic image." Lawrence retired to a cottage in Moreton Hamlet, 210 km southwest of London, after coming back from the desert, changing his name and re-enlisting as a Private in the Army. The motorcycle on which he was killed was to go on display in the church along with the *burnoose* or the Arab dress band which Lawrence wore in the desert.

Old Blighty

"They say there is a troopship just leaving Bombay for Old Blighty's shores..."

In the British Army, serving in India, from the Urdu word 'Bilayati' means 'removed at some distance'— which is where many soldiers wanted to be — back Home. Indian Army troops and also those who served in Egypt, where the word 'bilade' meant the village or the home town, came to Britain as 'b'lighty'.

One more explanation: in Hindustani, the word for England was 'Vilayat' and its corrupted English form became over a period of time 'Blight'. Blighty rhymes well with Vilayati meaning English.

Commonwealth Air Forces

The Runnymede Memorial to the Air Forces of the Commonwealth nations at Runnymede, UK, is dedicated to the men and women who served and died during World War II (1939-45). This site has a historic connection with King John of England as it overlooks the site of the signing of the Magna Carta.

"What Type of Man Makes the Best Pilot?"

"In the early stages of the development of aviation, it was, in some quarters, believed that a good horseman would make an expert pilot. This so-called belief was given some amount of credence, when it was pointed out that Germany's greatest air ace was Hauptmann Baron Rittmeister Manfred von Richthofen who was an excellent horseman, since the appellation "Rittmeister" (riding master) was a part of his title.

"However, there were quite a few gunners (artillery) who opted for aviation as there were also from infantry. Thus, the question as to what qualities are needed in a person to make him a potential good pilot, still remains a question.

"It is very hard to give a definite reply. The popular impression is that a special temperament is required for success in the air; it is rather assumed that an artistic temperament, a vivid imagination, carelessness and reckless daring are great assets in the psychology of a would-be pilot.

"Actually, this is not my experience. It is true that during the war, the air with its apparent romance and glamour appealed to the artistic side of society more vividly than either the Army or the Navy, but it does not follow that such men made the best pilots.

"I always found that the most useful pilot in war was the man who would have made the best officer in the old regular Army — the good old type which has won us the British Empire — unimaginative but absolutely reliable, courageous and honourable to a fault, rather solid, devoted to the hardy sports of the hunting field and the jungle and caring nothing for the artistic side of life — this type could usually be trained into a useful pilot at almost any age within reason.

"But most unexpected people turned into good pilots. Age was always a debatable point. Young men naturally learnt more quickly and easily than those bordering on thirty but they did not last as long under active service conditions. The demands of war forced us to train numbers of boys of eighteen, or even seventeen, to fly, and then send them straight off to the front, but I always said that the ideal fighting age was more like twenty-five.

"There is no doubt in my mind that for peace conditions, the younger a man starts to fly, the better, and personally I believe that the average man, trained properly and early, will go on flying all his life. During the War, it paid us well to teach a certain proportion of older men, because they were invaluable as Squadron and Wing Commanders, although possibly not star pilots.

"The fact is that almost any normal man can learn to fly passably well, and it is after that standard has been passed that the qualities of courage combined with caution, enterprise backed by reliability, and a spirit of self-sacrifice and *esprit de corps* bring the real good men into the front rank."

— Air Vice-Marshal Sir Sefton Brancker,
KCB, AFC, RAF (Retd)

Frontier Air Operations

"Most of the aircraft used by the RAF in the NWFP and elsewhere in India were conceived and designed and built in temperate climate and used mostly on the European battlefields. It was only when the aircraft were sent to Iraq, Egypt and India that the weaknesses became apparent.

"The thin air of the Frontier area made climbing to the required height difficult. While in Europe, it was the lack of power in the engine that made climbing to 8,000 ft difficult, in India, it was the weather conditions. Apart from that, aircraft of that period were bi-planes with fabric covering the wings, which the rains would thoroughly soak and the strong winds would displace.

"Most squadron fitters and riggers erected new aircraft after unloading them from packing cases, initially out in the open and later, with better organisation and some basic facilities, under canvas tents. Aeroplanes of that era had no parachutes; a proposal was mooted towards the end of the war that air crew, as we understand the term, that is, the pilot and observer, should have a parachute in the aircraft. Experiments were made, some were introduced but in far away India and on the Frontier, they were only heard of but not seen.

"For the RAF personnel stationed in India in the Twenties, life was peculiarly antiquated in certain respects. Steeped in centuries of long held customs (mostly British but blended and customised in native setting), the ritual of social life under the British 'Raj' sometimes contrasted quaintly with modern requirements of progress. To the newcomer, such customs gave a distinct impression of stepping into a bygone age — the Victorian era.

"And to the professional airman, these customs and outlook were linked directly with the equipment with which he was expected to carry out his duties. Aircraft were of elderly concept (some Bristol F2Bs of No. 20 Squadron still carried patched German bullet holes from 1918), while the maintenance situation in the early Twenties was not far short of a scandal.

"By virtue of Hugh Trenchard's single-minded if dogmatic, struggle to retain the RAF as a separate service, the RAF was granted, albeit reluctantly, an individual financial estimate (it was not even called a budget) in Parliament. But the RAF in India enjoyed no such independence. Regarded as merely one more formation of the Army and being a young and misunderstood and therefore, distrusted service, suffered accordingly."

— Chaz Bowyer

Teething Troubles

"Operating in tropical conditions, under the most primitive facilities, airmen had to use ingenuity, innovation, patience, and grit to fight the weather and the ability of the aircraft to survive in the mountainous regions where they operated. For instance, in No. 28 Squadron, they discovered that the entire engine rubber connections perished under old green paint.

"Changing them was a sticky finger job, but we replaced them with a complete set of plain and brand new rubber ones and by not painting them. This worked very well and we had no more rubber perishing. Other squadrons found similar problems and we informed each other via the Lahore depot.

"Routine flying started early in the morning around 4 am and went on till 10 am when it began to get hot, over 120 degrees in the shade. When not flying, we kept the aircraft in the hangars for as long as we could, some in the big canvas hangars and others in their individual shaped hangars. These were the same type of hangars used in the 1914-18 war, quickly erected and dismantled for movement. Flying only took place later in the day if and when anything special arose.

"Bristol fighters with which our squadron (No. 28) was equipped, were constructed mainly of wood and canvas. A tip from 'old hands' was to cut-off one side of our five gallon petrol tins, fill up the troughs with paraffin and keep the wheels and the tailskid in the trough. This kept the white ants off the aircraft because these ants would eat through the wood leaving only a thin outer shell of wood. The Bristol fighter proved very successful and I flew many hours with good pilots from the 1914-18 war and with young pilots from the post-war RAF flying schools at Home.

"On February 20, 1920, my aircraft crashed in some trees upon an approach landing and the two officers escaped injury. The mechanics had no flying logbook issued to them giving none of any official recording even when we (mechanics) were acting as observers. I did not enter all my flying in my diary, and on the Frontier, if any records were kept of mechanics flying, we never knew.

"Some pilots, when flying, wore a smart looking flying topee fastened with a chin strap, something like a jockey's helmet. We, in the cockpit did not. We managed with a flying helmet and goggles, sometimes wearing our topee fastened with the chin strap on top, but this was uncomfortable. Sometimes, we would fly in our shirt sleeves and while flying rather high at times to escape the heat was a relief, it became chilly flying in the open cockpits.

"The pilot's seat was a small wicker basket chair fixed on the rear petrol tank. Our (mechanic or the observer) chair was small and padded about a foot square. It moved backward by pressing two small levers at the side and it would slide along back down the fuselage out of the way. There was a petrol tank fitted on the top wing of the centre section which being gravity fed was turned on for take-off. The lower tank, positioned under the pilot's seat, was pressure fed by a pump at the right side.

"There were very few observers in the squadrons, so few, that there would often be two pilots in the aircraft, and on many occasions, mechanics in charge of the aircraft flew as substitute observers.

"The Bristol fighter was a very pleasant aircraft to fly. It was fast and manoeuvrable and in those days, as the saying went, 'You could chuck it about.' The squadrons had pilots of the 1914-18 war and many of these officers reached very high ranks as Air Marshals in the RAF in World War II and afterwards.

"The squadron began to experiment taking off in twos and then threes and flying in formation. Later, six aircraft took off in formation. The leader gave the signal and on full throttle, they roared away from us at the hangars leaving behind a dust storm nearly blinding us. What did it matter? The roar of the engines indicated to us that they were airborne and soon they were flying above us at a steady pace in perfect formation. It proved that our work and flying was proving itself.

"We heard that most of the squadron turned out to see them and the residents and other units and natives were thrilled to see such a wonderful performance. A lovely sight for us and we wished we were up there with them in this supreme effort. They circled the area over Ambala and split up, landing each aircraft independently. Then back to the hangars, a great performance for the squadron, the pilots doing a splendid job which they regularly repeated.

"Of course, there were hazards to face, but we all chipped in and did our bit. The dust storms that the aircraft caused did give us some concern, but they were not the only ones. Cavalry and artillery with horse-drawn gun carriages, out on practice, caused dust floating all over the flying field, making the landing of aircraft very dangerous. The dust could blot out the vision of the pilots. Sometimes, a ground mist would cover the aerodrome. From the air, you could see the ground, but as you descended, you entered this mist which blinded you. One aircraft landed on to hockey goal posts, the machine being a complete 'write-off' and the pilot and observer being injured.

"Smart turnout, precision parades have been and are a hallmark of the Army and this 'spit and polish' is more or less absent in the Air Force. Not that they do not have parades and do not insist on good turn-out, but, as the service was still in the transition phase of defining its relationship with the Army, many new innovations developed over a period of time by the very old method of 'trial and error'.

"On January 1, 1921, there was a big parade at Ambala known as Proclamation Day, a ceremony under the command of the General Officer Commanding (GOC) Ambala. Flying and too much ceremony did not go well with the mechanics who had much hard work to do in keeping aircraft airworthy, besides doing frequent guard duties as well.

"Most of the officer pilots had done little ceremonial drill, having been fighting in the air up to the end of 1918. The pilots were not so fond of ceremony with the comparable military efficiency of the Army officers, who were doing this sort of drill regularly.

"In discussion with the pilots in the hangars, we suggested that it would look good if the squadron supplied a fly-past in RAF salute over the parade, knowing it would keep us off the parade. It worked," recalls Aircraftsman Ross of No. 28 Squadron.

Their uniforms were slightly different from those of the Army, but their ranks were the same as the Army under which they served in so far as duties and discipline were concerned. But by virtue of their different role, they were separate. Every squadron, it was the objective, should get first-hand experience of flying in the mountainous area of the Frontier. Quite often, each squadron though based at either Karachi or Lahore or Ambala or Peshawar or Kohat or Risalpur had a flight of the unit, out on the Frontier, be it Miranshah or any other forward airfield.

"Some squadrons relieved other squadrons by 'tours' on the Frontier beyond Risalpur and Peshawar which was the headquarters for Frontier squadrons. We, in No. 28 Squadron, were to relieve No. 20 Squadron at Kohat which had outposts at Parashinar, Bannu, Dera Ismael Khan (DIK), Tank and other places.

"In fact, any point on the ground with a reasonably flat piece of ground, enough for an aircraft to land and take off became an advanced landing ground or outpost. A few tents for personnel and stores and tented accommodation, and they were in business, running an outpost. Aircraft, at such, were often parked in the open, exposed to the 'extreme elements'. There was no such thing as a control tower and wind conditions were tested by pilots prior to take-off by holding a handkerchief in the air and testing the wind direction and speed. Soon an innovation was adopted — the wind sock — which was visible to all as it was mounted on a pole adjacent to the landing ground.

"Upon arrival at Kohat, we were housed in tents, in fact, the whole station appeared to be under canvas except the general stores, bomb stores, armoury and headquarters. The whole place was not very impressive and the flying area, sandy and rough and bumpy, did not appear as good or secure as Ambala. The aerodrome was smaller than Ambala, a flat surface beneath the first range of mountains, with the Hindu Kush towering high in the distance.

"The guard duties were soon on orders and we had to undertake every type of guard, the squadron headquarters guard, the aerodrome guard, the quarter guard, the 'prowlers' guard. Between these duties, we maintained the aircraft and did flying duties as well."

Recalling these events in 1987, Ross says that there was no such thing as the luxury of a strong RAF Regiment — it did not exist at that time. The guard duties placed a heavy strain on their weekly duties, because they came so regularly, that it amounted to one guard duty within three or four days. That was not all. There was also a guard duty which lasted 24 hours and another a 12-hour all night duty.

"The mechanics in the hangars talked a lot to the pilots (officers). I was an instigator in suggesting that the Army, stationed not far away, should take over some of our guard duties. They were trained to do it, and it would relieve our air mechanics to devote their time to keeping their aircraft in good flying order. I also suggested to the pilots that in my opinion a unit of men should be enlisted (ex-Army) as a special job to do all the guard duties. They gave it a very sympathetic hearing and fully agreed to the idea.

"Who knows that the suggestions and ideas discussed on the unholy North-West Frontier outposts might have seeded and travelled upwards along the service ladder to higher authority? It might have brought about the need for forming an RAF unit for all special duties. Most of these pilots we spoke to gained high rank by the end of the war. Later, some were promoted to very high rank and knighted with power to use their influence and shape the issues with authority."

It did result in the creation of the RAF Regiment which took over all watch and ward duties and other duties that are unconnected to flying and maintenance work.

A few years ago (2008), the Indian Air Force (IAF) created a new force for ground defence and watch and ward duties at all air bases in the country (GARUD Force).

"In the early days, aircraft were fragile but efficient with only a mere handful of first class air mechanics to keep them flying. Flying duties could be hazardous and an additional demand was the open cockpit in which the mechanic doubled as an observer.

"Spares were practically impossible to get. We used any unbroken parts of crashed aircraft, even wire from empty boxes to use as split-pins to keep them flying. My Bristol fighter F2B at Kohat at one time flew without an exhaust pipe extension down the starboard side of the fuselage, and the flames were seen shooting out near the centre section.

"Out of the over 70 aircraft which were supposed to be airworthy, only seven aircraft were actually in flyable condition. Between January and June 1922, there were seven crashes. Despite having to face a critical shortage of spares, flying had to be continued. The magnitude of the task can be imagined when pilots had to fly 200 miles from the base day after day. 'The machines won't stand it,' lamented one, for the wear and tear on the already antiquated machines was terrible. There were forced landings and crashes all over the country. All our machines are old and patched up grids. There is not a single spare machine, neither is there a spare propeller in India."

Back in London, the Secretary of State for Air, Sir Samuel Hoare told the House of Commons on March 2, 1923: "All squadrons in India have been grounded for lack of spares." And privately, he spoke of these squadrons having received no new engines for seven years.

In terms of organisation, RAF India was initially a wing based unit. With the arrival of more squadrons, it became a group and in 1919, Air

Commodore T I Webb Bowen became the first Air Officer Commanding (AOC) RAF India, and continued in that capacity until 1923.

Sir John Slessor, Marshal of the RAF, who was a Flight Commander with No. 20 Squadron at that time, said:

"The RAF in India suffered less from the malevolence of a tribal enemy than the depredations of the Government of India. I think it was inevitable that among senior advisers to the Viceroy, the combination of ignorance about air matters, ingrained with tradition and the Englishman's national suspicion of anything new should have had the result, that, when cuts in military expenditure were required, they should fall upon this new service, which no one understood."

— Sir John Slessor in *The Central Blue*.

"The lack of spares in India and the scandalous state of affairs regarding equipment and maintenance of the RAF at that time was stated in a British newspaper as 'airmen were flying to death' to be entirely the fault of the Legislative Assembly and Council of State. They scared the life out of the Army Department and the Government of India would not buy from the vast supply of equipment available in this country. After much quibbling, the Government of India said they would buy 18 Bristol fighters with tropical radiators."

— Aircraftsman Ross, No. 28 Squadron.

The disastrous situation finally came to a head after Flying Officer Duncan and his passenger F/O Luard, both of No. 27 Squadron crashed during a take-off and were killed at Dardoni Fort on August 17, 1922. F/O Luard, the only son of a retired Colonel, had written several letters to his father explaining the state of the RAF in India. Following his son's death, Colonel Luard wrote many strong letters to the British national press on the subject.

Prominent names in the world of journalism such as C G Grey, editor of the magazine *Aeroplane*, wrote scathing editorials damning

Prime Minister Lloyd George and his Government for permitting such conditions to exist and as more details came to light, the body of influential opinion created a storm of protest which provoked heated exchanges in the House of Commons.

This public protest finally forced the Prime Minister to order an inquiry and Air Vice Marshal Sir John Salmond was sent to India in the summer of 1922 to investigate and report on the situation.

When the news of Salmond's impending visit reached India, mobilisation stores and a certain amount of finance were released and a thin trickle of long awaited spares began to filter through to the squadrons.

Here is an entry from John Ross' diary:

"June 28, 1922: We (No. 28 Squadron) are preparing for Sir John Salmond's visit and this squadron is providing transport for his tour, and owing to shortage of spares, we had to purchase inner tubes and a foot pump locally for his car, as the Air Force cannot supply them."

Little Gratitude

In the 1919-20 operations in Waziristan, the RAF contributed materially to the success of operations, "but they earned little gratitude for all they had done," complains Marshal of the RAF, Sir John Slessor, who served in the North-West as a Wing Commander, commanding the 3rd Indian Wing, RAF, in his book *The Central Blue*. He made some pungent comments on the state of affairs when he joined a squadron on the frontier in 1921.

"Air Force expenditure was shown as a sub-head of the Army in the budget and when cuts were made in the military expenditure, the Indian Stores Department in London was instructed to place a complete embargo on all air stores and spare parts," writes Major General J G Elliot, who spent ten years of his service life serving on the Frontier, in his very aptly titled book *Frontier — 1839-1947*.

The Air Ministry had in 1921 been given complete responsibility for the maintenance of law and order in Iraq, which it exercised through the medium of eight RAF squadrons backed by a relatively small force on the ground. Much of the opposition to the extension of air control on the Frontier stemmed from the conviction among senior Army officers — for that is what it amounted to — that conditions in the two areas were so different that to hand over responsibility for watch and ward on the Frontier to the RAF, lock, stock and barrel was a task that should not be undertaken.

The crux of the matter seemed to be in defining the object of the exercise and the final impact of responsibility if things did not go according to plan. The object was to protect the settled districts from the depredations of tribesmen from across the administrative border. Air action was admirably suited to strike fast and strike deep to nip trouble in the bud, but there was not, as there had been between Sind and Baluchistan in the early days, a broad strip of neutral territory, and if air action failed, trouble would very quickly have spilled over into administered territory and it would have been the Army that would have had to clear the mess.

This was perhaps the reason why the Iraq model was not followed in India by the Government and the middle path of the carrot and stick was utilised for better coordination among the Army, Air Force and civil administration.

Post-War Developments

The year 1919 began with peace in Europe, but in April 1919, came the first of a series of riots at Amritsar.

At this point of time, the political activity of the Congress Party led by Mr Gandhi transformed into a civil disobedience movement. Serious rioting broke out in several towns of Punjab. The local Army garrison was reinforced by the addition of more troops. Brigadier General Dyer of the Jullunder Brigade arrived and took command.

Proclamations were issued, forbidding all meetings and

declaring that violence would be dealt with by martial law. Despite this, a crowd of some 6,000 people gathered on April 13 at Jallianwala Bagh, an open space surrounded by houses, where they listened to inflammatory speeches. General Dyer, regarding this as a challenge, opened fire on the crowd without any specific preliminary warning. Some 400 were killed and many others were wounded.

His action was later severely criticised, particularly in view of the fact that it was difficult for the crowd to disperse quickly enough through the narrow exits, a fact which enormously increased the casualties. Meanwhile, this resulted in rioting and disorder elsewhere in Punjab.

Two BEs of No. 31 Squadron made a reconnaissance of Amritsar, reporting on the damage and burnt out buildings the pilots had seen. As the situation worsened, 'C' Flight was sent from Risalpur to Amritsar. The landing ground was situated in the fort area. It had been a polo ground. They landed and put a guard around the aircraft.

As the riots continued, a strong Army column was sent into the city to seize various strong points and they were supported by low flying patrols. Then fresh riots began at Gujranwala and No. 31 sent two BEs to help disperse the rioters and aid the civil authorities.

Captain D H M Carberry, MC DFC, who had been a distinguished flyer in France during the war, with Lieutenants Oddie and Vincent were the three pilots and on arrival, they found several buildings on fire. All three pilots began to fire on the groups of Indians they found in the open or towards nearby villages. Bombs were dropped on other groups. Soon afterwards, the riots died down and ended.

The next operational effort was during the Afghan War. Hostilities were declared on May 6, 1919, and the squadron was asked to keep two aeroplanes ready for operations. Patrolling started and the squadron's aircraft returned from sorties sporting bullet holes and flapping fabric, a sure indication of the shooting abilities of the Afridi tribesmen, although the BE pilots flew low and presented easier targets.

The tribesmen were occupying the high ground bordering the Khyber Pass and the area of Dakka which was successfully bombed on May 9, a total of 16 aeroplanes making continuous attacks throughout the day. Later reports indicated as many as 600 casualties among the tribesmen plus two elephants killed. Three of the squadron's aircraft were forced down, fortunately in friendly territory.

Daily reconnaissance and ground strafing operations continued and on May 13, a Handley Page bomber was flown from Lahore to fly in the campaign. Before it could be used, it was destroyed in a storm on the airfield. On a raid by the squadron on Jalalabad, three days later, Lieutenants Oddie and F E E Villiers had also to force land. Villiers spotted troops nearby and thought them to be hostile, but walked towards them, revolver in one hand and a 'ghooley chit' in the other. As he neared them, the sound of a broad Somerset voice came from behind a boulder: "I hope you ain' 'urt Zur".

Jalalabad was bombed on May 20 — the story of Jock Halley's exploits have been related earlier.

By now, the Afghans were completely demoralised by the constant bombing of the RAF. Large numbers of enemy troops and tribesmen began to retire from the Dakka front without taking any part in an offensive.

During the period May 4-17, no less than 264 hours, 55 minutes of flying took place. The total weight of bombs dropped was 5,868 lb, 62 photographs were taken and 4,475 rounds of machine gun ammunition were fired.

On May 26, 1919, a fresh development occurred involving the southern tribes of the buffer states, necessitating the active employment of aircraft. A leader named Nadir Khan, gained much support from many tribesmen. Three aircraft and crews, joined two days later by six more, flew over the hostiles continuously against the tribesmen and cooperated with a column of infantry and artillery against Thal.

Curses Galore, But Situation Normal

.On May 28, 1919, Lieutenants E G Keeping and Cox landed at Miranshah to refuel during a recce mission and crashed when taking off. When this became known, a local Mullah announced that he could cast spells over flying machines. In consequence, No. 31 Squadron sent a BE to bomb the area with the express reason of lowering the prestige of the Mullah. The pilot was Lieutenant R A Currey, who fortunately did not have to come down.

The effect of this raid was to produce gifts of sheep, milk, eggs and fowl from the villagers to the British. The detachment returned to Risalpur on June 15.

No sooner had the situation returned to normal, a new uprising began in June. The Mahsuds revolted in Jandola in the Darajet area. A flight was flown to Tank to assist the Waziristan Force which had to operate in temperatures of 123 degrees in the shade. Lieutenant C M L Vincent, flying a recce sortie on June 7, read part of a message signalled by heliograph, to the effect that the garrison at Jandola, under siege by the tribesmen, was running short of water.

The Waziristan Force commander instructed Vincent to drop a message into Jandola which informed them that he would fly to bomb and strafe the tribesmen. During this distraction, members of the garrison should obtain water from a stream some 200 yards from the fort. The operation was a complete success. Vincent inflicted several casualties on the tribesmen, and the fort obtained 15 days supply of water, without a shot being fired at them.

Owing to the presence and help provided by Vincent and his aeroplane, the relief column reached Jandola without any attack from the Mahsuds in the surrounding hills.

No. 31 Squadron also flew recce and bombing sorties each day in the area of Wana where the local militia forces had mutinied. Aided by the Wazirs and Mahsuds, they had seized the posts of Wana, Sarawaki, and Tanai. Lieutenant Vincent was again to the fore, with Lieutenant Curry, when they carried out daily raids on Wana between June 15 and 28. On the first of these raids, Vincent effected a surprise attack by gliding down 6,000 ft. to drop seven 20 lb bombs into the fort which was crowded with men and animals, causing many casualties.

Also in June, a detachment was sent to Bannu to fly against tribesmen until No. 20 Squadron took over early in September. During the squadron's period here, the aerodrome guard had to fight off an attack on the airfield by tribesmen and many bullet holes were found in the roof of the hangar. The tribesmen were evidently under the impression that aeroplanes would be 'roosting' in the roof.

Flying Bristol fighters after giving up the old BEs, the squadron continued operations at Yar Muhammed's Chara Fort near the Khyber Pass. He had been harbouring outlaws and intriguing with Afghan Headquarters in Kabul.

The first Bristol loss occurred on September 13, 1919, when Lieutenants Wells and G Winstanly, on a recce sortie, were hit by rifle fire and brought down. They were captured by Pathan tribesmen but treated well and later ransomed back to the British. The squadron lost Lieutenant F V Devonshire while on a recce mission in the Chora area. He was attacking retreating rebels, his bombs causing casualties and confusion. Then, as he flew across the open plain near the fort, a single man stepped out from behind a tree, fired his rifle and hit Devonshire below the right eyebrow. He was dead before the Bristol hit the ground. His body was not recovered.

The operation in which Devonshire was killed commenced on September 13 against Chora in the Khyber district. Aeroplanes cooperated with artillery and infantry and carried out aerial offensive measures. The fort, which was a very strong one, was built of stone and lime, and belonged to Yar Muhammed. This was the first operation in which Bristol fighters took part.

Being captured by the tribals brought forth the worth of the 'ghooley chit'. The following is the report of Lieutenant Wells who along with Lieutenant Winstanley was captured.

"On the morning of the 13th September, on my way to Chora, I flew over the hills to the South of the Bazar Valley in order to view the approaches from that side, including the Bara Valley. The engine was running smoothly and I heard a shot or two and later found boiling water coming back into my face. I glanced at the thermometer which registered well over boiling point. I immediately turned back being a little way west of Chora.

"Later, smoke commenced to issue from the cowling and the engine dropped revs, eventually seizing up completely. I made up my mind to land in a green patch of cultivation about one and a half miles east of Chora. This was as far as I could glide, it turned out to be terraced and walled. Finding that I had slightly overshot, I dipped my right wing to the ground. The undercarriage was swept off and the machine then rolled over to the right. Lieutenant Winstanley was thrown out of the cockpit and landed on his shoulder, fortunately only bruising himself. Beyond this, neither of us sustained any injuries.

"Lieutenant Winstanley immediately went to his cockpit to get a pigeon for release. He got hold of the pigeon box and his revolver and had just turned away when a Pathan slipped in and relieved him of both. We then found about six to eight Pathans by our side. Their approach was entirely concealed by the maize crop. They pointed to a *nullah* just below us and said '*Chelo*'.

"After crossing the *nullah*, in which there was a great deal of water, we went westward. Our troops were fighting with rifles and a Lewis gun at the time. Winstanley told me later that a good number of bullets came very close to him. We got out of sight, however, and started to climb a hill but what was a little more than a goat track. It was here that I came to grief by holding on to a piece of projecting rock. This turned out to be rotten and I fell about five feet on to a lot of scaly rock, tobogganing down some 50 ft, until I pulled up short on some boulders and bushes.

"I was a great deal bruised and sustained a rather deep cut on the knee. A Pathan who went down with me broke his collar bone. In the meantime, Winstanley had been taken on ahead. I eventually rejoined him about midday. We continued to march till about 4 pm when we halted by a stream and had a meal, consisting of *chapaties* and mutton, a *dumba* having been bought and killed. The warm skin was worn by the man with the broken collar bone for two days.

"At six o'clock, we again moved and after another three hours march, we camped for the night. They gave us a thick woollen mat to sleep on and one man threw a greatcoat over me. Another dressed my cuts with hot ghee and salt. The following morning, we moved on at about 6.30 am, arriving at the summer camp at about 11 am. There were no buildings, only crude branch shelters. We were told that we were going no further. We remained until the evening of September 15, when after a big *jirgah*, they removed Winstanley to the valley. I remained in the hills until the evening of September 18, when I was also moved down, about two and a half hours march. The village in which Winstanley was, was pointed out to me, and turned out to be about one and a half miles away from my show.

"The Malik of the Khyber had been sent out by the Political Agent to arrange for our release. A settlement was finally come to on the morning of the 20th. Within an hour, we were moving towards Landi Kotal. We put up in the village of Karamna or Karani and the following day arrived at Landi Kotal. During the whole of our time, we were well treated by the tribesmen, many of them, in fact, being ex-soldiers, and moreover there was nearly always a political messenger present from the morning of September 16, 1919."

— *History of No. 31 Squadron RFC /RAF*,
Naval & Military Press, UK.

The Twenties Saga

Three machines left Risalpur for Bannu to take part in a large raid on Dotanni Kot on the plain of Wanu. A total of 16 RAF aircraft took part, ten being Bristol fighters from No. 31 Squadron, one DH10 and five DH9s from No. 27 Squadron. The return flight was made with rapidly drying fuel tanks and some of the pilots glided the last few miles to Bannu aerodrome. Lieutenant Vincent was one of the No. 31 Squadron men, another being Lieutenant H R Junor. Lieutenant (now Flying Officers as RAF ranks were coming in) C M L Vincent and Flying Officer G S Oddie received DFCs for their action and Observer A J Cox received the OBE at this time.

On November 26, three machines were despatched to Bannu to work with No. 20 Squadron, at the beginning of the operations against the Mahsuds in the Tank Zam valley. They remained there till December 2, and carried out bombing raids and ground strafing in the neighbourhood of Marobi, Janjai, Makin and other villages.

The squadron was now completely operating Bristol fighters, the last BE2E being flown out to Lahore in February 1920. In April, the squadron moved to Mhow and stayed there for seven months. In October, the squadron moved to Cawnpore (Kanpur). On November 26-27, all eight Bristols made it via three landings to refuel. Earlier special landing grounds were prepared at Hoshangabad and Bina in addition to several intermediate forced landing grounds. At Cawnpore, the squadron occupied Nos. 8, 9 and 10 bungalows of the Wheeler Barracks. The aerodrome was on the old race course and was quite large. Four more Bristols arrived from the aircraft park to bring up No. 31 Squadron to a strength of 12 aircraft by mid-December.

In January 1921, Squadron Leader A D Neale MC left, his place being taken by Squadron Leader A T Harris. Arthur Harris had flown in the war with No. 45 Squadron in France, flying one and a half Sopwith Strutters and later Camels. In 1918, he received the AFC for his work. Meanwhile, the new RAF uniform began to be worn. The process started in mid-June 1920.

The service dress and mess uniforms were finally settled and officers were ordered to obtain these by December. The pattern of the tropical mess kit was changed from the open pea-jacket with the light blue cummerbund and dark blue shoulder straps to the old 'cavalry pattern jacket' with white waistcoat and shoulder straps. The shoulder straps were later changed back to dark blue with gold badges of rank.

Even as a Squadron Leader, he was known as 'Daddy Harris'. By the time World War II commenced, Harris was an Air Marshal and became famous as AOC-in-C Bomber Command. His nickname then changed. He was henceforth known as Bomber Harris.

The year 1921 dawned for No. 31 squadron with a complete complement of 12 Bristol fighters bringing the unit to full strength — four aircraft per flight. Cold weather training commenced — puff shoots, bombing, camera gun practice, photography and flying tests as laid down in the orders.

In January, 'C' Flight flew to Jhansi to take part in a 10-day Artillery Practice Camp. Shoots with live shells were carried out daily and much was learnt by both arms. At the Duke of Connaught's Durbar in Delhi in January, the RAF provided the Guard of Honour of three officers and 100 other ranks. Air Commodore T I Webb Bowen, AOC, RAF (India), was personally congratulated by the Duke on the smartness and turnout of this bodyguard.

In February, the squadron was inspected by Field Marshal Lord Rawlinson, Commander-in-Chief, Indian Army. On this occasion, the squadron did not parade with the rest of the troops on the station but was drawn up in front of the machines on the aerodrome.

To comply with standing orders on winter training, all pilots who had not taken part in the flight from Mhow had to carry out at least one cross-country flight. The route selected was from Cawnpore to Agra, with a landing at Etawah, a distance of about 150 miles each way. This flight was carried by Flight Lieutenant Coryton and Flying Officers Junor, Jackson and Davy.

At the end of February, two machines flew to Lucknow to demonstrate at a meeting which was being addressed by Mr Gandhi. The machines, acting under the instructions of the civil authority, circled over the meeting and dropped pamphlets containing the Duke of Connaught's speech.

The summer training programme started with all the usual flying practices. Experiments were also carried out with the high angle drift sight, and a great controversy arose as to whether it should be used by the pilot or the observer. In June, shoots were organised with 117 Battery using old 15-pounder guns, on the banks of the Ganges. These were carried out with considerable success, providing practice in the drill of both arms.

Preparations were started for the move of the squadron to Peshawar. It has earlier been mentioned that every squadron on the Frontier took initial steps at learning formation flying. Starting with two aircraft taking off together, they progressed to six and soon formation flying was nothing novel. Whenever a squadron moved base, the ground party would move a few days earlier so as to reach the new location earlier to receive the aircraft as they came in.

Recalls the then CO of the squadron A T Harris:

"The flight to the new base was far from routine. At the end of the first stage, F/O Vosper, landing at Agra, overshot and put his Bristol onto its nose, and Flight Lieutenant Watts was delayed with a broken fuselage fitting. After flying on to Delhi for the night, the Bristols flew into a rain storm on the way to Ambala and in the afternoon, flew through a dust storm near Lahore. It was impossible to see the ground from above 300 ft and then only by following the railway line.

"F/Os F G Robinson and J D Jackson missed the railway line and were forced to land. Jackson crashed trying to get down into a recreation ground while Robinson landed in a maize field but got away safely the following morning. The second formation led by Flight Lieutenant T F W Thompson fared better although F/O Vincent force landed twice between Cawnpore and Agra.

"Elaborate orders were issued for the flight — it was quite a long way. First stop was Agra, where we were able to look at the Taj Mahal. We stayed the night there so that we were able to see it at night as well as by day, as we flew past it. At Lahore, I had to have my propeller patched up. They should have changed it for I nearly came to grief when the patches came off while I was on a bombing raid later on."

In January and February, 'A' and 'C' Flights took their turns at the practice camp at Akora, where experiments carried out were perfected by the end of the training season. All the pilots in the squadron were able to handle all types of shoots, and the speed with which the pilots were able to direct the gunners on to the targets clearly showed the value of inter-service cooperation.

A large amount of infantry cooperation was also carried out, even in the mountainous district of the Khyber with the greatest success. The Director Arrow, the Popham Panel, and wireless were brought into play for this purpose, and owing to the keenness and energy of the officers and men of the squadron led by the OC Squadron Leader A T Harris, the other service, namely, the Army, was gradually convinced of the enormous value of the assistance which could be rendered by aeroplane cooperation.

On one occasion, an aeroplane machine gunning and bombing demonstration was given before an Indian battalion which astonished them greatly. On another occasion, during a contact patrol show near Naushera, the officer commanding the column with which the aeroplane was cooperating, received so much information as to the enemy dispositions and his own troops' progress, that he exclaimed, "How many more of these is he going to drop."

On March 4, 1922, HRH, the Prince of Wales, paid a visit to Peshawar. The personnel of the squadron helped to line the streets on his arrival and a formation of five machines met his train outside Naushera station and escorted it into Peshawar and then circled round overhead until the HRH entered the Government House.

On March 6, 1922, HRH inspected the pensioners in the city. Personnel of the squadron again lined the streets and a formation of three machines escorted him until the inspection was completed. After this, all the squadron officers were presented to him and an amusing incident occurred when HRH spoke to Flight Lieutenant Coryton, MVO. The Prince asked him where he got his MVO and Coryton replied that he got it for teaching HRH, the Duke of York, to fly. The Prince replied, "Good Lord! Fancy not remembering your face. I must write and tell Bertie about this."

On March 9, all serviceable machines in the squadron proceeded to Tank in conjunction with No. 28 Squadron, on a raid on the Jalal Khel Wazirs. The squadron left at 6 am and flew to Tank, did the bombing raid and returned to Peshawar the same day, arriving at dusk. The country was very mountainous and the targets bad, but bombs were dropped on flocks and villages, and a large number of rounds of ammunition fired.

Then on March 10, 1922, orders were received about midnight for the aircraft to fly to Tank. Khasadars, who were holding Kajuri Kach Fort, were being besieged by rebel tribesmen. However, when the squadron flew down, the trouble ended.

The Salmond Report

Air Vice Marshal, Sir John Salmond set out on a tour of RAF stations and outlying airfields in the frontier area of Punjab and the NWFP in July 1922 to acquaint himself with the problem of outdated obsolescent machines, total lack of spares and the Air Force being treated as yet another unit of the Army.

In his discussions with the high ranking Army and political officers, he pointed out the inherent added advantage of utilising the services of this new force in any of the Frontier campaigns. He stressed that the Air Force was a highly technical service where parade ground performance was not as important as maintaining the serviceability of the aircraft.

In terms of advantages, he stressed that the Air Force was an asset that ensured speedy operational effectiveness, low casualties and minimal expenditure in comparison with the traditional cumbersome Army columns which had been utilised for many years in the past in fighting the rebellious tribes in the Frontier region.

Salmond summarised his findings after a detailed, thorough inspection of all RAF units and presented his report to the Viceroy, Lord Reading, along with his recommendations. As to the existing state of affairs regarding the air service, Salmond observed:

- The RAF in India, to all intents and purposes, is non-existing as a fighting service at this date (September 21, 1922).
- The rank of the Air Officer Commanding RAF India should be raised and be on par with Army Commanders.
- A new organisation and administration should be formed with a definite stated policy for the Air Service.

This "on par with the Army" had a history. Initially, when the first squadron was posted to India in 1916 (No. 31 Squadron), it had to report in the field to the local Army commander, usually a Brigadier. After the war was over, and RAF units increased in number, they were grouped under a wing with a Wing Commander as the senior officer. After the units were formed into wings, they were grouped together under a group. The first senior commander of the RAF India group was Air Commodore T I Webb Bowen in 1920. He served till 1923, when, as a result of the Salmond report, which was accepted by the Government of India, the post was upgraded to the rank of Air Vice Marshal (AVM).

As regards equipment requests, newer aircraft and sufficient spares to keep the older aircraft flying until their replacements arrived, were made. A demand was also made that the budget for the Air Force should be separate as had earlier been done in England.

"'Elsewhere throughout the Empire, the RAF had been a separate autonomous service, with its own budget introduced to Parliament by its own Secretary of State. In India, however, the Air Force vote was still merely one of the heads of Army expenditure in the Military Services Budget, controlled by the C-in-C in India as the Army's member of the Viceroy's Council. It was not even shown in a separate section as was the expenditure on the Royal Indian Marine," says Clive Richards, Senior Researcher, Air Historical Branch, RAF.

"It is instructive to read about how pilots felt about the planes they were expected to fly against a formidable foe in a hostile and inhospitable mountainous country. The aircraft and engines were really very old and constantly requiring attention. There were numerous cases of a connecting rod going through the sump of the engine and some very nasty and horrible forced landings resulted. Often, as aircraft were taxiing out from the hangar, a tyre would puncture on the sharp camel thorn on the ground with the result that we had many patches on our inner tyres."

— Air Commodore S Graham, MC, GM (Retd)
Flight Commander, No. 27 Squadron, RAF, December 1923.

After the Salmond Report had been accepted by the Viceroy and the Commander-in-Chief of the Army, the rank of the Air Force Chief was upgraded to bring it on par with the Army Commanders, and Air Commodore Webb Bowen was succeeded by AVM Sir Philip Game who became AOC-in-C, RAF India, in March 1923.

In a fresh dose of reorganisation, RAF headquarters was moved in early 1923 to Raisina, Delhi, from Ambala, which had acted as headquarters, having moved there from Peshawar, headquarters of No. 1 Wing — the first such Air Force unit in India.

Meanwhile, flying continued and operations along with the Army were pursued with vigour and enthusiasm. On January 25, Nos. 27 and 60 Squadrons made history by undertaking the first long distance formation flight from Risalpur to Calcutta and the return one. For that, they had initially to learn and practice to take-off in pairs.

Early in 1925, bombing training was undertaken to prepare for a competition inaugurated by AVM Sir Edward Ellington, AOC-in-C India.

Organisational Structure

In the 1919 Trenchard/Churchill memorandum for the future organisation of the RAF, a total of eight squadrons was allotted to India. By 1925, ten years after the RFC made its appearance in Indian skies, the actual strength of the RAF India Group comprised three wings. Each of these consisted of just two squadrons, thus:

- No. 1 Wing — Nos. 20 and 60 Squadrons.
- No. 2 Wing — Nos. 5 and 27 Squadrons.
- No. 3 Wing — Nos. 28 and 31 Squadrons.

A recommendation of the Salmond Report made in 1922, for at least two more squadrons, came into effect only in October 1928 when Nos. 11 and 39 Squadrons arrived from England.

In 1925, operations were conducted and just after their completion, a full reorganisation of the Frontier squadrons was done, which now were distributed as follows:

NO.1 WING		
No. 20 (AC) Squadron	Bristol F2B	Peshawar
No. 60 (B) Squadron	DH9A (Ninaks)	Kohat
No. 2 WING		
No. 5 (AC) Squadron	Bristol F2B	Risalpur
No. 27 (B) Squadron	DH9A	Risalpur
No.3 WING		
No. 28 (AC) Squadron	Bristol F2B	Quetta
No. 31(AC) Squadron	Bristol F2B	Ambala

Communication and Weapons

The Message Hook

In the Twenties, though wireless had been used during the war for air-to-ground and ground-to-air communication and directing artillery fire, it took quite some time for it to trickle to the Frontier in India.

In the meantime, someone figured out a way to put a message on paper and then tuck it into a bag/ box with a rope tied to it and strung it from a rope hung between two poles, or lances or in an emergency, held in a upright position about 10 ft apart on the bayonets attached to the rifles.

The following is a first person account given in 1976 by Wing Commander H Millyard, MBE, of No. 5 Squadron, RAF, in India, deployed on the Frontier *circa* 1928:

"Our job was message picking with Bristol Fighters, which consisted of a long hook under the fuselage. They stretched a line with a message bag attached across two cavalry lances — we used this technique on the Frontier."

Adds Mathew Clarke, wireless operator, No. 5 Squadron, who

doubled as an observer in a Bristol fighter and took part in the message picking operation:

"About the message picking up, I will say, we had it. The bloody thing gave me one hell of a fright the first time I had to use it. A Brigade was meandering through a *nullah*, a lovely spot to be trapped in. The PBI had stopped — mules and all, when we noticed marker strips being laid out. Down we went to have a decko.

"At the rear of the column and well away from the others, a couple of soldiers were standing 30/40 ft apart, rifles and bayonets held upright and the pilot spotted the coloured streamers on the string attached to the bayonets. I hadn't a clue what was afoot until over the voice pipe, the pilot told me the score. Such was the standard of instruction in those far off days. Anyway, it seemed, we were to go down and pick up the message on the hook. I asked what I had to do and he told me. I wish he hadn't bothered.

"It appeared that I had to roll back the 'floor' of my cockpit, using the small reel attached to the side of the crate. To accomplish this, I had to first break the rules. That is, I had to detach the wire and clasp from my harness. This meant that I was no longer firmly fixed to the kite. Then, I was required to stand on the ledges on either side of the cockpit and work the wheel which unrolled the floor to the rear of the fuselage. Holding on to something, I then had to lean through the hole in the floor and undo the hook and let it hang down at an angle.

"It could have been the easiest thing in the world to have fallen out of the plane while carrying out this little chore. The ground slid past at what appeared to be a fantastic speed. Having got the hook down, the pilot then swung around and came up the *nullah* to where the blokes with the message were standing. I am willing to bet that they were as unhappy about the situation as I was.

"We got it first go and now came the difficult part. Getting the hook up and grabbing hold of the message tangled round the hook end. Standing on the ledges and leaning far out as possible, it was just possible to get it — but at the risk of neck and limb. It could have been so easy to fall out, and I reckon this little task was about one of falling out. If we had, I wonder what would have been the outcome. After all, we did break the rule book. And I wonder if one's next of kin would have been compensated in any way, if killed while carrying out this caper.

"Anyway, getting the bag untangled from the hook, I got the little bag and gave the enclosed message slip to the pilot. It seemed that the 'baddies' had got themselves into good sniping positions and halted the column and could we do anything in the way of bombs. The pilot scribbled out a message to the fact that we were bombless and that we would convey their request to base. And that, as far as I was concerned, was the end of the work for the day. Another kite took over and got the column on its way.

"I wrapped the message up and putting it back into the bag, we then swung over the column and I dropped the message bag over the side and watched the streamers float away. Gratefully, I then proceeded to close, what appeared to me at that time, the biggest hole I had ever seen. Giving air cover to a slow moving column as it wound its way through the valleys of the foothills of the Hindu Kush is, I think, one of the most boring tasks in an airman's life. Others thought differently — but then, they came home, bubbling with excitement after a good shoot-up. I never got into one of these, which probably is just as well — I might have shot half the tail (of our kite) off — as one poor sod done near Miranshah."

Weapons and Aircraft

Initially and later also, small arms, rifles, light machine guns were common to the Army and the newly created Air Force. The basic weapon of the infantryman was the rifle and the Enfield rifle had long been used by the Army, both in England and overseas in the far flung corners of the Empire.

But the Enfield superseded the Minie in 1856; in 1866, the Snider/ Snyder — the first breechloader — was issued. In 1871, this was succeeded by a hammerless rifle, the Martini-Henry and in 1889, the Lee Metford 303, the first magazine rifle, came into use. It had a range of 1,900 yards and was very accurate. Smokeless powder came in at the same time.

The first rifled field gun had been used in the First China War of 1860. In 1886, the first breechloader came to stay; in 1891, the first quick firing gun. The first machine gun, the Gatling, had been used in the Second Afghan War, 1878-79.

So far as the Air Force was concerned, weapons on the ground remained the same as with the Army. The gun fitted into planes like the Bristol fighter, or the Wapiti later, was the Lewis gun and for the bombers, the 20 lb bomb.

Technology was gradually filtering to the Air Force and more reliable and efficient wireless equipment was going to the squadrons.

The North-West Frontier XVT Close Support Code

During the Twenties and Thirties, as aircraft became more reliable and lethal with changing technology, giving the RAF reliable engines and wireless, there was a need to have a simple code that would be spread on the ground and would tell the pilot as to what was right with those on the ground and what was wrong and in which event what kind of help they needed.

It took quite a while to perfect the code and the kind of cloth strips that would be needed to show the message clearly to the pilot.

It was used in Waziristan by ground troops in communicating to the pilot their own position and the presence or absence of hostile tribesmen in the vicinity. This was done by displaying two fabric ground strips in the shape of an 'X', a 'V' or a 'T'.

'X' showed the position of the piquet or troops nearest the enemy and meant “all is well.” ‘V’ signified that the enemy was in the direction in which the apex of the ‘V’ was pointing. The letter ‘T’ related to an SOS signal and asked for assistance when a piquet was likely to be overwhelmed or when the troops’ withdrawal was being followed up by the enemy very closely. Used only in emergencies, it was put out with the top of the ‘T’ pointing towards the enemy. The great advantage of this code over previous methods such as the Director Arrow or the Popham Panel, was its speed and simplicity.

The pilot of a close support aircraft circled over the Army column at a height of 2,000-3,000 ft watching the country about two miles on each side of the route. As the piquets put out their ‘X’, he noted their position on the map. On seeing an ‘X’ change to a ‘V’, the pilot flew in the direction in which the ‘V’ was pointing and searched for the concealed tribesmen. On discovering them, he carried out a VBL (Vickers, Bombs, Lewis gun) attack.

A most successful action using the XVT was carried out in July 1938 by the Razmak Column of the 3rd Indian Infantry Brigade, several platoons of Tochi Scouts and No. 20 (AC) Squadron RAF, the objective being the destruction of the headquarters of the Faqir of Ipi in the Kharre cave area, North Waziristan.

Defending the Empire's Outposts

The Turning Point

What could, in 'officialese', be termed as peace prevailed in the early Twenties and although the year 1924 did not by comparison feature any major Army operations, it was not completely free from constant air operations. Even when there was no incident, aircraft had to fly on recce patrols across the length and breadth of most tribal districts of the Frontier, especially Waziristan.

However, trouble broke out in mid-1924 in South Waziristan where the Mahsuds rebelled. So, the Army set out on a campaign and air action went with it. Several squadrons took part in the bombing sorties against groups of Mahsuds. The campaign was brief and by October 1924, most of tribes had come to terms with their Political Agents.

"One particular tribe, the Abdur Rehman Khel, supported by Guri Khel, Maresai and Faridais, refused to submit to the Government terms and began a series of raids against the Manzai, Spli Toi and Gomal Scout posts of the Government. As these raids continued, the Air Officer Commanding (AOC), Sir Edward Ellington, decided that punitive operations against these rebel Mahsuds should be undertaken solely by the RAF units without normal Army formations in ground support," explains aero historian Chaz Bowyer.

This decision produced a campaign which drastically changed the status of the RAF as the junior partner to the Army in a Frontier campaign. It proved beyond doubt that the RAF could undertake any operation on its own, without the support of the Army. This was to be the first occasion in the Frontier's history when the air service was to conduct completely independent operations and, as such, its progress and results were to be scrutinised by both the Army and the civil authorities in order to formulate all future policy.

On February 20, 1924, Wing Commander R C M Pink, Officer Commanding No. 2 (Indian) Wing, was flown in a DH9A of No. 60 Squadron piloted by Flight Lieutenant J W Baker (later Air Chief Marshal Sir John Baker) to Rawalpindi for a conference with Northern Command Headquarters (which at that time, was in Rawalpindi) and the forthcoming operations were agreed to in principle between Pink and the Army commanders.

On March 3, 1924, eight aircraft each from Nos. 27 and 60 Squadrons were flown to the forward landing ground at Miranshah Fort, some 120 miles from Kohat. This was also the headquarters of the Tochi Scouts. Although, Miranshah had been used earlier by the Army for a number of years, the decision to extend its boundaries to include a permanent landing ground had only been taken in 1924 when an earlier and nearby forward airstrip at Fort Dardoni was razed to the ground and finance was diverted to improving Miranshah.

The aircraft (DH9As) belonging to Nos. 27 and 60 Squadrons were, therefore, the first RAF units to occupy Miranshah Fort, although aircraft had utilised it as an advanced emergency landing ground on several occasions in previous years. With its loop-holed walls, rifle watch towers and thickly-built surrounding defences, Miranshah was literally a fort in the true Beau Geste tradition but it offered the relative attraction of solid accommodation for the RAF crews instead of the tented billeting normally associated with forward airstrips.

Operational headquarters was established at Tank (pronounced as Tonk) and Wing Commander Pink moved his staff by road from Risalpur, the journey taking some ten hours. With him at Tank were the Bristol F2Bs of No. 5 Squadron and these in conjunction with

Nos. 27's and 69's Ninaks (DH9As), dropped warning notices to the intended village targets on February 25 and again on March 5, 1924. Despite the fact that hardly any Mahsud tribesman could read or write, warning leaflets were recognised as the normal method of giving the tribes ample time to either submit to terms or at least evacuate their women and children from the target areas before bombing commenced.

The pre-warning procedure may seem quaint to modern eyes but it was a part of the contemporary policy for avoiding unnecessary bloodshed and insisted upon by the British and Indian civil authorities. Once Nos. 27 and 60 Squadrons were settled into their new quarters at Miranshah, Pink flew to the fort and, seating all personnel around him, proceeded to explain the impending operations in detail, including the background reasons and importance to the RAF of the operations.

The hitherto unknown form of briefing was received so well by both air and ground crews that on the completion of his briefing, Pink was treated to an unprecedented and quite spontaneous applause by his audience. As one NCO, who was present, commented, "Pink went scarlet....but I do not think he was displeased really."

On March 9, 1924, operations began. Three types of operations were envisaged: villages were to be bombed; certain areas were to be 'blockaded' by irregular single aircraft patrols preventing hostile tribals from moving into safe harbours; and, finally, night bombing was to continue the offensive right round the clock. All targets were numbered on a master map at the Tank Headquarters and allotted to the squadrons in strict order.

The target area was between 3,000 and 6,000 ft above sea level, necessitating the reduction of fuel status to some 60 percent in order that the heavily laden Ninaks could gain the required bombing height of 3,000 ft above any target. Actual raids were made in flight formation with 112 lb and 230 lb bombs dropped in salvo on a signal from the formation leader.

In addition, pairs of Ninaks, loaded with 20/25 lb Cooper bombs, and occasionally 112 pounders constantly harassed the tribesmen, these raids being interspersed with night raids by Bristols of No. 5 Squadron. As the operations got underway, a further variation in technique was used whereby bombing sorties by Nos. 27 and 60 Squadrons' Ninaks were immediately followed by low strafing attacks by Bristols of No. 5 Squadron on nearby caves and hill refuges. On March 18, an additional flight of Army cooperation aircraft was flown in to Tank in support.

The only casualties to the RAF during this campaign occurred on March 21 when Flying Officers N C Hayter Hames and E J Dashwood, both from No. 27 Squadron, were hit by accurate rifle fire. Their Ninak spun down and exploded into flames in the resulting crash. Both men received fatal burns and in spite of the elaborate care and attention shown by nearby tribesmen, who slaughtered several of their precious goats and used melted fat and the goat skins to wrap round the dying men in an attempt to revive them. But both died and were buried with full military honours in Dera Ismael Khan Cemetery.

It was one example of the curious attitude sometimes displayed by some tribesmen to their British foes — a form of chivalrous mercy for brave men which was an inherent part of a hill tribesman's fighting code of conduct (although it should also be said that these tribes showed little mercy to any native troops in British uniform, regarding them as traitors).

On the night of March 30, a single F2B from No. 5 Squadron carried out a moonlight bombing raid which was judged to be so successful that two more F2Bs were flown to Miranshah from Tank on April 6 to increase the night raids. On April 4, Squadron Leader T F Hazell, CO of No. 60 Squadron, flew on his first sortie of the campaign, but once airborne, he noticed his engine cowling coming adrift.

Forced to land, he put the Ninak down at Sorargha, a sloping strip which ended abruptly in a sheer drop to a valley. With little option but to land down the slope, Hazell managed to save his life and that of his petrified air gunner by deliberately running the Ninak into a stone breastwork on the very edge of the prepice. The aircraft became a write-off but both crewmen walked away from the crash with mere bruises. Five days later, Flight Lieutenant Savery of No. 60 Squadron repeated this dangerous form of landing at Sorargha with the same result, while on April 15, a third No. 60 Squadron Ninak had to force land in open country with engine trouble.

By the end of April, the rebellious tribes had clearly had enough and on May 1, their leaders agreed to terms at a *jirgah* (meeting) held at Jandola. Rebel casualties had, in fact, been very few, a total of 11 men killed or wounded, while from the RAF's point of view, the whole campaign had been a complete success.

In 54 days of operations, a total of some 2,720 hours had been flown on 'war' flights, with only two losses. Several gallantry awards were made to individual crews, but all personnel of the No. 2 (Indian) Wing became eligible for what is regarded as one of the rarest campaign medals ever issued by the British authorities. This was the India General Service medal with a clasp annotated "Waziristan 1925" and only 46 officers and 214 other ranks were entitled to wear it.

Wing Commander R C M Pink, the unorthodox but highly regarded commander of the whole campaign, was accorded a form of immortality by having the operation referred to as 'Pink's War' by those who took part in it. His own reaction to the period was possibly summarised in a piece of rhyme which he composed during his many flights over the target area.

Waziristan — 1925

Oh big 9A, oh big 9A
What are you doing down Razmak way?
Why these bombs? The pomp of war?
Surely, your home is at Risalpur?
(chorus)
Pomp be damned, don't make me laugh
There ain't no pomp in this damned strafe
I am bombing the hell from the local Khan
To prove there is peace in Waziristan
Oh smart Brisfit, oh smart Brisfit
What are you doing in fighting kit?
I am praying hard I'll avoid a konk
On offensive patrols from a sink called Tank
(chorus)
Up the gorges and down Spli Toi
Sniped to blazes but attaboy
They call it war on the banks of Marne
But bless you its peace in Waziristan
If you ask me — what shall I say
To the folks back Home in England way?
(chorus)
Don't you worry there is nought to tell
'Cept work and fly and bomb like hell
With hills above us and hills below
And rocks to fill where the hills won't go
Nice soft sitting for those who crash
But war you call it? Don't talk trash
War is a rumour, war's a yarn
There is peace in Waziristan.

In November 1925, Pink was posted Home to England, promoted to Group Captain and in 1933, he became an Air Commodore. Unfortunately, he died soon after of cancer — a tragic loss of a brilliant and much respected officer. The legacy of his outstanding capabilities could be fairly said to be the change (albeit a grudging one) in the higher Army and civil authority's attitude to the potential of air power in India.

This campaign conducted solely by the RAF had proved conclusively that control and containment of rebel forces could be accomplished speedily and at a minimum cost in casualties and expenditure when compared with the hitherto traditional method of dispatching cumbersome and expensive Army columns.

In the words of the official historian:

"An instance of complete success being achieved in securing submission of NW Frontier hostiles by air action alone, thus, achieving the desired result at very small cost in casualties and money in comparison with a punitive expedition carried out by the Army….."

This grudging admission was, in fact, a carry over from the feud that had carried on for the four years duration of the war — when the air element had proved itself on the battlefield — that the RAF, which had been created as a separate service in 1918 even as the war was still on, was still facing stiff opposition from the other two older services. Right through the Twenties and Thirties, a campaign was launched by the Navy, followed by the Army, that the Air Force should be distributed between the two services as a subordinate part of the two services.

The effect of this controversy was naturally felt in India where, until the air element made its presence felt, the Army was the sole authority for peace-keeping and operations in the North-West Frontier. From 1916, when the first air squadron arrived in India, the air element had certainly been of great help to the Army, a fact testified to by the Army commanders on the ground.

Whether Pink's success had any bearing on the overall British policy or not, the fact remains that as early as 1920, the question of maintaining peace in Iraq, a League of Nation's mandated territory, faced Britain. At this point, after the war, Britain was facing economic difficulties. And an expedition to Iraq led by the Army would have been very expensive. At this point, Lord Trenchard, then RAF chief, proposed that the security of Iraq be handed over to the RAF with a minimum of the Army. This was supported by the Secretary of State for Air, Sir Winston Churchill and was accepted and implemented, saving the British Exchequer millions of pounds, while, at the same time, proving what an Air Force could accomplish in a much shorter span of time than the Army could in a much longer period, with more expenses and higher casualties.

In that sense, Pink's success was the success of the Air Force to have the right to claim equality with the other two services.

Miranshah — A Beau Geste Fort

"Miranshah Fort, about 120 miles south-west of Kohat, was the headquarters of the Tochi Scouts and at the end of 1924, Fort Dardoni, which lay just two miles north-west, was razed to the ground and the money diverted to the extension of Miranshah in order to provide a permanent landing ground and extra accommodation for RAF personnel.

"Of Beau Geste appearance, Miranshah was literally a fort, situated about a mile south of the old Dardoni site. Entry was by means of two gates in the loop-holed walls which were surmounted by watch towers at intervals around the whole perimeter of the outer wall. Surrounding these walls was an area bounded by a barbed wire fence, inside which some brick buildings provided sanctums for flight offices, workshops and the like.

"The whole area was some 500 square yards surrounded on the north and west by an L-shaped landing ground of small gravel on a rock base; the short arm of the 'L' running on the west side. A more realistic and picturesque description is given in the words of an anonymous poet, one verse of which runs:

> Steep hills, red rocks, grim boulders for the feet that do not falter,
> Clear crags and slender crevices, for eyes that see afar,
> A fight for life 'twixt man and man, that ages cannot alter,
> This prospect I would show you from on high by Miranshah.

"Nos. 27 and 60 Squadrons were the first RAF units to occupy Miranshah, each with eight aircraft in early 1925, while operational headquarters commanded by Wing Commander R C M Pink, was at Tank (pronounced Tonk) together with Bristol F2Bs of Nos. 5 and 20 Squadrons.

"On February 6 and 7, two British officers were killed during an ambush while they were on patrol. The Mahsud tribe as a whole was held responsible and a fine of Rs. 75,000 was imposed. As the Mahsuds refused to surrender the men responsible for the crime, aircraft from No. 27 and No. 60 Squadrons were deployed for bombing the villages of the Mahsuds.

"As both these squadrons were based at the Miranshah Fort, the constant movement of aircraft gave the airfield an appearance of perpetual motion. Overheated engines bellowed in a non-stop chorus, blasting a minor whirwind of dust and sand into the blistering sunlight and pasting a coat of sweat-streaked filth on the long-suffering ground crews."

— Chaz Bowyer, *The Flying Elephants*, 1972.

Wapiti Comes to India — 'What a Pity'

"A large, light brown or grayish brown North American deer having long branching antlers."

The name refers to the pale rump and tail of the American elk, a majestic deer that lives in National Parks.

"Right from December 1915, when the first Flight of No. 31 Squadron landed in India to about 1929, all aircraft operated by the RAF in India were BE2C, BE2E, Henry Farmans and even the old Bristol Boxkites, joined later by the Bristol fighter (Brisfit), the DH9A (Ninaks), and the twin-engined bomber DH10. Apart from the chronic shortage of spares, which led to the cannibalising of crashed, unserviceable aircraft, there was an acute need for new aircraft. The ones in use ten years after the war's end were all war-time products.

"Stemming from the 1927 general purpose aeroplane requirement of Air Ministry specification 26/27, the Westland Wapiti was in effect a compromise between the official desire for a newly designed aircraft to replace the ageing DH9As and Bristol F2Bs equipping most overseas squadrons of the RAF and the need for preserving finance in the relatively small budget allotted annually to the RAF at that time.

"In competition with at least seven other designs produced to bid for the official contract, the Wapiti eventually found favour because of its utilisation of certain DH9A components and spares, with which the RAF 'larder' was well stocked.

"The prototype Wapiti J8495, employed wing ailerons, struts and tail surfaces of the DH9A but its engine (Bristol Jupiter direct-drive) and improved form of undercarriage required a much sturdier fuselage than the older 'Ninak', being wider and deeper than its 'parent'.

"Accepted in 1928 for production, the major mark of Wapiti to enter RAF service was the Mk IIA (432 built out of all-mark production of 517 Wapitis) — the first all metal construction version. Power came initially from a Jupiter VIIIF engine, but later IIAs used Jupiter IX, X, Siddley, Jaguar and Panther engines.

"The first Wapitis to enter RAF service were a small batch of MkIs which were received by No. 84 Squadron at Shaibah, Iraq, in late 1928. In the following year, its sister unit, No. 30 Squadron began to reequip with 'Wops' and a third Iraq-based unit, No. 55, received their quota in 1930. By 1931, the Mk IIA was being produced in large numbers and the initial bulk went to RAF units overseas, particularly India.

"The first squadrons to introduce the Wapiti to the North-West Frontier of India were Nos. 11 and 39 Squadrons, both of which arrived from England in October 1928. In April 1930, No. 27 Squadron began exchanging its DH9As for Wapitis along with No. 60 Squadron and by January 1932, all eight operational squadrons were Wapiti-equipped.

"The change from their ancient 'Ninaks' and 'Brisfits', was welcomed by air crews. Its deeper fuselage offered a modicum of extra comfort (and stowage space) while the all-round improvement in performance meant an increase in efficiency. With a cruising speed in the region of 100 miles per hour, carrying up to 580 lb of war-load, the Wapiti's vastly-improved take-off and a rate of climb (1,100 ft a minute) when compared with the earlier DH9As meant a safer and confident start to any operational flight.

"Air gunners found little improvement in their 'rear office'. No seat was provided for any lengthy flight, but there was a detachable control column (although no duplicate rudder controls). Intended as a last-ditch form of emergency control in the event of any injury or indisposition of the pilot, the extra control column was usually utilised to give air gunners some practice in controlling the aircraft, thereby, offering some brief respite for pilots on any extended sorties.

"On May 17, 1930, its emergency use was demonstrated to the full when, during a sortie in the Red Shirts campaign, Fg Off Stroud of No. 11 Squadron was hit in the neck by an Afridi rifleman when 6,000 ft over a target. Stroud immediately signalled his air gunner, AC1 S Wiltshire, to take over the control and then collapsed and died. Wiltshire was faced with two grim alternatives. He could take to his parachute and be captured by the tribesmen (with almost certain prospect of torture and death by their hands) or he could attempt to fly the aircraft back to base.

"Being uncertain whether his pilot was dead or merely unconscious, Wiltshire chose to try and fly to base. With the barest minimum of flying experience, Wiltshire finally reached Risalpur, but, sadly, his total ignorance of the landing technique caused him to crash. Wiltshire died of his injuries the same night and was accorded the unusual honour of being promoted posthumously to the rank of Corporal.

"For long distance flying (such as annual long distance flights to Singapore) an extra fuel tank was normally fitted between the legs of the undercarriage, from which fuel was pumped by a wind-vane driven auxiliary pump and thereby, added two hours to the normal endurance of four and a half hours. In the event of a faulty pump, pilots were able to use a hand pump conveniently situated just to the right of their seats. For contents-checking of the long-range tank, a 'tele-level' fuel gauge was added to the pilot's instrument panel. This fairly primitive device was usually underread and more often than not became stuck or simply gave up the ghost completely.

"Ground crews soon accustomed themselves to the idiosyncrasies of the Wapiti but quickly discovered one worrisome innovation. The Jupiter engine required a two-man cranking start, entailing a man standing on each lower wing winding furiously to coax the engine into life. It was a particularly onerous job when carried out in the open during the 'blistering' heat of an Indian 'summer'.

"From a pure flying point of view, pilots found the Wapiti a thoroughly stable mount which responded easily to controls and, indeed, was fully aerobatic, if required. This latter capability was most welcome to men accustomed to carrying out a circuitous and highly dangerous form of operational flying among the razor-edged precipitous mountains and hills of India's North-West Frontier Province — an area described by one cynic as 'Nature at its barest — and lying on its side.' One of the aircraft's few flying vices was a permanent tendency to swing strongly on take-off and (especially) landing (stick right back and fully stalled if you want a neat three-pointer). With no braking system, this characteristic often led to 'expensive' landings by any pilot new to the Wapiti.

"For some 10 years, the Wapiti bore the brunt of almost continuous action along the never-peaceful Frontier bordering Afghanistan, although in steadily decreasing numbers. Newer designs such as Hawker Hart (India) and Audax replaced it in Nos. 11, 20, 28, 31 and 39 Squadrons by the end of 1935 but the remaining three RAF units soldiered bravely on with their Wapitis until (and after) the outbreak of World War II in 1939.

"Of these latter (three), No. 60 received its first Blenheim I bomber in March 1939; No. 27 re-equipped with Blenheim I 'fighters' at the end of 1940 (having flown its first operational sorties of World War II in Wapitis on anti-shipping patrols off Bombay), while the veteran No. 5 Squadron reduced by then to a mere third of its normal establishment, finally re-equipped in June 1940 — exchanging Wapitis for Hawker Harts.

"Nevertheless, the Wapiti continued to be used on operational sorties until the turn of 1942, piloted by men of No. 1 Squadron, Indian Air Force. Originally, created in 1932 by the Indian Air Force Act, the first formation of the IAF came into being on April 1, 1933 — with four Wapitis at Karachi. By the outbreak of the war, in September 1939, the IAF comprised just one fully-equipped squadron, although several Coastal Defence Flights (equipped with Wapitis) were in the process of forming to relieve RAF units engaged in protection duties at the five big seaports of India.

"It can, therefore, be said truthfully that apart from its valuable contribution to the RAF's history in India, the Wapiti can claim to be the foundation on which were built the present day Indian and Pakistan Air Forces."

— R C Norton, Aircraft (I), Illustrated No. 6, UK.

The Kabul Legation Siege — 1928-29

In the Salmond Report submitted to the British government in 1922, Sir John Salmond had recommended eight squadrons of aircraft for the RAF India, but the number remained at six squadrons for the next six years. However, in tune with a fresh reorganisation, two squadrons arrived in India, making a total of eight squadrons. In October 1928, Nos. 11 and 39 arrived in India.

"The reorganisation had hardly begun when RAF India was faced with a grave emergency. King Amanullah of Afghanistan had recently returned from an extended European tour and on comparing the relative 'backwardness' of his kingdom, had sought to bring in sweeping reforms. These well-intentioned changes merely served to cause an explosion of revolt among his people.

"In November 1928, nearly 3,000 tribesmen sacked Kabul in protest. The British Legation in Kabul was situated some two and a half miles outside the city and became isolated from all other Legations. By mid-December, the Legation found itself virtually in the middle of a battlefield, surrounded by rebel tribes and loyal supporters to the Afghan throne.

"The Minister, Sir Francis Humphrys, accordingly requested by wireless that the RAF arrange for the evacuation of British women and children resident in the Legation. The request posed a serious problem to the RAF in India. Possessing no passenger carrying aircraft, the only available aircraft were the DH9As of Nos. 27 and 60 Squadrons and these were incapable of carrying a large number of passengers over any reasonably short period of time.

"The nearest overseas RAF unit with proper troop carrying capability was No. 70 Squadron with its Vickers Victorias — some 2,800 miles away at Baghdad, Iraq. This unit was immediately sent to Karachi. In the meantime, DH9As (called Ninaks) of Nos. 27 and 60 Squadrons were stripped of military equipment (bomb racks, guns etc) in preparation for flying over Afghanistan, crews being hastily issued with visas to their passports.

"On December 18, 1928, Flying Officer C W L Trusk and his passenger LAC (Leading Aircraftsman) G Donaldson of No. 27 Squadron flew the 150 miles to Kabul, taking with them a Popham Panel, to be dropped to the British Legation there in order that the Ambassador could arrange for messages to be passed to the aircraft. Flying low over the Legation, Trusk's Ninak was hit 14 times by rifle fire from besieging rebels, damaging its radiator and oil pump and forcing Trusk to land at the nearby Afghan Air Force base at Sherpur, just outside Kabul city.

"Donaldson managed to transmit a signal to base before landing, advising HQ of the position, with the result that another Ninak from No. 27 piloted by Flight Lieutenant A R Prendergast, took off with a second Popham Panel for the Legation. This was delivered successfully within the Legation's walls and Prendergast was soon given a signal 'Don't land, fly high. All is well.'

"On December 20, Flight Lieutenant J L F Fuller Good with LAC Locke, from No. 27, made a morning reconnaissance of the Legation and dropped a message bag to Sir Francis Humphrys; while the following morning, another No. 27 crew, Flying Officer 'Square' McKee and LAC Steeres were forced to turn back from their recce flight by ignition trouble. Two days later, royalist forces in Kabul managed to drive off the siege rebels temporarily and Trusk and Donaldson were able to get into the Legation where Trusk was immediately appointed as Humphrys' Air Adjutant and Donaldson became operator of a wireless set parachuted into the Legation by a Ninak from No. 60 Squadron.

"On December 23, the first phase of evacuation commenced and continued till January 01, by which date the last of the 134 women and children from the Legation had been taken out safely. The same day, Fg Off G P Butcher and LAC Grellis from No. 27 were flown up to retrieve Trusk's Ninak from Sherpur and fly it back to Kohat.

"On January 10, 1929, the rebels advanced on Kabul again and four days later, King Amanullah abdicated in favour of his brother Inayatullah, who promptly fled to Kandahar with his harem on January 18 from Sherpur in two Victorias. The rebel leader seized the throne and assumed the royal title Habibullah II. The same day, Humphrys decided to close the Legation, resulting five days later in all other Legations in Kabul following suit.

"Permission was obtained from the new 'King' for two aircraft to land daily to evacuate 400 or so people from these Legations and the next phase commenced on January 28. During this phase, carried out in one of the worst winters ever experienced on the Frontier, Nos. 27 and 60 Squadrons flew escort to lumbering Victorias. Crews took off each dawn in temperatures as low as minus 20 degrees Centigrade and froze in their open cockpits while struggling to attain a height of 6,000 ft under full throttle. This was the lowest possible altitude needed to fly between towering peaks of 10,000-15,000 ft en route.

"The evacuation continued in appalling conditions of snow and ice and at last on February 25, 1929, the airlift was completed when Sir Francis Humphrys, Fg Off Trusk and LAC Donaldson were flown out — the last persons to leave the Legation.

"This historic first-ever air evacuation on any large scale had resulted in 586 people (a total weight of over 41 tons, including baggage, being airlifted) and involved a total of 57,438 miles of flying."

— Chaz Bowyer, *RAF in India* and *The Flying Elephants*.

Caught in Cross-Fire in No-Man's Land

Given below is a first person account of the siege of the British Legation in Kabul in December 1928 by Squadron Leader Bill Burley who was at that time on deputation to the Legation Staff.

"In 1927, while serving at Peshawar and like all good 'bods' at that time, ticking off the days from my boat calendar, I was suddenly offered a post in the British Legation at Kabul in a civilian capacity — that is, seconded from the RAF.

"I accepted, subject to three months leave at Home, for the blanks on my boat calendar had become very few by then. After the leave, I sailed back to India in the *Neuralia* and entered Afghanistan via the Khyber Pass.

"I found the work at the Legation very gratifying. I had a house to myself, three servants and a part time gardener, and pleasant social company.

"King Amanullah of Afghanistan went on a world tour in 1927 or early 1928 and absorbed lots of ideas for westernising his country. On his return, he began to put these ideas into practice."

Resentment

"The first thing that I noticed was the dressing-up of his Cabinet Ministers in suits which resembled a cross between a US Mormon preacher and an orthodox Jew.

"After a few more royal ideas had percolated into practice, a good deal of resentment among the population became apparent. The decision to unveil the women of his strict Muslim domain was the final straw.

"I remember so vividly attending a cine lecture given by the King to the diplomatic corps on his return from abroad. Seated close to the royal party, I was fascinated by the clear beauty of Queen Soraya, who was one of the first women to unveil in public.

"Little did I think that within a few months, she and her royal spouse would have fled the country and that a child of a water-carrier — for that is the meaning of the name Bacha-i-Saqao — would reign in his place.

"The unrest over westernisation was most apparent in the Jalalabad area. There, the people's frustration took the form of shooting up and looting vehicles coming from India via the Khyber Pass.

"I think we were denied access to the Khyber long before the final rebellion and the march on Kabul, and this was probably why the Military Attache could not get back from leave.

"The first I knew of the rebellion was while walking up a gravel path from my house in the Legation grounds to the Chancellory. I was suddenly aware of spurts of gravel in the path ahead of me. Looking up and wondering how it was possible to have a sudden heavy hailstorm out of a cloudless sky, I immediately heard the rattle of machine gun fire.

"I think I did the 100 yards to the Chancellory in ten seconds. I blurted out that some sod had turned a machine gun on me.

"I got the 'You have been drinking, old boy' sort of look, but it did not last long, for there was soon a clamouring at the Legation gates, with hordes of Bacha's rebels demanding access.

"Sir Francis Humphrys went to the gates and tried to reason with them, but eventually allowed them to enter. He had no option, for besides our complement of 13 staff, we had only a dozen Indian soldiers of King George's Cavalry as bodyguards."

Rebels Gatecrash

"Once inside, their leader — it might have been Bacha himself for all I knew — dived into the entrance lodge, carefully removed a fire extinguisher and gently deposited it into the stream which ran past the Legation grounds. That tricky business over, he announced that his troops would occupy the Legation buildings and compound to conduct the war against the King's troops.

"After a lot of diplomatic talking by the Ambassador, punctuated with mild reminders of British military and Air Force wrath should harm come to us — plus their own childhood tales of what 'Roberts Sahib' did after the last massacre of Britons — the rebels intimated they would leave us alone provided we furnished oil for their rifles.

"Whether they got the oil or not, I never knew. From then onwards, for about three weeks, we were in no-man's land, being clouted by both sides — each believing the other was using the Legation as a sniping post.

"We had a big Army W/T receiver in store, but no transmitter. It had never been used because no one in the Legation could take Morse code.

"To me, the thing was just a Chinese puzzle and it took hours of trial and error before we had it going. I was then able to tune in to the outside world to hear what was going on."

Sinking Heart

"The strongest station was Peshawar (civil), belting out the Foreign Office five-figure code at over 20 words a minute, and I listened with a sinking heart, vainly trying to cope up with that speed.

"Fishing around for RAF stations, I was able to identify them and their call-signs by the simple means of intercepting aircraft movement signals between stations, mentioning pilots by name.

"'BFD8092, Flight Lieutenant Smetham, left for you at 0800 hours' — was definitely Peshawar, so the call-sign was logged. 'DH9A, Flight Lieutenant Jordan, left for you at 0900 hours' — that must be 'Rizzy' (Risalpur), and so on. It is quite possible that Group Captain Cocks' trip to Karachi was logged by me.

"RAF W/T was not only slower but in plain language, so a word or two which I missed could be guessed with confidence and I could cope. Imagine my delight when tuning in to RAF Peshawar, I found them tapping out messages to us, tapping out messages at eight words a minute.

"Gawd, it was slow, but I could have hugged the brainy soul at Peshawar who remembered me. As an air gunner, eight words was my qualifying speed.

"I cannot remember how or when I was given a call-sign — may be it was allocated to the Legation when the set was acquired — but I can clearly remember the slow and steady VWR, VWR, VWR, that came from Peshawar. Forsaking all others, I stuck to them like glue which was perhaps as well, for I was able to intercept a message that a DH9A was leaving for Kabul to find out what was happening to us.

"Being aware of the trigger-happy crowd around us, we divested the servants of their *pughrees* and laid them out on the lawn, during darkness, spelling out the words 'Fly high, don't land'."

No Life

"Next day, the 9A duly showed up and the crew clearly read the message, for I tuned in on the aircraft and heard them describing it. However, they added: 'But there is no sign of life in the Legation.' This immediately set us waving from an upper window to correct the report. One might ask why we did not go out on the lawn to wave, but the fact was that Amanullah's troops on one side of us were convinced we were all dead and that the rebels were in occupation. They, therefore, fired on anything seen moving in the Legation grounds.

"Before this time, we were all housed in the main Chancellory, with a set installed in my house. I could go down in the dark early mornings in safety to tune in, but it was not funny dashing back in daylight. Eventually, the Ambassador decided it was too risky and in darkness, we had the set moved to the Chancellory.

"The pilot of the DH9A must have seen some movement, for he came down to within small-arms range to investigate and was promptly shot down. Later, we received a message stating that a Vickers troop carrier from Mesopotamia was flying to Kabul to evacuate the women and children. In darkness, we obtained safe passage through the King's lines for Lady Humphrys and two wives and a child of the Legation staff to the Kabul aerodrome, where they were evacuated to India the next day.

"Eventually, the King's troops managed to clear the rebels from the Legation area and we were able to proceed with the main task of evacuating European and Indian civilians to Peshawar in Vickers Victorias.

"On my own return to India, I was given a spot of local leave, which was why I was not in Peshawar to say goodbye to the Ambassador. However, he left a note, which I very much appreciated and still have today.

"It said, 'I have given orders that Rs 125 compensation should be paid to you for the loss of the dinner jacket destroyed by a shell. The question of compensation for loss of crockery, etc left behind will be disposed off later.' Thanking me for my services in Kabul, he brought them to the notice of Sir Geoffrey Salmond and the C-in-C."

— RAFA Journal *Air Mail*, Spring, 1973.

Group Captain Adrian Cocks, RAF, recalls an incident during the Kabul air evacuation, 1928-29:

"In the winter of 1928-29, there was a bit of a 'do' going on in Afghanistan between troops loyal to the Crown and a bunch of revolting insurgents under the leadership of a character called Bacha-i-Saqao.

"At the time there were two squadrons of Ninaks (DH9As) on the North-West Frontier, No. 60 Squadron at Kohat, where I was stationed and No. 27 Squadron on the other side of the hills at Risalpur, popularly known as 'Rizzy'.

"Just before Christmas of 1928, the Afghan 'do 'had got close to Kabul, and the British Legation had become a place of refuge for a variety of other nationals, including Russian princesses, Italian counts and Arabian knights.

"Rizzy were told to send a 9A to do a reconnaissance over Kabul. At Kohat, we were told to open up a W/T watch, to back up the watch at 'Rizzy'. Air-ground-air wireless communication was a bit of a variable quantity.

"In addition to being a 9A chauffeur, I was the unit signals officer at Kohat during the morning of the recce from 'Rizzy'. I was in the wireless cabin to see what luck we should have. My Flight Sergeant was 'on the key'.

"I remember watching over his shoulder as he was writing down a signal from the aircraft over Kabul. The message gave the aircraft's height and position and I watched flight's pencil write down the word 'shot'. Then there was an abrupt wireless silence.

"We later learnt that a good, if lucky, shot from a ground marksman had punctured the aircraft's water pump. The pilot made a successful forced landing on the bit of ground outside Kabul, which served as an aerodrome, and he and his wireless operator managed to scuttle into the Legation and join the throng.

"The next day (I think), 'Rizzy' sent up another aircraft to try and see what was going on, and what did the pilot see — laid out on the green Legation lawns, using every bit of white fabric which could be enlisted and large enough for the pilot to read from the air, were the words: 'All is well. Fly high. Do not land'.

"The aircraft returned safely and we subsequently learnt the reason for 'Don't land'. The opposing ground parties had taken up positions on opposite sides of the landing area and were conducting carefree Bisley practice at each other.

"However, it was decided that, as soon as the landing ground was free of hostilities, an air evacuation of refugees in the Legation would take place. Ninaks were to fly to Kabul in ballast, land, ditch the ballast — lead weights — embark one passenger without stopping the engine and return to base.

"For a few days, including Christmas Day itself, we put our Ninaks out on the aerodrome at Kohat, first thing, ran them up and shut them down, and then just waited for an order to take off for Kabul.

"If no order came through by midday, then the plan was off for that day, because there would not be enough daylight left for us to get there and back before dark, and Kohat aerodrome, on account of its size and approaches, was not suitable for night landings."

Christmas Moans

"During those few days of marking time, a Vickers Vernon troop carrier had been flown in from Mesopotamia. I knew the pilot well and I remember his moaning about his Christmas Day, which had mostly been spent, for a refuelling process, at some remote hot spot along the Persian Gulf. Apparently, the only shade that the crew could find was under the wing, although the design seems to have allowed for precious little ground clearance.

"The Vernon could take about 25 passengers and so do the same degree of evacuation, in one trip, as could be done by all the Ninaks of Nos. 27 and 60 Squadrons combined. And so, as it happened, that one 'Mini Jumbo' — and what a Jumbo the Vernon did look — did most, if not all, of the relief of Kabul.

"I had to go to Karachi immediately after Christmas, to ferry back, a new (reconditioned) Ninak and by the time I returned to Kohat on January 2, 1929, the evacuation had been successfully completed."

— Group Captain Adrian Cocks,
Air Mail, Autumn, 1972.

The Frontier Shows

Organising Frontier Wars

The tribes of that era looked on war as an honourable, exciting and manly exercise. When they had no quarrel with the British or the Afghans, they arranged one among themselves. Many of them clearly thought that the Government of India organised Frontier wars on the same basis. At least, there seems no other reasonable explanation of the fact that when a Frontier campaign was over, scores of Pathans used to apply to the Political Agents for the Frontier Medal with the appropriate clasp.

"I think their request was reasonable. As they pointed out, they were British subjects and they had fought in the battles organised by the King Emperor across the seas. Indeed, without their cooperation, the war would have been a complete fiasco and no one would have got any medals," says John Masters.

To this, adds Chaz Bowyer (*The Flying Elephants*): "They applied in all seriousness for the India General Service Medal with the clasp for the campaign in which they had fought. Denied this, they could not see the logic of it. They had fought well and bravely, providing much useful training for the King Emperor's Army and they surely deserved a reward."

Indeed, without their active cooperation, there would have been no war and no training for British soldiers and airmen.

Rules of the Game

John Masters, the famous and well known writer on the 'Raj' years in India, was commissioned as a 2nd Lieutenant from the Sandhurst Military Academy in the British Indian Army and allotted to the 2nd Battalion of the famed IV Gurkha Rifles in India in 1934.

He was his family's fifth generation member to serve in India. He served in the India for 14 years, which included field service in Iraq, Iran and Burma during World War II, apart from seven years of regimental duty on the North-West Frontier of India.

Having experienced and participated in the well-oiled machinery of the Government of India, he saw at first-hand the civil-military equation at its practical level. How British Political Agents tried hard to keep their eyes and ears open to any sign of trouble from any of the tribes in the entire 'unadministered' area, adjacent to the Durand Line, the border with Afghanistan which is now a part of the Frontier folklore.

May be, the British Army units now deployed as part of the North Atlantic Treaty Organisation (NATO) coalition forces today (2010) in Afghanistan did get a briefing from the old-timers or even read regimental histories of earlier campaigns. Basically, nothing has changed in Afghanistan, whether it is the terrain or the tactics. Perhaps, one thing has changed — the enemy is better equipped and is trying to unite the tribes.

The introduction of the air element seemed a little strange and 'unsporting' to the tribals at first, but they soon got used to it as it posed a challenge to their marksmanship and 'manliness'. However, in the hallowed halls of European Chancellories and in the League of Nations and the Western press, there were loud protests about the use of bombing planes on the Frontier. True, aerial proscription was unthinkable against a European populated city, but on the Frontier, the tribal was not a helpless person as would be the unarmed population of a city.

Aerial proscription was subject to many rules that were quite rigid. In most incidents, the Political Agent would be the one getting credible information about the wrongdoings of a tribe. He would warn the neighbouring tribes not to get involved by giving shelter to anyone from the renegade tribe. To add punch to the warning, Scout units would carry out *gasht* (patrolling) in the surrounding areas and with increasing numbers and frequency. The next step: the aerial proscription request would then work its way up through various layers of the Government from the Resident in Waziristan to the Governor of NWFP and perhaps, to the Viceroy.

If sanction was given, aircraft at once dropped notices printed on White Paper all over the tribe's territory, warning them that proscription would begin one week thence, unless the tribe surrendered and paid a fine, sometimes in terms of rifles or money itself. The notices also defined a safe area, a small enclave big enough to hold all the people of the tribe with their flocks, but not big enough to graze the flocks or to live in with comfort.

Twenty-four hours before proscription was due to begin, aircraft dropped thousands of more notices, on red paper, to say that since the required action had not been taken by the tribe in question, proscription would begin as promised, barring a last minute compliance. As with the 'ghooley chits', hardly anyone among the tribals could read either Pushtu or Urdu, but the red colour of the notices conveyed the message louder than words.

From H-Hour, aircraft continuously patrolled the proscribed area and attacked with machine guns and 20 lb bombs any man or animal seen outside the safe enclave. The pilots were not allowed to attack buildings unless they could clearly see that the buildings were being actively used at that moment for hostile purposes.

Ideally, aerial proscription sent all the tribe members into the safe enclave and forced its surrender, without bloodshed, by complete disruption of its normal life. In practice, the threat alone was often enough. If not, the tribal determination went still further. Aircraft attacked sheep and goats surreptitiously sent out to graze or fired on groups of people, sometimes having women, as they scurried about in the forbidden territory.

The tribesmen would tie up a few useless old women in the hope of collecting 'blood money' for them, and sometimes, the airmen could not see the ropes or the disguise of male clothing and duly killed them.

The Air Force (RAF) also acted in direct support of the Army under another and equally rigid set of rules. They could take offensive action only in a proscribed area and against bodies of armed men, specifically pointed out to them by the soldiers on the ground as a legitimate target or against bodies of armed men indubitably hurrying to, or away from, a fight, whom the Army could not see.

Even with the speeds of bumbling old Audaxes, Harts and Wapitis, this caused considerable strain to the pilot, who flew miserably along at low level in fierce mountains, his thoughts muddied by a host of instruments, his responsibility to the soldiers, a lapful of instructions, and dire thoughts of castration, should he crash.

It may not be out of place here to chart out the imaginary verbal or written exchanges between the civil authority and the armed forces regarding putting down a tribal rebellion, or fighting a skirmish or going on a hostile mission called 'Barampta'.

Decision-Making and Decision-Taking

- Get there fastest with mostest men.
- Do not get there at all until we have referred the matter to the Governor General-in-Council, which will take months.
- Shoot first, shoot fastest, shoot last, and shoot to kill.
- Do not shoot unless you have been shot at, and then try not to hurt anyone, there is a good chap.
- Mystify, mislead and surprise the enemy, then never leave him a moment to gather himself again, but fall on him like a thunderclap and pursue him to his utter destruction, regardless of fatigue, casualties, or cost.
- Announce your intentions to the enemy, in order that he may have time to remove his women and children to a place of safety — and time to counter your plan. At all events, stop what you are doing as soon as he pretends to have had enough, so that he may gather again somewhere else.
- Casualties, damage, losses, cost, are only some of the many factors to be considered when making a battle plan. If any factor is given undue weight, the plan is likely to fail.
- Pardon us, but your plan does not interest us. We are happy to say that that is your business. However, casualties cause questions in the House, damage brings complaints in the Assembly, losses get into newspapers, and cost we cannot stand, in view of the depleted state of the country's finances.
- Remember all that, and get the war over quickly. And if you

should fail — Ah! but there, you won't fail, old chap, will you?

Almost every month of the 150 years that the British Indian Army battled the tribes of the North-West Frontier Province, one fact remained paramount in the policy of the Government of India.

- Treat the tribes fairly but firmly, should they break the rules of the game.
- Ultimately, face the fact that the tribals are British subjects as you and I are.

Today (2010), is such a policy feasible in that area? Yes, they are trying, but the tribes are more organised, better equipped and with more radical religious frenzy and more political savvy.

Air Operations in the Thirties

In 1919, the disturbances in Punjab had resulted in widespread protests and rioting. The situation had been brought about by the firings on an unarmed crowd by the Army at Jallianwala Bagh. At that time, the RAF had been called out and had succeeded in putting down the rioting and the demonstration.

Just 10 years later, the Air Force was again called upon to quell riots and disorder. In 1929, the Indian National Congress, inspired by Mahatma Gandhi, organised a massive civil disobedience moment. They received support in the NWFP from Khan Abdul Gaffar Khan of Utmanzai who organised the Frontier Youth League who became known as the 'Red Shirts'. Khan Abdul Gaffar Khan was arrested. This sparked off an agitation which spread and resulted in rioting in Peshawar and in Kohat.

In Waziristan, the Madda Khel tribe captured the Datta Khel Tochi Scout post on May 11, 1929. This was the signal for the Army and the Air Force to go into action. Ninaks (DH9A) of two squadrons, Nos. 27 and 60, were detached to Miranshah for the operations which lasted three days after which general unrest spread through the entire Peshawar Valley.

In June, aerial patrolling revealed a crowd of 7,000 Afridis at Tendal which was immediately bombed and strafed, while another group, several thousand strong, went towards Peshawar. Aircraft went into action and after several hours, the crowd was forced to retreat across the Khajuri Plain on June 6. They suffered casualties and for the air crews, it was impossible to bomb fleeting, moving targets accurately. Flying at low levels and strafing targets was extremely dangerous, especially for the crew as the Afridis were extremely fine marksmen even at comparatively long ranges. One of the casualties was Flying Officer Stroud who was shot through the neck during a 600 ft bombing run. On October 3, the Afridis submitted and hostilities ceased. Gaffar Khan was arrested and deported from the province.

The Red Shirts protest campaign ended. No. 27 Squadron had flown 202 operational missions and 100 reconnaissance sorties in this period. In early 1932, a fight broke out between the Upper and Lower Mohamands. Whenever they were not fighting against the Government forces, they would settle scores on some other issues and this flare-up was due to that. In July, the Lower Halimzai Mohamands appealed to the British for help in subduing their enemies and this was granted, resulting in the withdrawal by the Upper Mohamands. This support was given so that the Government could get help in building a proposed road into the Gandab Valley.

Refuelling and Flying Hazards

During the hot season, as was usual among North Waziristan tribes, during the idle period between sowing and reaping their crops, inter-tribal feuds were renewed and the Faqir of Ipi first became prominent in the news, particularly in the Razmak region. The RAF maintained a forward landing ground at Razmak at 6,600 ft above sea level — the strip sloped alarmingly at an incline. The actual take-off strip was only some 500 yards in length and all landings had to be made uphill with no overshoot. The technique for take-off was decidedly energetic, not to say dangerous, for air gunners.

After a Wapiti had taxied to the top of the strip, the air gunner was required to pivot the aircraft by one wing-tip and then run to gain his cockpit, as the pilot necessarily opened up his throttle. With no wheel brakes, it was essential for a pilot to have full boost in order to clear an Army occupied fort at the far end of the strip. The fort, the Queen Alexandra Picquet, was reported to be the highest Army outpost in the British Empire. Perched precariously on the edge of a knife-edged plateau, its occupants usually turned out in large numbers to cheer and wave at air crews as they flew past on their way Home.

On August 23, 1929, a composite formation of Nos. 27 and 60 Squadrons flew to Arawali to carry out refuelling exercises. Due to water pollution in the petrol lines after refuelling, two aircraft made crash landings and another one a forced landing. All three aircraft belonged to No. 60 Squadron. The contemporary method of refuelling was by four-gallon drums of petrol being handed over, up from the ground and poured into the tanks by hand via a large funnel covered with chamois leather as the only external means of filtration. It was a wearying job at the best of times and particularly, in the open during the hot season. Oil was taken from a 50-gallon drum and poured in directly by means of a hand can.

Railway Carriages for Travel

A glimpse of the prevailing conditions of service for RAF personnel at this period is provided by the comments of No. 27 Squadron, R 'Dicky' Bird, who was posted to this squadron in October 1932, having just completed two years of service with No. 55 Squadron in Iraq. In those days, it was normal for some airmen posted overseas to split their five years' tour in this fashion.

"The outstanding thing of note in my first two days in India, which set the seal on a very happy stay there, was that on our journey to Rawalpindi from the troopship, the travelling arrangements included railway carriages, whereas in Iraq, the Government could only afford open iron trucks. By the odour emanating from those trucks, I should think they were not normally employed for transporting RAF personnel. The journey from the railhead to Rawalpindi was made by Leyland lorry to Risalpur where we stayed overnight and then continued on to Kohat by Leyland. I was posted to 'C' Flight as part of the ground crew to an aeroplane piloted by Sergeant Stamp (later Squadron Leader) and it did not take me long to realise that here was a very happy squadron and I think I might say the same for No. 60 Squadron and the Kohat station generally."

Operations Against Mohamands

"Two separate series of operations against the Mohamands and Bajaur occurred in the area just north-west of Peshawar at the same time. In May 1933, the pretender to the Afghan throne, who was being sheltered by the Khan of Kotkai in Charharmung Valley, was trying to raise a rebellion against Nadir Shah, Amir of Afghanistan. The latter demanded action by the Indian Government to suppress this movement.

"By July 20, 1933, all political measures had failed and four days later, air leaflets were dropped demanding acceptance of terms issued by July 29, with a warning that air bombing would start in default of such acceptance. The Khan of Kotkai would not submit and, therefore, plans were made to raid Kotkai.

"This village was situated on a steep hillside and measured a mere 112 yards by 54 yards in perimeter — an exceedingly small target to pinpoint. Using 112 lb bombs, Nos. 27 and 60 Squadrons from Kohat with Nos. 11 and 39 Squadrons from Risalpur (flying Hawker Harts) attacked Kotkai heavily. The first raids were deadly accurate and by August 10, only demonstration flights were made over the rebels to intimidate them. The result was an agreement to terms by August 13 and the expulsion of the pretender."

Outlaw at Large

"In August 1935, serious trouble cropped up again in the Mohamand region. It was fomented by an old outlaw, the Hadji of Turngzai and his three sons. On August 14, the eldest son led a force of nearly two thousand Upper Mohamands to destroy the Gandab road built in 1933. Three days later, warning notices of intended bombings were sent out to the tribes and were followed by demonstration flights of 38 aircraft over rebel villages.

"The show of power failed to impress the rebels who remained in their camps and villages. To minimise casualties, the first bombing phase was limited to small smoke bombs but within the hour, two high explosive bombs were dropped, giving emphasis to the serious nature of impending air attacks.

"On August 20, Nos. 27 and 60 Squadrons raided Khel and Isa Khel villages. After two days, a series of consistent bombing flights was started and these continued for a week. They included the dropping of several delayed action bombs which discouraged villagers from returning to their homes after each raid. On August 31, further three squadron formations, comprising 39 aircraft, again demonstrated over rebel areas.

"With the decision to advance further into Mohamand country over the Aahakki Pass, a notice of the Government's intentions was dropped to the tribes on September 7 and two nights later, bombings recommenced in conditions of clear moonlight. This form of operation proved extremely dangerous to air crews — and yet paradoxically, exhilarating from a purely flying viewpoint. Winging through the black menacing gorges and towering rock-faced mountains bathed in shafts of silver moonlight inspired at least one pilot to burst into song, much to the astonishment of his air gunner who could, henceforth, claim to have been serenaded at 7,000 ft in the early hours of the morning.

"Operations continued without let-up until September 29, 1935, when a pitched battle ensued between the tribesmen and two Army platoons on a high point of a mountain ridge known as Point 4080. It was during this hand-to-hand fighting that a Victoria Cross was so deservedly won by Captain G Meynell of the 12th Frontier Force Regiment (FFR), when he was killed leading a magnificent defence against overwhelming odds. This battle became the turning point of the rebel's campaign and on October 1, they finally submitted."

— Chaz Bowyer, *The Flying Elephants*.

Coming of Age in the Air Age

By 1930, and right through the Thirties till 1941, the RFC/ RAF had been in India for nearly 25 years. Beginning with one squadron that was later split into two and with the arrival of more squadrons, it had in all, six squadrons divided into three wings, operating about 75 aircraft. Practically, all the machines were of World War I vintage, with the exception of the Westland Wapiti which was a post-war product that came to India in 1928. Along with that came two more squadrons, raising the RAF strength in India to eight squadrons.

The post-war scenario for the RAF in England was a desperate fight for survival as an independent service. Many vital ingredients of a new service had to be introduced: the service ensign, squadron markings, integration of gunnery and wireless, use of parachutes, more reliable engines, the service motto, the new rank names and structure, the introduction of the double wing for pilots and the vertical organisation such as the wing, group formation along with that of command.

In India, the RAF was concentrated in the North-West Frontier Province and the neighbouring state of Punjab. Army cooperation was the main task. Initially, it involved flying aerial reconnaissances to get information to the Army units on the ground, either before the attack or during the operation itself. As wireless was in its infancy, message dropping via a special hook and signs on the ground to alert the pilot about the condition on an isolated piquet were slowly developed.

What the RAF in India proved to the world and more especially to the sceptics in the Army was that it could provide the tangible part that would help the Army column on the ground achieve its objective. Immediately after its arrival on the Frontier, the RAF began to train its pilots to direct artillery fire against objectives seen from the air and transmitted via the wireless to the Battery Commander.

The British used balloons and man-lifting kites during the South African War 1899-1900 for reconnaissance, in order to see, as General Edward Swinton put it, the other side of the hill. Their organisation under the command of Colonel B J Templer of the Balloon Factory at Farnborough, was mobile.

It was this ability of the balloon to see the other side of the hill that prompted the Army to utilise the air arm to pinpoint targets for the artillery. The only improvement was that on the Frontier, at this time, they began using the aeroplane.

Once the utility of the aeroplane as a spotter had been established and acknowledged by the Army, no single mission on the ground was commenced without a general aerial reconnaissance and likely targets for the artillery.

This was further enhanced by demonstrating that the Air Force could on its own mount air operations, without the Army with its cumbersome bag and baggage and its comparatively slow pace. To the parsimonious Government of India and Whitehall in faraway London, it showed how the cost of land operations could be reduced considerably by using the air element, either independently or in conjunction with a smaller Army unit or units.

This was acknowledged by the Army in the field but those who sat in the headquarters needed foolproof convincing. This was provided by Wing Commander R C M Pink when he offered to conduct operations without any support from the Army. This he did in 1925 and proved conclusively that control and containment of rebel tribes could be accomplished speedily and at a minimal cost in casualties and expenditure when compared with the hitherto traditional method of despatching cumbersome and expensive Army columns.

During this campaign, all three forms of operations were carried out. Locating the tribals called for constant reconnaissance flights. Once *jirgahs* (collection of tribals at one point) were pointed, ground attacks took place by machine gun fire, and then bombing of targets was resorted to apart from directing artillery fire from the air against targets considered vital to the operation.

This brought a grudging admission from the Army and civil authorities about the potential of air power in India. This was also buttressed by the example of the RAF under the command of Air Marshal Sir John Salmond who was given full authority to take control of Iraq in the Twenties, which saved the exchequer millions of pounds.

Starting with one squadron in 1916, the RAF presence in India, especially the North-West Frontier and Punjab, increased by stages to six squadrons which were operating old and obsolete relics of the last war. In 1922, the Salmond Report recommended eight squadrons for India, but it took six years to implement that. However, by 1928, the RAF had eight squadrons in India divided into three wings under one umbrella group.

Thus, by the mid-Thirties, the RAF had acquired the skill and the experience of mountain flying, ground attack, bombing and directing artillery fire. A stage was reached when, before starting on a major campaign, the Army commander would consult the Air Force about the various aspects and request its help. It was, perhaps, the Frontier experience that helped pilots to fly in the mountain and jungle conditions of Burma in World War II.

It is held that this development overall laid the foundation of what during World War II were called 'combined operations'.

Squadron Identification Markings

"It was around this time that No. 27 Squadron began smartening up their aircraft to a very high degree. All wing and fuselage was silver-doped and under the aegis of Squadron Leader Ralph Whitehead, who had taken over command on March 15, 1923, unit identification markings were standardised in conjunction with their sister unit, Squadron No. 60.

"Although such markings were by local authority only (there were no official unit markings in the RAF at that time), the practice stemmed from a natural desire for a squadron's individual identity, thus, stimulating unit pride. A rather hump-backed green elephant profile began to appear on aircraft fins — a direct reference to the squadrons first operational aircraft in 1916 in Europe, the Martinsyde G 100 Elephant.

"It was during May 1924 that RAF squadrons officially began to include the unit role in their titles, thus, 'No. 27 (Bomber) Squadron'."

— Chaz Bowyer, *The Flying Elephants*.

Aircraftsman L H Smith, who joined No. 5 Squadron as a Warrant Officer in June 1917 in France, confirms that "an order was issued to all units of the RFC (RAF) to take to themselves a crest after the manner of Army regiments.

"As I recall, the maple leaf that was taken by No. 5 Squadron was due to the fact that it was mainly Canadian officers who formed the bulk of the officers of the squadron."

— L H Smith, 1976.

Quintus Fructus

Mr Mathew Clark of No. 5 Squadron, RAF, has penned down some more on the squadron crests and markings.

"I met Squadron Leader K A Bennett of No. 5 Squadron a few days after my arrival in India. For starters, we got involved in a discussion regarding the crest and motto of No. 5 Squadron. "Let us straighten out the matter of Quintus Fructus, etc" — which was the motto of the squadron crest prior to the earthquake (in Quetta). Then, in 1936, Squadron Commanders submitted crests for approval by the Sovereign through the College of Arms.

"On my pewter pot, the badge then used had the numeral V superimposed on the maple leaf. The motto meaning, 'Bend but not Break' was inspired by the squadron's experiences through the earthquake.

"According to Walter J Verco, CVO, Norroy and Ulster King of Arms, Inspector of Royal Air Force badges, in a letter to me, dated June 10, 1936, the numeral V was omitted when the badge was agreed upon and sanctioned in 1937 and it was then noted that the maple leaf had been adopted because the squadron during the Great War 1914-18 was attached to the Canadian Corps, especially during the Battles of Vimy, April 1917 and Amien, August 1918.

"The new badge was submitted by the Squadron Leader commanding No. 5 (AC) Squadron, RAF, in a letter dated April 22, 1936, and addressed to the then Inspector of the Royal Air Force Badges. The badge was approved in June 1937 and that date was on the badge in the RAF Club when we had a look at it on May 31, 1974."

The Service Ensign

Today, we take it for granted that every military service or even paramilitary service will have its own insignia — an ensign to signify its own separate identity. First, we have the national flag that takes precedence over all other flags, then the service and then the regimental or the unit flag. For the Army, there was its own ensign that came after the Union Jack.

When military aeroplanes appeared for the first time in the Indian skies, there was no separate Air Force, it was a corps of the Army. After April 1, 1918, though the RAF was a separate service in England, in India, it was under the control of the Army. Gradually, many new innovations were introduced — uniform, ranks, organisation and one of the first was the RAF ensign.

The RAF ensign was approved and issued in 1921.

Orders are Orders

Lieutenant C M Eastley was an Army officer from the Royal Field Artillery (RFA) who volunteered for observer duties from Allahabad where the Wessex Brigade, in which he served, was stationed.

He joined No. 31 Squadron during the winter of 1916-17 and was soon flown over tribal territory in a small operation against the Mohamands.

Lieutenant Eastley says: "On one occasion, I flew with a pilot named Taylor to Shabqadar on a reconnaissance. After doing the job, we landed and when taking off, he took off with tail down and we landed on a rye plantation and the machine collapsed with the naked exhausts spluttering at me.

"The fanatical tribesmen believed anything that their leaders told them. For instance, they were told that they had only to flash mirrors at us and we would fall from the sky. Though mirror flashes were seen, none of us fell. One of the Mullahs announced that any of his followers could get through the electrified wire fence between Peshawar and Abazai by carrying a copy of the holy book under each arm.

"In due course, our soldiers on patrol found a couple of dead tribesmen in the wire defence, with the holy book under each arm and with burns upon their backs.

"I should also mention that on the Frontier we carried revolvers to destroy ourselves in the event of a forced landing in tribal territory, as it was said that the tribal women, after extracting gold from false teeth, would remove one's genitals while the victim was still alive," recalls Lieutenant Eastley.

Trust British ingenuity and innovation. What guns could not achieve, gold could. It was during this period that it was widely publicised after the induction of aeroplanes into the tribal area that any airmen who crashes or has to land with engine trouble should be rescued and returned to the authorities without any physical injury done to him. Anyone doing this would be rewarded, with no questions asked.

Thus, was born the 'ghooley chit' which contained the above message. It served its purpose, for all that the airman had to do was to show his 'ghooley chit'. Though the tribals were illiterate, they all knew what the chit said.

Fighting the Faqir of Ipi — 1936-39

The year 1936 proved to be 'relatively' peaceful in that the entire tribal belt known as the unadministered territory did not see any major revolt. Peace in terms of the Frontier was a pause because the volatile nature of the relationship between the Government of NWFP and the Government of India and the tribals of the region was so unpredictable that an unknown cleric could cause a rebellion by inflammatory speeches. Thus, while 'peace' prevailed, the Army and the RAF continued training.

The RAF squadrons maintained routine aerial reconnaissance flights over the length and breadth of the area, patrols over the proscribed tribal areas and contact flights over the remote Army garrisons and Scout posts. As part of their on-going training, all Frontier squadrons sent their detached flights to Karachi (Drigh Road) in November 1936 for a three-week armament training camp where live bombing and air firing practices were pursued against armoured target boats in the sea off Manora.

Enters the Faqir

A relatively unknown cleric named Mirza Ali Khan openly proclaimed himself as "Champion of Islam" and called for a *jehad* (holy war) against the *firangi* (infidel British). He gave himself a name by which he was known — Faqir of Ipi. His influence among the highly superstitious tribesmen was such that, for the first time, he achieved a fighting cohesion among three major tribes — the Mahsud, Bhittani and Tori Khel Wazir tribes which normally devoted themselves to bitter inter-tribal feuding.

A member of the Bangal Khel clan of the Madda Khel section of the Tori Khel Wazirs, the Faqir was born in 1897 in a village near Khajuri Post at the western end of the Shinki Defile, his father owning some property in the neighbourhood. In 1922, he and his brothers sold their property in the Khajuri Post area and purchased some land near Spalga and also in the Sham Plain area, building a house and a mosque on their property.

They lived for a while near Spalga and during this time, Mirza Ali Khan frequently visited the village of Ipi to get further religious training under the Mullah of that place. In 1926, he took up permanent residence at Ipi. In 1928, he performed the Haj pilgrimage and on his return, continued to live a purely religious life, visiting shrines and religious leaders far afield. He, thus, acquired a reputation for saintliness and gained considerable influence on this account among the Daurs and the Tori Khel Wazirs.

He first came to the attention of the authorities in the "Islam Bibi" case. A Hindu minor girl had been kidnapped by a Muslim and reportedly converted to Islam. When the parents of the girl complained and sought her return, it was refused. A court case followed and on an appeal, she was returned to her family. It was this incident that catapulted Mirza Ali Khan to fame as he practically took over the leadership of the agitation.

When he left the Daur Lashkar, which had collected as a result of the "Islam Bibi" case, he laid his curse on the Daurs for what he perceived as their defection, and on the Tori Khel for not supporting him. He then departed with his personal followers to his property in the Sham Plain area. He did not stay here long and on May 11, 1936, at the invitation of the Zarinai Tori Khel tribe, he moved to Kaskai on the Khaisora river and here he built a house and a mosque and set himself up to actively foment trouble. He persuaded his brother Sher Zaman to give up Government service and Sher Zaman now became his right hand man.

Support Intensifies

In his subversive activities, the Faqir, as he began be known as such, received strong support from certain sections of the Tori Khel who had supposed grievances about the distribution of the ordinary allowances and the fresh allowances arising from the agreement of 1935 with the Government. He also gained further influence by bringing about a semblance of peace between the different tribes bordering the Khaisora. In this, he received the support of the Tori Khel Wazirs, the Mahsuds and the Bhittanis who normally were in a constant state of fueding with each other.

He also received support and help from three well known men, Khonia Khel, a Malik of the Jalal Khel Mahsuds, Din Faqir, a Bhittani Mullah, and Mullah Fazal Din, a Shabi Khel Mahsud of Lataka, son of the late Mullah Powindah and a spiritual leader of the Mahsuds.

In early autumn of 1936, he openly adopted the role of "Champion of Islam". He made his grouse known about the "Islam Bibi" case and also made wholesale allegations of Government interference in matters of the Islamic religion and acquired supporters who rallied to the cry of "Islam in danger". He claimed miraculous powers and promised his followers many things, among others that gas and bombs would be made ineffective and that a few loaves of bread would become enough to feed a multitude. He threatened everlasting disgrace to informers and promised rewards to the martyrs in his cause. The credulity and superstition of the tribesmen was such that all his promises were received with credence in the tribal areas.

All attempts by governmental authorities to prevent this uprising by diplomacy failed and on November 25, 1936, two Army columns from Razmak and Bannu advanced southwards, heading for Biche Kashkai. RAF units were requested to air-supply both columns, No. 27 Squadron being allotted solely to support the Bannu column.

The Army's clash with the Tori Khel was because this tribe was responsible for harbouring the Faqir. A brief but bloody clash left 24 killed and 107 wounded, while the tribe had 41 killed and 31 seriously wounded. The Army operations were assisted by Nos. 5 and 27 Squadrons, RAF, and the Faqir was temporarily forced to take to the hills for refuge. By early December, however, he had gathered a force of about 800 Afghans, Wazirs and Mahsuds around him at a fortified village, Arsal Kot, situated deep in the midst of particularly deep mountainous country.

The headquarters of the Faqir was promptly and most accurately bombed by No. 60 Squadron's Wapitis and again he was forced to take refuge in nearby caves. Bombing operations continued throughout January 1937 inside a proscribed area of two miles and by February 2, these operations were officially considered ended.

It was to be a temporary respite because four days later, two British officers were ambushed and killed by the Mahsuds. Fined Rs 75,000, the tribesmen refused to give up the killers and in consequence, air operations recommenced. Two flights each from Nos. 27 and 60 Squadrons, along with two Valentias of the Bomber Transport Flight were employed in bombing two villages in the Kazha Valley on March 10 and 11.

Although not directly involved in the two murders, the Faqir of Ipi was at the same time gathering support among the Bhittani tribesmen and directed an attack on the Wana Army Brigade. On March 7, 1937, Nos. 27 and 60 Squadrons began a series of air blockade flights over a three-mile radius of an area centred on Arsal Kot, still the main centre of the Faqir's activities.

Air Operations

This operation continued through April, mainly in the form of relays of single aircraft from dawn to dusk over the proscribed area despite the start of the hot season. By mid-April, with some 45,000 regular and militia troops in Waziristan engaged in the campaign, operations reached a peak of effort.

The RAF was fully committed with Nos. 11 and 39 Squadrons operating from Arawali, Nos. 27 and 60 plus the Bomber Transport Flight of Valentias based at Kohat (refuelled and rearmed at Miranshah) and No. 20 Squadron based at Miranshah itself. No. 5 Squadron soon relieved No. 20 Squadron which returned to Risalpur, and towards the end of April 1937, No. 28 Squadron brought its Audaxes from Ambala to Manzai.

Among its many other commitments, No. 28 Squadron provided one novel feature of operations by flying close support escorts for railway trains running from Manzai and Shabbaz Khel through the Pezu Pass.

Miranshah Fort with its three 'resident units' and other occasional visitors, soon assumed the appearance of an extremely busy RAF station. The almost constant traffic served to throw up near-permanent dust and sand storms over the fort and the noise of bellowing engines became a normal background to the daily routine. Toiling in this hell-brew of dust, sand, blistering heat and blinding sun glare, the ground crew remained amazingly cheerful and were always ready with a word of humour and encouragement for the stiff-legged air crews as they climbed out of their aircraft between sorties.

Despite sun-burned, sun-blasted arms, legs and faces, the 'erks' set a minor record for maintenance under comparatively primitive conditions, no aircraft being declared unfit for operations for lack of servicing throughout the campaign. Refuelling was a laborious and sweating business, being accomplished entirely by hand, using four-gallon tins, while oil was drawn from 500-gallon tanks and poured in from a hand-tin. Filteration comprised merely a chamois leather stretched over the access cap and could not prevent the insertion of one consignment of petrol which was polluted with water. This led to several forced landings and crashes during April.

One pilot of No. 27 Squadron slewed on take-off and in the resulting crash, the Wapiti's bomb load exploded, killing the pilot and his gunner L A C Gibbs, while Pilot Officer Johnny Darwen of No. 27 Squadron had a complete engine failure on April 18 when flying over the besieged outpost at Ladha. Landing safely in open country (with his two 250 lb bombs in their racks), Darwen was isolated for days before finally being rescued.

Operations Peak

As the overall situation intensified, the Khaisora proscribed area around Arsal Kot was extended widely to include some near 200 square miles of territory between the Khaisora and Tochi rivers. Nos. 27 and 60 Squadrons were then asked to maintain fighting patrols over the whole terrain. The area was further enlarged on May 5 to include the Sham Plains, north of Arsal Kot.

Ground and air operations continued to escalate, one example being the air effort on February 7 and May 6, when Nos. 27 and 60 Squadrons between them flew a total of 1,350 hours on operations. In June 1937, the Bomber Transport Flight of Valentia was reinforced by 'A' Flight from No. 70 Squadron detached from Iraq to assist in supply and troop airlift sorties.

Bombed and harried from village to village, the Faqir of Ipi was kept constantly on the move and, by July 1, the Indian Government permitted bombing of any village suspected of harbouring him or his immediate supporters. On July 8, 9 and 10, aircraft of No. 27 Squadron bombed Razin with 230 and 250 lb bombs under particularly difficult conditions, having to fly dangerously close to 12,000 ft high mountains on the run into target. In these three days, a total of 130 flying hours and some 11 tons of bombs were dropped.

On August 16, 1937, some 4,000 tribal chiefs (including the Faqir) got together at Shawal to decide the future tribal policy, but some of the lesser tribes had already been deeply impressed by a demonstration flight carried out by 30 RAF aircraft flying in three line-astern formations of 10 aircraft over the Shawal area, intended to intimidate the Faqir's followers.

In August and September 1937, both the Western Mahsuds and the Tori Khel tribes had agreed to submit to terms, and all operations became concentrated against the Bhittanis. For these, 'A' Flight of No. 27 Squadron was detached to Miranshah and 'C' Flight of No. 60 Squadron to Manzai in early September.

This forward airstrip already enjoyed a reputation as the hottest forward landing ground on the Frontier, being a bald desert plateau with no relief from temperatures which rose habitually to 120 degrees in the non-existent shade. Accommodation was tented and the paralysing heat claimed many victims of exhaustion, apart from several minor landing mishaps due to misjudgment of height in the simmering heat-haze covering the landing strip.

Nevertheless, in 70 flying hours, the Manzai flights dropped 11 tons of bombs on Saruna, causing extensive damage. At Miranshah, the No. 27 Squadron Flight and No. 60 Squadron's 'B' Flight expended

119 flying hours, 12 tons of bombs and 16,000 rounds of ammunition on the Faqir's latest hideout Gambakai, at the end of September.

By the middle of September 1937, the Bhittani tribe agreed to terms, and although operations continued in other sections of Waziristan, the Faqir's influence among the tribes had greatly diminished. By December 1937, government casualties amounted to 245 killed and 684 wounded and 73 deaths from disease. In the eight months period, January 15 to September 15 of the same year, RAF losses were three killed and three injured, all in flying accidents.

A total of 11,000 hours had been flown on operations and these included the first participation of 'A' Flight of the newly-formed Indian Air Force.

In support of the bomber units, RAF transport aircraft had carried over 260 tons of supplies and 4,400 personnel, including 100 sick and wounded during the last eight months of 1937 alone.

For several weeks, little was heard of the Faqir of Ipi, but in February 1938, he was discovered stirring up an active rebellion in Madda Khel country and on March 3, bombing raids recommenced on targets at Sarrum, Wucha Kazha, Stara Khaza and Sar Kalai. This latter target was a specially difficult one to attack and the recently appointed No. 1 Wing Commander, J O Oliver decided to fly the first sortie as a form of pre-briefing exercise.

With L A C Fudge of No. 27 Squadron in the gunner's cockpit, Oliver flew in very low over Sar Kalai and was greeted by a veritable barrage of rifle fire as he released his two 250 lb delayed-action bombs. The Wapiti became literally riddled with bullet holes and on his return to Miranshah, Oliver put the battered aircraft down to a perfect three point landing. As the wheels touched the earth, the whole undercarriage collapsed and subsequent inspection showed it to have been hanging by a solitary fitting, the remaining structure being completely shattered by small arms fire.

Early in April 1938, operations were flown in the Main Toi, Spli Toi and Baddar Algad districts while the Madda Khel, at that time, hosts to the Faqir, incited local sub-tribes into raiding several isolated Scout posts and Army convoys. With the rising tensions of international affairs in Western Europe, every endeavour was made to finally curb the Faqir's influence so that the RAF could be prepared for a seemingly unavoidable war with Germany and her allies.

Accordingly, all RAF leave was cancelled throughout India and from May 16, Madda Khel villages came under very heavy and concentrated attack from the air and ground. For these raids, Nos. 27 and 60 Squadrons' aircraft were refuelled at Arawali and a minimum of two raids were made by each aircraft every day.

By the end of June 1938, intensive operations caused the Madda Khel to agree to terms and they evicted the Faqir of Ipi from their territory, the latter fleeing to Kharre for refuge. It was virtually the end of his major rebel activities although he continued to create dissension throughout the 1939-45 war, albeit on a gradually dwindling scale.

— Haltonian, RAF in India,
Official History of Operations on the NWFP (1936-39).

Air Operations on the Frontier — 1936-41

The unadministered areas of the NWFP were the only regions in the British Indian Empire where peaceful conditions eluded the rulers. The hard earned experience of fighting the tribals for over a century had made the armed forces, through a process of trial and error, able to confront the hostile actions of the various fiercely independent tribals.

The British authorities, however, had to concede that the tribals, east of the Durand Line in what was called the 'unadministered' area as distinct from the administered settled districts, were indeed British subjects.

Here it is pertinent to recall the assessment made by General J G Elliott of the Indian Army, who spent a third of his service life on the Frontier:

"The whole British approach to the problem of raiding from across the border differed radically from that of the Sikhs, whose only concern had been the amount of revenue they could collect, and as long as the raids did not harm their interests, did not consider them to be their problem at all.

"If the villagers did not like being raided, it was up to them to do something about it, and if the methods they employed were such as would be frowned on in humane society, that again was no concern of the ruling power.

"The British not only assumed the burden of protection but felt it incumbent on them that it should be as complete as possible: making themselves responsible for every cow that was lifted."

By 1936, with more than a hundred years of experience behind them, the British were faced with the dilemma of confronting a lone cleric who raised the oft-repeated cry of *jehad* against the '*firangi* infidels'. As soon as the trouble erupted with the Tori Khel tribe which had been supporting and sheltering the Faqir of Ipi, the political authorities tried to bring pressure on them to control the activities of the Faqir for which they would be held responsible.

The ideal thing at that time would have been for the Tori Khel to surrender the Faqir to the authorities, failing which they should have expelled him from their territory. The Government-appointed Maliks admitted their responsibilities but professed themselves being unable to control the Faqir and his supporters. They could not even guarantee that the entry of an Army column into the Lower Khaisora Valley would be unopposed by the tribals. They explained that while they and the majority of their tribe would help the Army to get into the valley, they could not guarantee the safety of the troops. They said that the Faqir's supporters, a collection of malcontents from various sections, would certainly offer opposition.

At that time, the Government assessed that certain factors existed as being the underlying causes of the unrest among the tribesmen, which tended to favour the activities of the Faqir. In 1936, the Congress was negotiating with the Government for a share in participating in responsible government which eventually took place in the aftermath of the elections that resulted in the Congress forming and running the governments in nine provinces of British India for two years from 1937.

The feeling among the tribesmen about this development was that making constitutional changes in British India indicated the progressive weakness of the government. Added to that was the attitude of the younger elements in most of the tribes. War and fighting was manly and many who had not tasted action were eager to espouse any cause so that they could get an opportunity to show their ability to fight the infidel.

The boredom, due to the prolonged period of peace in Waziristan stirred the irresponsible and restless elements in the tribes. Such men welcomed the chances of trying to match their strength with the forces of the Government, both for the excitement and for the chance of securing rifles and other loot. In addition, there was widespread dissatisfaction on account of the existing distribution of allowances.

In November 1936, the Resident in Waziristan recommended that troops should visit the Lower Khaisora Valley. At the political level, it was felt that this would hasten, and result in, the expulsion of the Faqir from Tori Khel limits, and would then force him to possibly go to the Mahsud country, where the risk was that he would gain wider support. This risk had to be accepted as otherwise the gains made so far by penetration into the Khaisora Valley would be lost. If the operation was extended further into winter, then there was less likelihood of trouble, especially in Makin and Kaniguram areas.

The Government, thus, decided on November 25, 1936, that troops should visit that portion of the Tori Khel country which lies south and east of the Central Waziristan Road between Asad Khel and Khajuri Post. This move, it was hoped, would strengthen the hands of the loyal Maliks and check the Faqir's propaganda. It was a purely peaceful demonstration and no offensive action was planned, except defence in case they were attacked.

RAF Steps In

By this time, a stage had come when the importance of the air component had been fully recognised. No Army operation was planned without prior air reconnaissance and later cooperation from the air, in direct support.

Accordingly, on November 25, 1936, one flight of No. 5 Army Cooperation Squadron, with one aircraft allotted to each column for the first two hours of the march of the Army columns. After that, one aircraft had to meet the needs of both the columns but with such a wide area to cover, it was difficult. Besides that, radio-telephonic communication between the Army column (RAZCOL) and the aircraft failed as the pack set with the Army was damaged during the march. Communication of air reports to both the columns was done by the older system of message dropping.

Close support duties were undertaken by 'A' Flight of No. 27 (Bomber) Squadron but any air offensive was to be resorted to only on instruction by the column commander. Such air support was given to the other column (TOCOL). Next day, apart from reconnaissance, ammunition, food and medical supplies were dropped by aircraft to both the columns.

To ensure enough close air support during withdrawal from Biche Kashkai, an additional flight of No. 27 Squadron was deployed. The earlier restriction on air operations in support of troops was withdrawn by the OC, No. 1 (India Wing) who ordered close support to troops which was given on several occasions. In all, five air reconnaissance and six close support sorties were flown on November 27.

Air operations were conducted in aid of the Army in Tori Khel country from November 28, 1936, to December 27, 1937.

In an operation on the divisional level, with several brigades operating in different areas, better coordination was needed with the Air Force. Accordingly, the Army Commander General Sir John Coleridge placed Wing Commander J Slessor, commanding No. 3 (India) Wing, RAF, under operational control as air adviser or to accompany columns as required. His headquarters was established at Mir Ali with the Waziristan Force Headquarters.

The RAF units at Slessor's disposal were: a detached flight of No. 5 Squadron, reinforced by another flight of the same squadron; two flights of No. 20 Squadron at Miranshah; Nos. 27 and 60 Squadrons of No. 1 (India) Wing at Kohat.

By 1936, with two decades of air operations in tandem with the ground forces behind them, the pilots and the air crew of the RAF had fully become conversant with the process that preceded the commencement of a combined operation. Official records show to what extent care was taken not let any extraneous factor creep into the conduct of operations.

Instructions Regarding Air Action:

Proscribed area — work commenced on the new road from Mir Ali to the Khaisora river — over this area, the warning to be given from the air — composition of the Faqir's *lashkars* — ground forces' advance to the Khaisora river, observing activity of the enemy.

Operations of the 2nd Infantry Brigade on December 22, 1936, — arrangements made for one aircraft on the front of the advancing brigade throughout the day from sunup to sundown, one close support sortie from 0830 hours to 1100 hours during the approach march and another from 1230 hours to 1500 hours to cover the withdrawal.

On two days, flying was not possible due to rains. After that, continuous close reconnaissance was provided daily from dawn until the columns returned to camp in the evening and, frequently, two aircraft were in the air throughout the hours of daylight.

Initially, reconnaissance was carried out every morning and afternoon to report any unusual activity in the neighbouring tribal areas, particularly the Mahsud and Madda Khel country and to supplement other intelligence sources in obtaining early indication of the movement of *lashkars* and of the spread of unrest to adjacent tribes. Later, reconnaissance was carried out once a day only. The Scouts' posts at Madda, Sorarogha, Dosalli and Datta Khel were visited daily.

A daily air service was also instituted for the picking up of orders at Waziristan Force Headquarters and dropping these orders on different camps. Generally, this proved to be the only way of circulating written orders in time, as the road was closed daily by about 1600 hours.

During this period, 98.40 hours were flown in addition to a number of occasions on which support action was taken by aircraft. A further 137.10 hours were expended on other duties, including 39 hours of flying on photography. Four tonnes of supplies were dropped by parachute during the few days when the new road proved impassible owing to rain.

During operations on January 8 and 9, 1937, the RAF attacked villages where it was thought that snipers might be concealed and also took action against small parties of the enemy in the open, besides giving close support, called for by the Air Force Liaison Officer at Bannu Brigade Headquarters, to the piquet of 2/13 Frontier Force Rifles (FFR).

Directed from the air, artillery harassing fire during withdrawal was resorted to. The objective, apart from driving out the Faqir, was to ensure that the Army's lines of communication were kept open.

Trouble broke out again in February 1937, and the Army was invested with political control as the GOC-in-C, Northern Command, took over control from the political authorities and conducted operations from February 6 to April 21 in the proscribed area.

The trigger for this phase of operations was provided when the tribals brutally murdered two British officers, namely, Captain Keogh and Lieutenant Beatty. Initially, the Tori Khel Maliks went to see the Faqir in the Shaktu area. They did not get an assurance of peace and rumours were rife about the commencement of hostilities.

It was reported that the Faqir had declared that he would do nothing for a month, but he openly voiced his hostility to the British. To counter this, reinforcements were sent to Waziristan. By March 1937, the Government was trying to persuade the Tori Khel to expel the Faqir from their area, failing which they would have to face the consequences.

To give force to the warning, an air blockade was mounted around Arsal Kot. This involved keeping a standing air patrol over the proscribed area. This resulted in a hostile attack on the Damdil camp piquet. All over this area, the Faqir's propaganda was having effect and many flocked to his side.

Meanwhile, the 1st Infantry Brigade went into action at Asad Khel on March 29 when units of the brigade were attacked by the hostiles. Aircraft of No. 5 (AC) Squadron were active over the area throughout the day on reconnaissance and close support duties and assisted the Army through the operation.

When the Utmanzai Maliks again approached the Faqir, he set his terms. Meanwhile, supplies that were reaching the Faqir were destroyed by action from the air. Intelligence reports indicated movement of hostiles in the Shahur Tangi. On April 9, the hostiles ambushed the Army convoy. Three lorries were able to leave the Tangi. Those following were attacked by the hostiles.

Armoured cars following the lorries were attacked. One section of armoured cars arrived from Sarawakai and attempted to extricate the lorries. A force of Khasadars also arrived and an advance party of the South Waziristan Scouts also arrived on the scene. It was a difficult situation.

When a section of a tank company arrived from Manzai, they faced an impassable block at the tail of the column. More troops arrived at Changamalai. After some hard fighting, the lorries were extricated which left for Sarawakai.

Three platoons of South Waziristan Scouts arrived and captured point 3940 at the fag end of the day at 6 pm. The next day, troops in strength advanced and extricated the remaining lorries.

Air Support to Ground Troops

Once the action began on April 9, one aircraft of No. 5 (AC) Squadron was cooperating with the Army convoy. Later, more constant support was provided until 7 pm when it got dark. Even after dark, aircraft flew over the area, bombing and machine gunning any enemy that could be seen and smaller groups seen from the air and pinpointed by their fires. Earlier in the day, at 2.30 pm, an aircraft made a forced landing near the Chagmalai Post having been shot in the petrol tank by hostile ground fire.

Minutes after the pilot landed, two armoured cars arrived on the scene and with the help of some Sappers and Miners, the aircraft was dismantled and except for the main plane, was loaded on to a lorry sent from Manzai and removed to safety. During the latter part of this operation, the rescue party came under increasingly accurate fire from tribesmen coming from the direction of the Tangi.

With the arrival of the 2nd Brigade on April 21 the Spinwam Post was invested with the tribesmen being in the vicinity—just two miles away. In retaliation, the hostiles attacked the Tiaraza Post and a piquet on Alexandra Ridge Post. Meanwhile, the police station at Tajori was also attacked. This was the serious situation on the ground. With the political control having passed from the civil authorities to the GOC-in-C, Northern Command, preparations were made for operations.

No. 3 (Indian) Wing Headquarters at Mir Ali ordered Nos. 20 and 28 Squadrons to Waziristan. The former relieved No. 5 Squadron on April 20, and the latter arrived on April 24 at Manzai. No. 20 was placed under the operational control of headquarters 1st division and No. 28 under that of headquarters Waziristan district. Two more squadrons, Nos. 27 and 60 of No. 1 (Indian) Wing at Kohat, were also made available for the operations.

Offensive action in the proscribed area was to be carried out from April 23 by No. 1 Wing but, in order that air crews cooperating with the ground forces should have the latest information, it was arranged that air operations in the immediate vicinity of the line of advance should be the responsibility of the OC, No. 3 Wing, under the direction of the commander 1st division, a portion of the proscribed area being withdrawn from the area of operation from No. 1 Wing and taken over by No. 3 Wing. From April 23 to 29, operations by the Army continued.

During these operations (1st Indian division), No. 20 Squadron flew close support and reconnaissance sorties. This was done on a selective basis when good targets were obtained. The squadron also provided photographic, supply dropping and other travel sorties.

The Khaisora column was accompanied throughout its march by the OC of No. 3 Wing, who acted as a Liaison Officer with the column commander and, at the same time, attempted to control and coordinate the operations of Nos. 20 and 28 Squadrons. He was also accompanied by an intelligence liaison section. However, the RAF Liaison Officer found himself unduly isolated from his squadrons. As a result of this experience, it was decided that in future, an experienced officer from the Army Cooperation Squadrons should replace him with the column.

Contrary to popular belief, both the Army and later, from 1916 onwards, the RFC/ RAF, were expected to do their fighting with both their hands tied behind their backs. The moment a trouble spot was cleared, unrest developed somewhere else. The Government of India in its official pronouncements did not like the rebellious tribals to be called either hostiles or enemy.

With the threat of the *jehad* propaganda unleashed by the Faqir, which refused to abate in spite of action taken against him and any tribe that gave him shelter or supported him, the Government found in the current campaign that "the instructions regarding the control of operations, including the employment of the Air Force, which limited air action to within two miles of the force engaged, resulted in missing of several chances of inflicting damage on hostile tribesmen."

On the urgent representation of the political authorities, after the operation had been completed, the regulations were modified to the extent that aircraft were permitted to continue to operate against such tribesmen, except in villages, without strict adherence to the two-mile limit provided that the crews were able to keep the offending tribesmen in sight throughout the engagement.

Pursuit of hostile tribesmen by aircraft beyond the three-mile limit of the Durand Line (the line that demarcated the official border line between British India and Afghanistan), was not, however, permissible in any circumstances.

The situation on the ground continued to deteriorate. While all this was happening in the tribal unadministered area, the hostiles further escalated the situation by carrying out a daring raid on Paharpur, a settled district.

In May 1937, troops were concentrated for an advance on Sham Plains which was completed by May 10. A further reorganisation of forces was undertaken and authority for the conduct of operations was vested in the commander, Waziristan district. For the RAF, the area proscribed was now extended.

When the 1st Infantry Brigade moved and camped near a village, it was attacked but the attack was repulsed. It was decided to mount a two-pronged attack. The Bannu Brigade advanced by Iblanke Spur and the 1st Infantry Brigade by the Sre Mela Algad. Night advance started on May 11 and, for the rest of the day, the fighting continued, with snipers as an additional threat, and the camp was established by 1.30 pm on April 12.

Cooperation by the RAF from dawn was very effective and the pilots engaged several good targets successfully. The RAF used up all their bombs and ammunition in two sorties, being immediately relieved by other sorties which were standing by in the air above them.

A first person account of the march to Sham Plains and the action that preceded it is given below:

"Fifty miles to the south, the Mahsuds ambushed a truck convoy in a savage gorge called the Shahur Tangi. The escort of armoured cars got sandwiched on the narrow road so that they could use neither their weapons nor their mobility. Seventy officers and soldiers were killed or wounded. The Government decided that the time had come to take the offensive. Our brigade (of which 2/4 GR was a part), hovering in reserve off the north of the storm centre, was ordered into battle.

"We marched on May 5, 1937, and spent the night at Talin Tochi. The camp site was on a bare bridge above the Tochi river, and no matter how carefully a commander sited his camp piquets, it was impossible to prevent the enemy from sniping on to the face of the slope at night.

"The crawling sweet smell of death pervaded the place when we arrived, and as I marched in, I passed three mules rotting in the open graves at the foot of the camp. It was late and we had no sufficient time to dig properly, but there were some shallow holes already and, we used them.

"At two minutes after 11, something exploded in the air over my head with a sharp whip-crack slap. A second later, a dull thump sounded from the dark ridge to the west. Both sounds were rapidly repeated several times. At last, I was wearing the real crack-thump. We were under fire.

"Unhurriedly, the sniper searched the camp, firing 20/ 30 rounds. I heard men moving about near me and called to them to be still. A mule snickered, and water was splashed on the dim ashes of a cooking fire. The sniper killed nine mules as they stood in their tethered lines just below us on the slope.

"Next day, we moved on upto the road to Damdil and the day after, to Dosalli. All along, I saw traces of battle. Dead mules lay in the ditches, bloodstains splashed the white stones, twigs and whole bushes lay broken on the road, and shell blasts pock-marked the ridges.

"On the right of the road, just beyond the Damdil camp, stood a low knoll crowned with a *sangar*. We stopped and examined it with respect, for here, on the night of March 20–21, there had been a fight. Eight Gurkhas of the 2nd Battalion, 5th Gurkha Rifles (Frontier Forces Rifles), had been left without support to fight all night against 50 crazed Wazirs. By dawn, two of the eight were dead and each of the other six had been wounded many times. They had fought with rifles, bayonets, khukris, stones, boots and fists and they held their piquet until, at dawn, relief came.

"We went straight into fighting around Dosalli. Two brigades began to force their way slowly up the Sre Mela, towards the centre of the enemy's resistance, the Sham Plains. At the head of the short stream, the brigades faced giant precipes and steep ridges that swept up from the valley, and the tribesmen held their crest line in strength.

"The Divisional Commander decided to leave one brigade facing the ridges, to contain the enemy, and to outflank the position by moving the brigade — ours — round behind the enemy's right. The operation was to be carried out at night over the Iblanke, a long, steep and unreconnoitered mountain.

"We went back to Dosalli and prepared in secret for the battle.

"On May 11, 1937, at 9 pm, in full darkness, we moved off. Eight platoons of Tochi Scouts led the advance, wearing grass-soled sandals. At first, the pace was painfully slow. I covered six hundred yards in the first two hours, while the Scouts far ahead, picked their way across the Khaisora river and faced the black slopes leading up the Iblanke, and the rest of the brigade struggled after them.

"Enough water flowed in the stream to wet me to the knees, so I started the night's work with wet feet — not cold though. I was enjoying this so far. All along, it was start, stop, sit down, get up, move on a yard, stop, and sit down again. The river valley was warm and the air felt stuffy.

"At last, they got going in front. Soon we were all launched on the ridge. Movement became a steady grind of climbing, one foot after the other. I could see only a few yards off, a dim whiteness in front where the officer at the tail of the company ahead wore a white band on his hat. Fixed bayonets flashed faintly against the mountain side and I climbed in the strong mixed smell of sweat and the cardamom seeds the Gurkhas chewed.

"We tried to be quiet, but our passage boomed indescribably loudly in the silence of the hills. Boots clashed on the stones, the harness of the mules creaked, and their hooves struck sparks from the flints. There was no path on the knife-edged spine of the ridge, and men and animals floundered on up, panting among the bushes and concealed rock outcrops.

"Sudden storms of noise burst over us as mules loaded with shovels or radio sets lost their balance and crashed down 200 ft of mountain among us. Twenty times I dived for shelter and listened, appalled, pressing into a thick bush, while the heavy animals thundered down in the darkness, their loads rolling beside them. I thought any tribesman within five miles must have heard each one. As the night wore on and men and animals grew tired, the falls became more frequent, more cataclysmic.

"The ragged, disconnected column forged painfully on for eight hours. There were soldiers everywhere — on the ridge spine, lost along the sides, down in the dark gullies looking for fallen mules. I heard swearing in 10 languages and saw soldiers cut mules' throats and manhandle the loads on the mountain.

"In the wind that blew before dawn, there was a long check. No one moved in front. The clattering and banging behind, down the hill, came up and closer. I was in the middle of a lot of men. Light began to silhouette the far hills, then to show grey on us. We were well up the ridge, but near at hand on both sides, other ridges converged on ours. And at this point, they were somewhere higher than ours. What if the enemy were on them?

"As far as the eye could see in both the directions, our ridge, the Iblanke, was dotted with men and animals. The trees and bushes had thinned out, and there was no cover. I took my binoculars from the case, hung them around my neck, and lay down. Shivering from exhaustion and nervous strain, I waited. There was nothing else to do.

"Ahead shooting began, very loud and close-seeming in the dawn. The bullets came over our heads — crack, pause, thump. The enemy's range was about 600 yards. This was it. Here we were, strung along a knife-edged crest with no power of manoeuvre, about to be attacked on all sides. I remembered what happened to the Guides when they were caught just like this, three years before, on another part of the Frontier. I braced myself for a long waterless day of slaughter.

"A runner came down with a message. The Scouts had made contact and were in action. The tribesmen and the Scouts knew each other well — many by name. The tribes knew the Scouts' only weapons were rifles. They were confident in their own strength and the strength of their position at the top of Iblanke. They were confident that no one but the Scouts could climb that ridge at night under arms.

"They started shouting insults, and, for a few minutes, barrages of Pushtu invective and innuendo flew back and forth between the uniformed Pathans and their unreconstructed cousins on the crest. Both sides interspersed the shouts with shots, but the Scouts deliberately weakened their fire, and the tribesmen's taunts grew more strident.

"The two leading companies of the leading battalion, 2nd Royal Battalion, 11th Sikh Regiment (the Ludhiana Sikhs) deployed behind a roll in the crest. Back down the ridge mountain, guns clanged off the mules on to the ground. Machine gunners dragged themselves forward on their sides, the heavy guns or tripods rested on their lower legs, until they were in a position behind rocks and ledges.

"In full dawn, shells rumbled through the air, machine gun bullets rippled along the ridge crest, and the Sikhs and Scouts went into the attack together. The tribesmen stayed only a moment in the face of this powerful, determined, and totally unexpected assault. Then, we had taken the crest of the Iblanke. Ahead lay the Sham Plains. We were behind the enemy.

"The day was May 12, 1937. Back in England, the Archbishop of Canterbury was crowning King George VI, King of England and Emperor of India, and we named our new camp, 'Coronation Camp'."

— Lieutenant Colonel John Master's Autobiography
(2/4 Gurkha Rifles, Indian Army).

Fighting the Faqir — Strategy and Tactics

Throughout this period, when the Sham Plains' fighting was on (the first person account shows how different Frontier campaigns were from conventional combat), the RAF provided continuous air support to the ground troops.

Air cooperation with ground troops was provided by No. 20 Squadron of the No. 3 (Indian) Wing and 'A' Flight of No. 28 Squadron moved from Manzai to Miranshah to assist them between

May 24 and 31. During the four days of advance to Arsal Kot and the subsequent withdrawal, No. 20 Squadron averaged over 48 flying hours per day and during the month of May, it flew 919 hours. No. 28 Squadron, with a strength of two flights during this period, flew a total of 808 hours.

A vital part of the long-term British strategy was to get access to those high points, hill features, *tangis*, passes, so that they could keep watch for any wrongdoing and, at the same time, maintain garrisons in the tribal territory. The most important practical aspect of this policy was the need for roads to connect, not just for animal transport but also for the Thirties' motor vehicles. However, in retrospect, it can be seen how the tribals saw the ingress that roads were making into the tribal heartland. They did not believe the officially proclaimed announcement that the road building was a part of ensuring that peace prevailed and no raids into the settled districts took place. They believed, more the propaganda of the clerics, that the British Government was trying to merge their tribal lands with the rest of British India. They were stoutly opposed to it and this opposition was buttressed by the propaganda of the *jehadi* Mullahs.

Thus, road building was of great importance but what was of equal importance was Road Protection (RP). It speaks volumes for the tenacity of the troops and their frontline commanders that RP was developed into a fine art, science and an essential part of an infantryman's duties. It was this practice that helped the British to keep the lines of communication open, though such was the 'fragile' nature of peace that a single malcontent or a few could disrupt the smooth flow of men and supplies by sniping at a column from heights.

After the Sham Plains campaign, the troops were ordered to move to Razmak via Sorarogha in June 1937. Learning the lessons from this campaign, there was a thorough reorganisation in the command and control of troops on the ground and the aircraft that they now needed constantly for reconnaissance, close support and artillery deployment.

While the Government at the highest level sanctioned the road construction programme, detailed instructions were issued and tasks assigned to the 1st Division and the Waziristan Division. Allotment of air support was detailed — from June 8, 1937, No. 28 Squadron was allotted to the Waziristan Division. For better command, control and coordination with ground troops, No. 3 (Indian) Wing shifted its headquarters to Miranshah Fort.

All this preparation was for protecting the Sappers and Miners who were to be deployed on road building activities through the Mahsud country. Soon after the work commenced, the Razmak Brigade had to go to the aid of a road piquet at Gaj. This attack by the Bhittanis was repulsed and troops of the Bannu Brigade marched out to Madamir Kalai on June 4, reaching Sorarogha on June 7. Meanwhile, the 1st Brigade marched to Ghariom where they met the Bannu Brigade. Soon, peace conditions were spelt out to the tribal leaders.

In all the operations of the advance to, and withdrawal from, Arsal Kot, and of the march to Sorarogha, reconnaissance and close support duties were carried out by the RAF not only for the formation concerned but also for road trains in the area of the Pezu Pass. In addition, the supplies of the Wana garrison were carried out by aircraft of the Bomber Transport Flight of the 70th Bomber Squadron which arrived at Risalpur from Iraq on May 31. Although lorries had been running to Wana, there had been no regular Motor Transport (MT) convoy for some weeks and there was an accumulation of personnel and stores at Manzai which could not be taken earlier. These were all conveyed by air.

Road Protection — A Hazardous Task

The need for roads linking various areas, especially for supplies of men and materials, was acute, especially since the old Indian Army was slowly but steadily coming into the modern age where the internal combustion engine powered lorries could move faster from settled districts and other cantonments to the scene of action, compared to the earlier system of using animal transport. However, the earlier system was still used in tandem with the automobile.

A system was evolved whereby supplies and men either coming or going in lorries or on horseback or on foot could safely use the roads without being ambushed for weapons and loot. The planning for operations on the lines of communication had to take into account many factors as the following account will amply demonstrate.

"Two days later I went out on RP duty. This was the hardest task the Frontier offered, and we did it three times a week. The battle area in these parts was so close that we could not risk letting our convoys go along the roads under the doubtful protection of Khasadars alone. The convoys ran every other day.

"RP meant getting up very early and marching out along the road in battle formation. As we went, we searched each place where an ambush might be lying in wait, and on every vantage point, we dropped off one of the clusters of men called piquets. At the end of our sector, we met troops from the next camp who had been similarly working backwards towards us.

"Then signals were sent to the higher authority that the road was clear, and at once the convoys set out from both terminals. RP was hard because every day we covered the same stretch of road, and every day it became more difficult to obey the cardinal Frontier principle of never doing the same thing in the same way twice running. We had to fight against fatigue and carelessness because someone was watching. Someone was always watching — someone with an inborn tactical sense, someone who missed nothing.

"The watcher might see that every day a piquet of half platoon strength (about 15 soldiers) left the road at Milestone 27, and moved 400 yards to the top of a hill. Every day, two machine guns waited among the boulders near the milestone, ready to support the moving men until they were in position. There was one little dip in the ground near the bottom of the hill, perhaps 15 yards wide. The watcher never went near it, but his feel for the country told him that the machine gunners could not see into the dip.

"The first four or five times the piquet went up, it split at that point. Half the men lay down near the bank, ready to shoot, and half crossed the little dip. Then that half lay down on the far bank and covered the others while they crossed in their turn. Then, they all went on together, again in the view of machine guns.

"But the sixth time the soldiers got bored, because nothing ever happened and they could not see any Pathans, and they trailed across the dip in one tight bunch. They talked and laughed because it was such a small dip, they were out of sight of the machine guns for only 20 seconds. An RP had become a peaceful monotony.

"The next night, twenty tribesmen arrived in the dip at 3 am, scattered among the rocks, and lay still. They were hard men and had control of their bodies. Not one of them coughed or cleared his throat, but all lay utterly still among the boulders. The nearest soldiers were four miles away but if an undisciplined young tribesman had moved a pebble, his elders would have withdrawn the whole ambush, just in case. They would have crept away, to return again three or five nights later — never the next night. Every man carried a straw so that, if he had to, he could urinate silently down the stem."

Ten Lethal Seconds

"Around half past six or seven in the morning, the soldiers walked into the dip. One blinding volley — one rush, two seconds of stabbing and hacking, and it was done — six soldiers dead, six left for dead, twelve rifles and 600 rounds of ammunition gone, one tribesman dead — another typical Frontier incident.

"It might have happened to us, any and every day, but it did not. Our Battalion was not careless, not with Lieutenant Colonel David Murray Lyon, DSO, MC, known simply as ML, watching through field glasses, and nothing ever exhausted the resources of his tactical ingenuity. We never did the same thing in quite the same way twice running. It might look the same to an untrained eye, but the watching tribesmen were not untrained.

"They noticed that the covering machine guns were in a different position every day, so that no one could be sure on any particular day what they could or could not cover. Or the soldiers would not move on to the hill by going north-east from Milestone 27 but by going north-west from Milestone 27½. Or no one would go to the hill at all.

"But the next day, the piquet would consist of a whole company — 132 men. It is impossible to plan a safe and certain ambush in these conditions, and we were never ambushed. The tribesmen knew our hat badge and kept away.

"In the afternoon, when all the convoys were through, we got the signal to start pulling back to camp. This was the dangerous part of all the Frontier operations. Except on the rare days of major battle, the tribesmen knew that the Army was strong enough to get forward and up the hill regardless of pinpricks. There would be no rifles or loot, because the troops would press on past their dead and wounded. At the end of the day's work, when we went back and down the hill, it was different.

"From their eyries, the tribesmen saw the last of the convoys go through, and knew we would soon be off. They gathered in creeping silence towards the ridges, and worked up snake-like into hidden positions near the piquets. If the piquet commander had been careless in his search of ground, or if he had sited his sentries badly, they (the tribesmen) would crawl up dangerously close.

"When the men of the piquet start down the hill, the tribesmen would be on the crest before they have gone fifteen yards. The supporting guns open up but a man has been hit in the back and falls unseen in the scrub. A dozen tribesmen are inextricably mixed up with the piquet, shooting, yelling and hacking at the wounded man to get his rifle and ammunition.

"The whole piquet must turn back and recapture the hill-top — if it can — and then stay there for an hour, until the wounded have been carried down and away, safe from mutilation. Sometimes, a reserve company has to be thrown into battle before the hill-top can be re-taken, and several more men are wounded and a couple killed in the process, and then the whole business of pulling the piquet had to be gone through again, and it would be dark before the Brigade is once more on the move towards the camp.

"The tribesmen follow hard on their heels in the night, and shots flash out, and more men are killed and wounded. All this happened because one *jemadar* (in post-47, Indian Army, this rank has been renamed as Naib Subedar) put one sentry one yard too far back, because one man walked when he should have run, because one machine gunner pressed his thumb-pieces one second later than he should have. War on the Frontier was not very dangerous, but it was exacting, personal and merciless!

"A resourceful commander like ML used many ruses to ensure that the Pathans treated his piquets with respect. Sometimes our men pretended to be careless. Sentries moved about instead of lying still; men walked idly and talked loudly. When the moment came to withdraw, the rear party got up and trotted back over the crest in no hurry. Fifteen seconds later, suddenly reverting to their true skill, they crept back upto the crest and met the confident, rushing tribesmen with a blast of fire at point-blank range."

Enter the Tanks

"Sometimes, a small piquet would seem too weak to hold the big feature to which it was allotted, but behind the hill was a concealed section of light tanks. The country around the Brigade's base camp at Miranshah was a stony plain split by low ridges and dry watercourses, all sparsely covered with sagebrush and scrub. This was perfect terrain for the most popular of all Pathan sports, night sniping.

"To protect us against this, the Brigadier used tanks. About 9 pm most nights, two or three of them would rumble out through the barbed wire, crouch hull down behind a ridge and wait. In darkness or faint starlight it was difficult to tell exactly where they were, though they could be heard for miles. After 20 minutes, they would suddenly switch on their searchlights, examine the ground all around them, switch off again, and rumble on through the darkness to another place.

"It worked, we were sniped only once. It was comforting after the long menacing silences to see the flashes of light and hear the thunder of tank engines and the muted clank of treads. These tanks were old fashioned things, useless for 'real' war, but we liked them.

"In all these activities on the ground, the Army started getting a helping hand from the Air Force. An aerial patrol would pinpoint for the ground troops, via the wireless or even a message box, the location of the hostiles. From 1916 to 1920, the RAF was, so to say, on probation so far as the Army brass was concerned. Once they (the pilots) showed their worth, the new rule followed religiously was that no operation could commence without an aerial reconnaissance.

"At every stage, the mere presence of the aerial guardians was enough to give a sense of confidence among the ground troops and if any untoward incident took place, the guardians in the sky were armed enough to deter the ambition of the hostiles."

— John Masters, *Bugles and the Tiger.*

Tactics — Lessons Learnt

In Frontier combat conditions, it was the cumulative experience of generations of British and Indian troops that paved the way for operational instructions to the troops engaged in combat.

The first lesson was that eternal vigilance is the price of survival.

Combined together, the methodology of Frontier warfare can be summed up in one word — tactics.

There are three factors that influence combat operations' tactics:

- The nature of the ground — the actual physical features.
- The character of the enemy — aggressive/ consistent/ brave/ risk parameters.
- The weapons available to the troops — infantry weapons/ mountain mobile artillery/ light tanks/ armoured cars/ aircraft.

Any infantry soldier will want to know what the ground looks like over which he would have to traverse and fight before he actually commits himself to battle. Reconnaissance is a word that comes to mind with the prefix 'prior'. The entire North-West Province on the Frontier is dotted with dominating hills with very few open spaces and was not "within effective rifle range of high ground."

Hills were steep surfaces with loose stones and huge boulders, side by side or separately, loose scrub, straggling bushes and even those areas dotted with trees. Knife-edged ridges, towering cliffs, or short precipices, and with such an irregular lay of the land, movement for ground forces was difficult. Movement from one valley to another would be by a path over which a goat would hesitate to walk and usually such access from one valley to another was only known to the locals but the Army had to gain such knowledge of the topography through very expensive trials and errors.

Status of the Pathan

A look at the enemy: here one must first define the status of the Pathan, a native of the NWFP, which was divided into two distinct regions — one, the settled districts where British law prevailed and the other, the unadministered area where the Pathan lived by his own tribal code, did not pay any taxes and would brook no interference from the *firangi*. Since the British had left this area adjacent to the Durand

Line that marked the border between India and Afghanistan to the tribals, the Pathans resented any presence of the Army in these areas. In their eyes, the building of roads and railways was an encroachment amounting to invasion of their homeland.

Question: Why did the British venture into the unadministered area of the Pathans? The answer to this question lies in the Pathans' passion for looting, attacking, kidnapping *kaffirs* for ransom and regularly sniping at British military camps. As long as they stayed on their side of the border, the British authorities had no cause for worry. However, when the looting and killing forays extended to the settled districts and cantonments such as Peshawar, the Government had to react in the form of military expeditions thrusting into the Pathan territory, thereby conveying to the fiercely independent Pathans that the Government could, if it so wished, reach any corner of the tribal land.

The irony of it lies in the terminology used by the officialese.

The Army in its battle reports always referred to the militant Pathans as the 'enemy' but the Government of India, in its wisdom, referred to the Pathans as 'misguided' subjects of the Empire, who should by stages be brought into the mainstream of life within British India. That they (the British Indian Government) failed is a fact. When the British left the subcontinent, after partitioning it, the Pakistan Government inherited the area and the problem. Despite withdrawing all military units from the Frontier area (this was done under the advice of the last Governor of the NWFP, Sir George Cunningham), there was no change in the situation although now, with the *firangi* gone, the new enemy was the Pakistan Government.

All that the new post-1947 Pakistan Government did was to rename this area as Federally Administered Tribal Area (FATA) and later (2010), the name FATA was abolished and the whole province renamed Khyber-Pakhtunkhwa. It needs to be explained that after 1947, the distinction between the settled districts and the unadministered area west of it, adjoining the Durand Line that marks the border with Pakistan, disappeared, and it was treated as a separate area administered directly by the Pakistan Government.

To those familiar with the conditions that prevailed in this area during British rule, what happened next was shocking. Till 1947, no Pathan could come into the settled area with a firearm. But in October 1947, the Pakistan Government opened the flood gates and gave the latest service rifles, machine guns and even artillery to the tribals, appointed experienced Pakistan Army officers and many ex-servicemen who volunteered and invaded Kashmir so that it could be annexed to Pakistan. It is inconceivable that the British Governor of the NWFP did not know about the plan to invade Kashmir, as he was, even after the creation of Pakistan, still in the saddle as the Governor of the province.

Of course, the Pakistan Government maintained a facade of not knowing, and inspired media leaks spoke of the Pathans marching to Kashmir to free their Muslim brethren from the tyrannical rule of the Hindu Maharaja. Pakistan maintained this charade until the Indian Army started pushing the tribals back, inflicting heavy losses on them. It was only in June 1948 that the Pakistan Government openly came out in support of the tribals.

A Shrewd Tactician — Mobility his Other Weapon

He (the Pathan) was at home on his own ground. He could cover the most difficult hillside at top speed as he knew every yard of the way. He was not bogged down by any baggage and knew how to live off the country — water and food. He knew where every stream lay and knew that food was always available to him in any village whether he was coming or going.

He carried on his person a rifle, a knife and about 50 rounds of ammunition. His physical capacity was enormous. He was tireless, as fresh at the end of the day as he had been at the beginning. With a highly developed sense of caution and cunning, he was a born tactician, with a keen eye open for opportunities which might present themselves in the course of his movement.

The Pathan's estimate of an 'even battle' was an advantage of six to one in his favour. Patient to the extreme, he always reconnoitered the ground, always choosing high ground from where he could be sure of hitting an Army column before committing himself to battle. He also had the inestimable advantage of choosing his battleground. Surprise was always on his side. He sniped at the troops at a time of his choosing. All that the Army and even the Air Force could do in response was to react with an expedition which was always a slow process. The air element helped to pinpoint trouble, saving time and energy.

He knew that once the surprise element had passed, he could not match the firepower of the Army as also the discipline of the regular Army columns, in which firing discipline was most important and decisive in many of the engagements against the Pathan's various *lashkars*. He was shrewd enough to understand that he had to make do with smaller gains and quick returns. "Half a dozen casualties, crudely mutilated, the same number of rifles, and a few hundred rounds of ammunition, would count as a huge haul."

While individually he was brave, based on carefully calculating the odds, he did not possess the discipline and training that a regular soldier underwent before venturing into the Frontier areas. The lack of collective discipline and the command and control that a regular Army unit had, proved to be his undoing. But the number of times such battles took place when thousands of Pathans gathered as a *lashkar*, were few and far between.

On such occasions, the Pathan discovered that he could not, even in the company of several hundred or thousand compatriots, withstand a cavalry charge made by a disciplined force. "He disliked having his enemy on high ground above him, such as the top of a hill feature, having his line of retreat threatened by artillery fire as he had no guns of his own. He thought this was always unfair," says General J G Elliott, who did a number of tours of duty on the Frontier.

Enter the Warbird

Once the aeroplane made its appearance over the skies of the Frontier in early 1916, the tribals could not at first believe that a man could fly and later that he could use guns from the sky to rain bullets on an enemy. He held that attack by aircraft was most unsporting until he discovered that his sharp shooting expertise could bring down an aircraft and that a crashed aircraft would provide enough loot to keep him satisfied for the season.

Although he did not know this, the authorities were also considering how to protect the pilot and air gunner should the aircraft be brought down by ground fire and have to make a forced landing in hostile territory. To make sure that the scheme worked, it was advertised that if the tribals returned an airman unharmed to the authorities, a cash reward would be given. This was printed on paper and circulated. Though the Pathans did not know how to read or write, all recognised this piece of paper as being lucrative and profitable.

To ensure that pilots were not physically harmed and returned unharmed, it was mandatory for every pilot and air gunner to carry this chit, named as "ghooley chit," in his pocket when flying, in case he needed it.

Looting weapons, especially service rifles, was the Pathan's favourite occupation. Over the years, whenever he organised, along with his own people, such successful ambushes, he collected enough weapons and ammunition to become even in the military sense a formidable foe. This tremendous increase in his weaponry was a source of great worry to the powers that be. In 1902, there were about 2,000 rifles estimated to be in Waziristan, and by 1921, there were 20,000.

As more modern weapons fell into his hands, his tactics also changed. His early weapons were inefficient and were used just for giving covering fire at short range to support a group attacking an objective such as an Army piquet by swordsmen. Right from 1890, when the Pathan honed his skill as a sniper, his favourite hobby was sniping columns, camps and as for individual targets, there were British officers and any other Indians whom they identified as infidels.

As soon as the military aeroplane appeared over the Frontier skies (No. 31 Squadron, RFC/ RAF), after the first shock and disbelief, he realised that the enemy had an eye in the sky with which he could with impunity track his movements and there would soon be no place left where he could hide. After seeing the 'war bird' at close quarters his eyes would gleam with envy and then greed as he wanted the Lewis guns with which the aeroplanes of that era were equipped. The next step was to gain height and stand on a hill feature and snipe at a patrolling machine. A crashed aeroplane would yield a lot of loot and the ghooley chit with the pilot and the air gunner would provide enough ransom money to keep him in good living and humour for months on end. And the bonus would be: no action would be taken against him.

Mobility and Movement

The Indian Army on the Frontier suffered from one inherent weakness — limits to its mobility. As the Pathan was on home ground, he knew every *tangi* and piquet, knew where the passes between valleys were and when they would be open, keeping in view the weather conditions. On the other hand, the soldier had to familiarise himself with the ground, the access to it and learn through trial and error (sometimes fatal) where the Pathan would strike, his favourite time for attack or ambush and his tactics. Here, mobility of the forces became a crucial factor in the operations.

An even greater brake on the mobility of regular troops was the length of the administrative tail which imposed a collective handicap, for it slowed down almost every stage of operations. All loads were perforce carried on packs and the pack animal (mostly mules and some horses) was extravagant in space and its own demand for forage, baggage, tools, stores, ammunition and rations. Mules were needed for everything and more mules or camels to carry ration for the mules. The deeper the advance into tribal territory was, the longer was the accompanying column, every yard of which had to be protected throughout the twenty-four hours.

Almost all Frontier expeditions that the Army mounted were in the nature of a punishing exercise because the Pathans had wantonly attacked, looted, kidnapped in the settled districts for the sake of loot, money and weapons. The inhabitants of the settled districts, where British law prevailed, expected the Government to protect their lives and limbs and property. Since the attacks were carried out by Pathans from the unadministered districts, the Government had to use the stick to punish them. This was always the last resort after all attempts at holding talks with *lashkars* and other conciliatory measures, even bribes, called 'allowances', failed.

Since this had become almost a routine, the Pathan knew when and where the blow would fall. In almost all cases, the Government would restrain the Army when the Pathan indicated that he had had enough and would submit to terms set by the authorities. The numbers of pitched battles were few, ambushes were frequent, and even a single individual could disturb the military by sniping from a safe distance and slip away when he was satisfied that he had done his bit.

In this, the Army was hampered as all expeditions carried with them the Political Agent who often advised restraint, because it was his duty to deal with the Pathans, in both peace and war. One can, with hindsight, say that political considerations outweighed the immediate military objectives. Moreover, the presence of the Political Agent in the camp permitted a cluster of Maliks, spies, agents to enter and this prevented concealment of plans as there were too many doubtful ones among them who had a leg in both the camps.

Intelligence Gathering

When the Army ventured out of the cantonments or camps into the field, the natives viz the Pathan population, viewed them with suspicion. An Englishman would be spotted a mile away and a Gurkha, or a Sikh or a plainsman would be spotted as spies. So none ventured and getting information about their 'hostile' brethren from the Khasadars or even the Scouts was next to impossible. The Scouts would fight if it came to that but betraying their kind would land them into blood feuds.

It was not that information did not come into the camps or the Political Agent's office. It was just that according to the Army's doctrine and practice, the information had to be verified. In the Frontier area, the usual channels — prisoners, deserters, signal traffic were just not available and under such circumstances, the Intelligence person had to rely on political sources which, viewed objectively, were suspect: "Someone somewhere along the line had an axe to grind and quite often important information never came at all," observes Major General J G Elliott, an expert on Frontier warfare.

On several occasions, it has been recorded, the Army, basing its operations on such information found itself very much at a disadvantage because the commander had gone by the information (intelligence), that, though given in good faith, proved to be completely misleading. "On three occasions — the battle at Point 4080 in September 1935; the Khaisora Valley, November 1936; and Shahur Tangi ambush, April 1937 — full warning of enemy strength and intentions were given and totally disregarded, on each occasion at great cost to the troops involved," says the Frontier expert General Elliott.

One source had the remote possibility of providing intelligence from among the tribals itself. During the early part of the 20th century, keeping in view the 'martial theory' of Lord Roberts in mind, Pathans were recruited into paramilitary forces as also regular regiments of the Army. Apart from that, the 'Maliks' who worked for the Political Agents were themselves Pathans and could provide information on the goings-on in the villages.

With this in mind, a start was made in 1906 with the raising of the Frontier Intelligence Corps, to train a small body of independent observers, but no effective step was taken to bring all available sources under one single control until 1933 when a central bureau was established in Peshawar.

Rear Guard Sting

On the ground, the Pathan enjoyed a unique advantage of staging an attack at a place of his choice and a time most suitable to him. He would refuse to fight, pretending that he had had enough and was willing to submit to government terms. Thus, it was easier for the Pathan to achieve surprise than for the Army. A stage was reached in the Thirties when the Army did not even make an attempt at achieving surprise.

Frontier operations were, in one sense, one-sided. In the conventional scenario, one Army fights the other Army. But in the Frontier areas, what opposed the Army was the entire population and all its armed males. To understand the difficulties that the Army faced, one has to imagine an entire brigade of three battalions of infantry with artillery and engineering support, out in the field. A brigade column advancing would have five miles of transport and supplies and every yard of that had to be protected.

"In Frontier warfare, there was no enemy Army but the enemy was the whole population. A column advanced through a stretch of tribal territory like police forcing its way through a mob; the crowd closing in behind them. The enemy was always there, and there was immunity from attack only in areas protected by piquets on the high ground," says General Elliott.

Even when the Army advanced in force, say in brigade strength, with artillery and cavalry, it was understood that the move was in response to some hostile acts of the tribals. A punitive expedition, once it had done its work of punishing the tribe, had to return to its base. That is where the Pathan took his revenge. Whatever the task ahead of the advanced guard, upon completion, it fell to the lot of the rear guard commander to protect the tail of the column.

It was the rear guard commander's duty to withdraw piquets which were put out during the advance. He had to get the men down from the piquets in the right order, ensuring that they were not withdrawn until the rear party was clear of the stretch of road they were established to protect. The tribesmen could be counted to disturb the tail-end of the withdrawing column by attacking stragglers in close shoot-outs or hand-to-hand fighting with knives. A few slashes on the soldier — stab, stab, and the tribesmen would take his rifle, ammunition and anything worth taking. It was in these withdrawals that the rescue and clearance of the casualties presented the most difficulties. To rescue a soldier, the rear guard had to counter-attack and, bringing a casualty first to safety and then the camp/ hospital was indeed a difficult task.

Once back at the base, which was the day's camp in the field, it was to be protected by two, quite separate, defensive systems.

Apart from sniping at the camp, a favourite sport of the tribals, especially after the evening meal, around the entire campus perimeter, a low ditch and a wall had to be built. When the alarm sounded, a platoon of infantry based outside the wall of the actual camp would provide protective fire. This platoon strong piquet outside the camp had to have a stone wall (*sangar*) built around to provide protection to the infantry.

Under favourable conditions, with no opposition dogging it, a brigade level column of all arms could, at best, cover eight miles a day. This gave enough time and scope for small bodies of tribals to prepare ambushes at the spots of their choosing.

Combined Operations

The operations on the ground cannot be seen in isolation but neither can the air operations in support of the ground troops be so considered. After all, before the coming of the aeroplane, every artillery observer would search for high ground to check out the enemy's disposition of its troops.

It was during the Boer War (1899-1901), when aviation was still in the balloon stage, that an aerial reconnaissance by a balloon was ordered, in order to see, as General Sir Edward Swinton puts it, "the other side of the hill." As the aeroplane replaced the balloon, this became a norm, with the need to see beyond the obstacle in front.

At first, the Army on the Frontier was sceptical about the air element, but by 1915, the aerial machine had already proved itself in the business of aerial reconnaissance. After a lot of hesitation, air support was demanded by the Viceroy from the Home Government and the first air squadron of the Royal Flying Corps (RFC) made its appearance over the Indian skies.

Initially, it was observation of the hostiles from the air. Gradually, it came to direct ground support to the troops aside from gathering intelligence. Once it was proved that the air element could actively help and support the ground forces, a stage was reached within a few years that when a ground operation was planned, aerial reconnaissance was a must. If a land battle was on, an aircraft could observe and report back to headquarters of the Army, either by the old type message box or later by air-to-ground wireless.

Air action was admirably suited to strike fast and strike deep to nip the trouble in the bud, and it gave time to the Army to prepare itself for the land battle, in which, at a later stage, bombing of targets was also resorted to.

Overall, air operations fell into three categories:

- Air blockade.
- Destructive action.
- Direct attack.

The first two were exclusively the concern of the RAF. Air blockade was directed at the morale of the enemy. He and his wife and his ox and ass and everything that was his were denied all access to the house, grazing grounds, water, and all other amenities of life.

What the RAF and after 1933, the IAF, gained from flying experiences over the Frontier stood them in good stead when flying over the mountains and jungles of Burma, acting as the "eyes of the 14th Army."

This narrative closes with 1941 and is confined to facts relating to tactics, and expansion of the organisation of the RAF in India, especially the north-west. The IAF, from its inception, learnt and worked in the shadow of the RAF, proving itself on the Frontier. But the big opportunity came from 1939 onwards and from 1942, the expansion was spectacular. From January 1942, when the lone No. 1 Squadron went to war with antiquated obsolete aircraft, there was no looking back. The IAF soon matured and by 1946, had 10 squadrons at the time of independence but the deeds of valour by IAF squadrons need a separate telling. For that is another story of cold hard courage under fire over the skies of Burma.

While none can deny the role of the Army on the Frontier, assistance by the air arm has made a great deal of difference in the conduct of combined operations against the hostiles.

It is relevant here to echo the words of an expert who, as a keen observer of developments, concluded that the RAF did indeed assist the Army in quite a few ways: "The coming of the aeroplane has made a great difference to fighting on the Frontier. As a Scout, it is invaluable, for it can tell the Army General where the tribesmen are waiting on the hillsides, though they are invisible to the troops. It can also attack them with light bombs and machine gun fire; the Pathans are scattered among the rocks, these weapons have only a limited effect; the Pathans do not resent losing some of their men if they have had a chance to kill some on the British side; they resent being attacked from the air, as they have no means of fighting the aeroplane on equal terms. Occasionally, they bring one down with a rifle, but not often."

— F A deV Robertson, 1940.

Compare and contrast this with what is happening in the same area today (2010). In the place of a single-engined Wapiti or an Audax or a Hawker Hart or a Lysander, we have today the helicopter gunships hunting the hostiles. As for returning fire, in the place of a stolen Lee-Enfield rifle, the hostiles now are armed with Stinger missiles!

Puff Shoots — In the Words of an Airman

Flight Sergeant L Smith of No. 5 Squadron, when it was at Quetta, has written about how the RAF was cooperating with artillery batteries in trying to make their shooting accurate by monitoring the flight path of a shell on its way to the target. Such exercises and training were conducted not only in the Frontier areas but also other places in India wherever artillery batteries were based.

"We had a dug-out on the blue and an exchange switchboard but not for telephones, having field telephones in action. These wires lead from the switchboard to various parts of a circle radius. These were connected to a detonator and buried with a small bag of explosive powder (that was self-rising).

"By means of the box, the charge was set off from the dug-out. Meanwhile, a Bristol fighter overhead would observe the position —

believe me, the bang shot a mighty cloud of dust and reported by radio where the shell would have struck. By this means, the pilot would guide the gun — which was supposed to be at the dug-out in stages to a certain target. It used to be interesting fun and if any natives happened to pass near, as it was a free country, the bang soon set them on the run.

"All this was organised by the Signal Section and somehow got the name puff shoots. This was considered good tactics for training erks (airmen) to cooperate with artillery batteries. It came in useful too when I was posted to Kutwa near Calcutta as Wireless Operator for active and real cooperation with the artillery and their heavy guns.

"The radio receiver was known as the Short Wave Tuner and was controlled by crystal, a cat's whisker and carborundum. Each time a gun went off, so did the cat's whisker, then there was panic to get it tuned again in time to receive the pilot's signal for which an impatient Battery Commander was waiting.

"To get to the shoot, we had to travel by mule cart handled by a native soldier. These mules took everything in their stride and never went round a ditch. It was a case of holding on for dear life and on one occasion, the tuner went round and round the floor and was quite useless on arrival at the destination. But it somehow got patched up.

"It was not possible to answer the aircraft by wireless in those days, so we had to use ground strips. I can only remember two (he recalls it after more than 50 years) — 'H', I believe, was for receiving 'You OK' and, 'L' for telling the pilot to land.

"For reception on the ground, we had a telescopic, 30 ft mast and a copper mat for earth. In the aircraft — and I did a few of these trips — one had a reel of seven-strand copper wire attached to the side of the aircraft and passing through a fair lead then attached to a 7 lb weight of lead. The aerial had to curve below the aircraft for 150 ft or so.

"The HT generator was constantly running on the wing, giving 1,500 volts. The transmitting set was called a T23, I believe, and was with me in the rear cockpit. The sending key, 'Morse key' was on the pilot's gun ring and he did the transmitting. Funny, really, because I could do over 30 words per minute, while it took the pilot all his time to do his required seven words a minute.

"But I was glad that he could control the aircraft. On cooperation, we would fly from the gun position to the target and when overhead, the pilot would do a sharp left hand turn and that would be the moment when the Battery Commander would fix his sights. You see, he knew the height of the aircraft, say 2,000 ft and could, therefore, drop his first salvo right bang on target. And it was real shells this time.

"My first flight was with F/O Wheatley at Ambala and the ground station could not receive our signals. The pilot blamed me for some reason, so I wound in the aerial and down we came. The fault was in the tuner on the ground. So we went up again and all was well. Anyway, I got an extra flight and was quite happy. F/O Wheatley eventually became Chief Test Pilot at RAF, Manston, Kent (UK), but sad to say, a Gamecock plane he was testing, broke up at 4,000 ft and so, I deplore the loss of my first ever pilot."

Camera Obscura

"At Ambala, we had what was known as a Camera Obscura. It was a hut with a glass dome in the roof centre. Below was a table with a large map and passing overhead an aeroplane of No. 5 Squadron. On the map, one could actually see the aeroplane, red, white and blue markings and all. The plane would flash a light from underneath and this would be on the map at the point where the light could substitute for a bomb. This arrangement was apparently an improvement on, and no doubt prompted by, the aforementioned puff shoots at Quetta."

Supply Dropping — RAF Style

"Military aviation developed, under war-time pressure, reliable engines, better firepower and mobility as the priorities. No one paid much attention to the carrying capacity of an aircraft. As the war progressed, the long-term objective of carrying men and materials in a peace-time world slowly emerged. Necessity being the mother of invention, gradually aeroplanes began to appear capable of carrying four, five, then ten, and later, may be twenty passengers."

"Logically came the idea of having air units solely for transport, but, before that was the practical experience of seeing first-hand small units of the Army desperately short of ammunition and signalling to the pilot their plight. In such cases, the pilot would throw his own ammunition taken from the Lewis gun and rush back to base for help.

"From this, emerged the idea of supply dropping, as we understand the term today, from the air and having special units to undertake this task. Experiments were carried out by private companies, as also by the services, not always successful, but still a learning process that would result in success one day.

"One such enterprising officer, Flight Lieutenant Anderson, based at Kohat, started experimenting in supply dropping from the air on the authority of Mr G F McConnell of the 2nd (Indian) Wing, RAF, Risalpur.

"The primary objective of the exercise he and his assistants carried out was to devise some system of getting supplies to the various Frontier posts and forts which were in the danger of being cut off from normal means of provisioning if the tribals on the Frontier got out of hand.

"Anderson and his helpers spent a long time devising and having made in the station workshops, various types of containers suitable for dropping food, water and various other stores, including, medicines and radio equipment. One of the most elaborate of these containers, which I recall, was made up to convey carrier pigeons, and if memory serves me right (this was written in the Seventies, almost fifty years later), consisted of two cigar-shaped aluminium canisters about 6x2 ft, one fitted into the other and the intervening space was filled with water to act as a shock absorber and insulation when the containers hit the ground.

"When pigeons were seen coming from a camp, a drop was made with this live load at Kohat. The pigeons must have been in one piece as they flew back to Rissy (Risalpur), in fact, there was a camp sweep on the first birds back. From what height, this load was dropped, I have no idea, but I do know that these experiments consisted of dropping simulated loads from various heights, consequently, the outer edge of the aerodrome was littered with broken cases, sand and split sacks.

"However, when the correct heights had been worked out for the various types of loads, Flight Lieutenant Anderson apparently demanded that he be allowed to drop the real things — flour, biscuits, canned goods. The Indian Government, as we know, was very parsimonious and they were very reluctant to release the real thing for this purpose.

"However, permission was eventually forthcoming on the condition that all items should be returned to the ration stores after the drop. The funny thing was that the last few dummy loads had always landed in one piece but when the run was made with the real things, some cases burst and damaged the contents.

"Consequently, for a couple of days, our rations were augmented with corned beef and corned mutton, which strange as it may seem were luxuries to us – they made a change from the usual Indian meats and normally we only had tinned meat about once every 12 months when the Army stocks in the various outposts were changed — turned over — for fresh stocks.

"The cases of broken biscuits were not appreciated so much and the broken sacks of flour scattered on the 'drome' gave the appearance of a snowfall. I do not recall any further drops of the real thing and I am sure there was not very much of the original issue returned to the store — dented tins would not keep for long in that climate.

"As far as I remember, these drops were made from DH9As. However, oak trees grow from little acorns and it is obvious that from these small beginnings, the massive air drops over the Hump, the Berlin aircraft, etc of later years, developed."

— G F McConnell, Headquarters,
2nd Indian Wing, Risalpur, 1929-30.

Adds the Official History of No. 31 Squadron:
"At the beginning of 1928, a significant step was taken, in that experiments were made during January in the dropping of supplies from the air. It was in this role that some of the squadron's most stirring exploits took place later in World War II on the Burma Front. The containers were apparently slung below the main plane and parachuted down from a height of 500 ft, whilst the aircraft was flown at an air speed of 90 to 110 miles per hour.

"In October, an opportunity came to enable these supply dropping trials and experiments to be put to the test when a patrol of armoured cars and lorries became stranded on the Toba plateau, owing to a breakdown of one of the vehicles. Headquarters, Western Command, anxious as to the position of this convoy, requested that aircraft should endeavour to locate it. The convoy was duly found, supplies were dropped, messages were picked up, and it was maintained generally from the air for several days before it was able to proceed."

— *The History of No. 31 Squadron, RFC/ RAF 1915-50*,
Naval and Military Press, London.

Airlifting Troops — The German Experience

"By 1936, the second generation of German aircraft, the ones to replace the initial, interim types had begun their flight testing. The standard single-engined intercepter fighter was the Messerschmitt Bf109, and for the long range destroyer role, it was the heavier twin-engined Me Bf110. The standard bombers were the Dornier 17 and the Heinkal 111 and for short range dive-bombing, there was the lighter and simpler Junkers 87.

"In August 1936, the new German Air Force (Luftwaffe) went into action for the first time, in support of General Franco's Nationalist forces against the Spanish Republican Communist Government. Initially, the German air support comprised a mere 20 Junkers 52 transports, together with an escorting force of six He51 fighters. But these few aircraft were able to have an effect on events far beyond their meagre numbers.

"General Franco desperately needed to move troops loyal to him from Morocco to mainland Spain and move them quickly. By flying as many as four round trips a day and carrying some twenty-five fully equipped men on each trip, the Ju52 force rapidly moved in 10,000 fighting troops.

"It was the first time that an airlift operation on such a large scale had ever been mounted. It was sufficient to consolidate Franco's shaky position."

— Alfred Price, *Birth, Life and Death of an Air Force*, 1969.

Airlifting an Army Division

For the first time, in the history of Allied military operations, an entire infantry division was airlifted from one spot on the Burma Front to another, along with all its animals and other vital accessories, several hundred miles away, during World War II.

The 5th Indian Infantry Division (Ball of Fire) commanded by Major General Briggs, fresh from its victory in the North African desert, was flown in Dakotas and Commandos of the Allied Troop-Carrier Command from the Arakan to Dimapur. Within a few hours, the entire infantry division was in position on a new part of the front facing the coming Japanese onslaught on Imphal/ Kohima in 1944. The speed with which this was accomplished was indeed breathtaking and its consequences became clear when the Japanese attacks were repeatedly repulsed and the Japanese were eventually driven out of Burma.

Life on the Frontier — 1916-39

As in Britain, so in India, the RFC initially and the RAF after 1918, was treated by the Army as a poor country cousin which had to be tolerated, especially in the NWFP area where, even in peace-time, battles and skirmishes were constantly fought with the restless tribals. Not a single week passed without some tribe or the other shouting *jehad*.

Into this complicated scenario stepped in the No. 31 Squadron, RFC, in 1916 with the vague orders that it had to provide aerial recces, cooperation to the artillery batteries and protection to the Army columns battling the hostile tribes and the more hostile elements.

Through the eyes of aircraftsmen and pilots, we see the scene as it was in the winter of 1915-16 when the war in Europe and the Middle East was raging. The entire north-west of India which included Punjab, Sind and UP, comprised the bases where cantonments had been set up. It was into such units of the Army that Air Force units had to be accommodated. It, of course, implied that the newcomers had to conform to the Army discipline and methodology.

What did it look like to the Air Force boys, especially those who came to India for the first time in their lives? When the first Flight of the first unit, No. 31 Squadron, arrived in December 1915, it was sent to Naushera, then a small village close to Risalpur, a big Army cantonment.

Subsequently, other squadrons came, but life on the Frontier was primitive, crude and very difficult. Any flat piece of ground adjacent to an Army cantonment became an aerodrome, as it was called then.

Following three years of service in the Air Force, 1st Air Mechanic, George Haynes, of No. 31 Squadron was suddenly uprooted from routine work by being ordered to go to Afghanistan. Specifically, he was sent to Dakka by the Khyber Pass, to level out the primitive flat piece of ground that in those days was called a landing ground so that the squadron's planes could land and take off from there.

John Ross of No. 28 Squadron, RAF, who came to India three years later, was luckier as his first posting was at Ambala where his unit No. 28 Squadron was stationed.

"At the railway station, we were transported by lorry to No. 114 Squadron on October 3, 1919. On January 31, 1920, this squadron became No. 28 Squadron, RAF Ambala. The airfield was part of the huge cantonment known as the British Cavalry Lines. As we young regulars were arriving, the older (for the duration of war category) ones were ready for going Home.

"For the British Army in India, going on leave and fresh posting was always done in winter from October to April — trooping season.

"Our quarters were in the large barracks known as the Lord Roberts' bungalows because they were of Lord Roberts' design, built of Indian hand-made bricks and very substantial, with thick walls, one large main hall with a high roof, an inside verandah and a wide covered outside verandah with stone steps down to the sandy ground. These outside verandahs had open archways. The middle main hall was entered through huge doorways at each end with a large porch and the middle side had two large wooden doors to both outer verandahs. Each doorway had two large thick heavy doors of wood with a long heavy plank of wood to secure it, mounted on an axle to be lowered into a big iron cup, resting in a horizontal position over the door.

"Our bed, 'charpayee' was iron framed, with a vertical pole at each corner and a wooden frame around it. On top of it was hung from each of the corners and sides a mosquito net, covering the bed which was tucked in at the bottom. The night patrol was a native 'sentry' who patrolled outside the bungalows with a duty to examine the mosquito nets and if one was kicked open by its occupant, he tucked it in again.

"One necessary visit to the native bazaar was to purchase a strong trunk. A native travelling sign writer painted, in white paint, on the lid your name, number and RAF squadron. In those days (*circa* 1920) there was no lighting, gas, electricity and radio and certainly no television (this was written in 1920 and published in 1987). All airmen had a large oil lamp known as a 'Hurricane' lamp and when going outside at night, we took the lamp, accompanied by a pal.

"Because of the need to adjust to the weather conditions, flying was carried out from 4 am to 10 am when it grew unbearably hot, often 120 degrees F in the shade. In the afternoon, by 4.30 pm, flying would be resumed as long as daylight lasted. After morning flying, aircraft were pushed into hangars and checked well before noon. Our latrines at the hangars were a trench with canvas around.

"A regular custom in India was 'tiffin,' a light tea for all, taken in the afternoon and a ritual on the cantonment. We were warned not to drink a lot of water and never from a tap. Mineral water and lime juice, of which there was plenty, was easily obtained from the Ambala Cantonment British Mineral Water Manufacturing Plant made by British management and equipment. Beer was supplied mainly in barrels and recommended to be consumed in the evenings.

"All of us were issued with what was called a spinepad and a neckshade. The spinepad laid on your back was tied by tape loosely around your neck and the bottom of the pad was tied by tape around your waist. These garments were filled with what looked like 'kapok'. Not to wear them or the topee when outside in the daytime was a punishable offence.

"At Ambala, there was an Electric Rink and Cinema managed by two Europeans in partnership. We were entertained with a gripping serial 'The Voice on the Wire' or a comic film 'A Bandit's Wager.'

There was also a place across the desert beyond the hangars, 'Sandes Soldiers Home' run by a white man and his wife. Here, you could buy cups of tea, biscuits, rock buns and most delicious custards and have a comfortable chat in quiet surroundings, meeting some of the troops.

"The 'Raja' of Patiala often visited the Ambala Cantonment in state procession and his elephants looked spectacular. He used to visit the squadron and watch the flying. The Maharaja of Patiala, Bhupender Singh, was the first among the Princes of India to take interest in aviation and, as early as 1911, purchased a BE and a Maurice Farman plane. By the time World War II came, he was a qualified pilot and an Honorary Air Commodore in the RAF. Already in his forties, he cheerfully went through the rigours of training, both on the ground and in the air, to earn his 'wings', once a Flying School was opened at Ambala in 1942-43.

"During the long British rule in India, the Englishman's language, English, underwent a subtle change, in that, Indian words crept into English and English words began to make inroads into the many vernacular languages. One of the most frequently used was the word 'wallah', used as a suffix to an English word.

"The 'wallah' soon became respectable when 'box' was the prefix and 'wallah' was the suffix. A new word emerged, a new species was born — the boxwallah.

"Apart from the Army and the civil servants of the ICS and educationists, engineers, doctors, lawyers, those Englishmen who became part of a new constituency called business and trade, soon got this name or designation — the boxwallah.

"But the humbler types of 'wallah' served the airmen and the pilots to make their life a bit more pleasant and bearable. They came in all shades, did different jobs on nominal payment, performed various roles and provided variety when boredom during off-duty hours was the biggest enemy. They were the Native wallahs.

"The wallahs were a part of our lives and sustenance, playing a very significant part of the daily routine affecting all of us. They were useful associates in many ways. When our Pay Day arrived, they came along with all sorts of marketing.

"The snake charmer with his basket of snakes, sitting on the sand, playing his pipe, like a tin whistle, his snakes obeyed his tune and with varying twist of his arms, performed as warranted. It was fascinating. They all had helpers, like a team. The magician with his cups and peas, beans, small pebbles, was clever in making them disappear and come back again. The jugglers were clever and amusing to watch, the tatooist brought his designs and patterns. The fellows who wanted badges, squadron wings and personal designs got me to sketch them on tissue paper.

"They (my colleagues) then visited the bazaar and had the chosen design tattooed upon them. The fortune teller with his books about the stars would tell you: 'Sahib will be going on a long sea voyage. Nice lady write letter to you soon. You have got a lucky face, you pay me more, get lucky number.' The music maker with old trumpets and drums like large coconuts slung round his neck, the weird tunes went up and down the scale with an ear piercing melody.

"The native bazaar road was narrow, about the width of a cartway, with a nasty stinking channel in the middle which slowly drained refuse away from the place, including the contents shed from humans and animals. Shops on both sides were doing business, with sacred cows wandering about amongst everyone.

"All this was for the Pay Day or a visit to the bazaar. But there were other 'wallah' comforts that did come at a price during the working of the airmen when they had to work on a rigorous time-table."

The Mochie Wallah (The Cobbler)

"The mochie was very popular, squatting in a small kitchen sized workshop, with models of his trade hanging from nails on the wall.

Drawing round your feet on pieces of paper for a pattern, he made some excellent footwear by hand, from officers' riding boots to running pumps. He made pumps for me, wearing which I ran."

The Munchie Wallah (The Tailor)

"The munchie was the camp tailor, using a small place for a workshop. Cloth and cotton all over the place, with his treadle machine racing away, he did competent repairs to servicemen's clothing. He made outfits of the drill tunics, slacks, shorts and shirts for officers and airmen of all ranks. The tailor had plenty of work in his shop because we bought lighter drill outfits for wear after parades which conformed to regulation pattern but were smarter. Drill shorts were always extra kit, and shirts that needed mending helped to keep him busy."

The Bhasti Wallah (The Water Carrier)

"It was forbidden to drink water from the tap (if it was running). Drinking water was brought in by the carrier known as the 'Bhasti wallah', a native who carried, over his shoulders in sling fashion, a goat-skin or a leather bag containing water. He grasped an opening or released his hand at the bottom of this bag and poured out water. Pure water came from the British Mineral Water factory on the cantonment. This water was poured into large earthenware receptacles in the barracks each day and it kept nice and cool. On his rounds, he would sell some of his precious liquid if we wanted extra."

The Nappie Wallah (The Barber)

"We rarely shaved ourselves, the native barber, the 'nappie wallah' a craftsman, was in our employ, sanctioned by the squadron. He came on his rounds before reveille with his hot water in a small can shaped like a milk can or churn with a charcoal fire underneath.

"He would lather your face and shave you with an open (cut throat) razor, often one would wake up with him lifting your nose in order to shave your upper lip, even waking up to find you had already been shaved. We trusted him and paid him his weekly wage of a few annas even though the water must have been rather murky before he changed it.

"In the bazaar, I bought a German 'Crown and Sword' razor, and I gave him my issue razor and he was pleased with it."

The Chah Wallah (Tea Supplier)

"The native confectioner would be found at any place where the troops were. He visited us at the barracks and in the squadron hangars during the morning flying hours.

"We could tell when he was on the long trek from the barracks as he was followed by 'kitehawks,' a ravenous bird which seemed always hungry. These birds swooped down at the tin box being carried on his head in order to get at the buns, tarts and cakes he had made. He did his best to scare away these birds by slashing at them with a long stick around his head. His ('chicku') boy and helpmates carried his large milk churn type of tea can with the charcoal fire at the base. With our own mugs, we would buy our cups of 'chah' and also pastries, paying him on the spot.

"It was a much brewed tea but acceptable in the heat and dust. Not having a canteen or a 'naafi,' we were thankful for this and the odd things he would bring us from the bazaar."

The Dhobie Wallah (The Washerman)

"This was the laundry man who would collect our laundry. Each of us had been given an indelible mark of his own pattern of dots and dashes on our garments. He never got mixed up with any of them, always bringing back to us our own individual items. Off he would trudge with his load in his *gharry* or by foot and he would bring them back clean and nicely folded and place them on your bed.

"His women helped him with the work and the laundry was at the local river side, in the water. These dhobie wallahs did the washing by bashing the garments on large stones at the riverside, while singing a tune of their own. They performed the actions of bash-bash, knocking the dirt and sometimes the stuffing out of the wash load, but they always did a good job of it, sewing any buttons which were missing."

The Book Wallah (Books and Periodicals Man)

"At Pay Day and off duty time, the book wallah and his two or three staff arrived. His books would be laid on the floor along with an assortment of small knickknacks, like a model of the famous Taj Mahal, brass ornaments, toys, small swords and magazines, periodicals, old British newspapers and Indian newspapers in English.

"*The Onlooker* was an Indian periodical with military news, advertisements, cartoons and caricatures. One would find a book or other items for sale that the wallah had purchased from some other soldier. He was wise enough to keep his better books in the trunk, allowing you to glance at them one at a time. On post cards he produced a lady's face, 'Pretty lady, yours in Britain (Vilaayat)'. Looking at it, the card said, 'Printed in Calcutta'."

The Fruit Wallah (The Fruit Seller)

"There was plenty of fruit and the wallah with his 'chicku' brought his basket of fruit everyday, consisting of nuts, oranges, bananas, dates, etc."

The Wood-Carver Wallah (The Carpenter)

"The native wood carver was clever and I have a specimen of his work cut into a part of a broken propeller."

The Punkah Wallah (The Hand-Operated Fan Operator)

"To keep the barracks cool, the 'punkah wallah' would be kept busy all day and night. The punkahs were fastened one to another by a length of rope in a row over the beds, the end rope being long enough to go through a hole in the wall to the outer porch. Here, the punkah wallah would sit down, squatting, pulling the rope towards him and then he let it swing away from him causing all the punkahs to swing in rhythm with an acceptable swish of air over each bed."

Living Conditions

"For Englishmen, born and brought up in the temperate climate of England, the hot, dusty and disease ridden countryside of India was initially a nightmare, but taking lessons from their Army cousins, the airmen slowly learnt to fight it and survive.

"In the tropics, there is always an acute amount of sickness. I recorded three dates when we were inoculated against cholera, June 7 and 12, 1920, and May 15, 1921. On June 26, 1920, I was put in the Ambala Military Hospital with slight dysentery and was discharged on a milk diet on July 8, 1920. I was told it was to make way for some bad malaria cases.

"The flies were a nuisance and whilst we were constantly swatting them, they would be crawling all over the faces of some natives who did not seem to bother. Some of the ants were huge, wobbling about as they ran. When we put all sorts of fruit peel on the ground, an ant would approach, give it an inspection, race away, then come back with an army of them organised and they set about the peel and carried it away.

"Small animals like squirrels, when approached, shot to the other side of the tree and went up it in a flash. A big, greedy-looking bird looking for scraps, we called it a 'kitehawk'. It was like a wild fowl, it snatched food out of your hand, a wing scratching your face, swooping around like a single seat fighter doing aerobatics.

"The flying beetle was something you got used to. But the mosquito was a deadly insect and they buzzed about in plenty and your best friend was the mosquito net over your bed. The busy insect would fly at you at any time, any place and sting you. You could hear the devilish insect, even if you could not see it. The night patrol or the orderly native on their rounds made a tour of the beds and if they found a bed with the net pushed out, they would tuck it in for you.

"The female of the mosquito species was reputed to be the one that injected you with the malaria germ. Spiders were a nasty thing and it was wise to be clear of them or destroy them. We would always shake out the sheets and examine underneath the bed. A towel hanging up or lying down on your locker was a haven for creepy crawlies and as a precaution, we would shake out our clothing.

"The worst and the nastiest insects were the scorpions and the centipedes. The tail of the scorpion was its weapon of attack and it would grasp its prey between the front claws and very quickly bring the tail over putting a sting on what was between the claws. The centipede was a nasty and dangerous crawling insect with a fair turn of speed and before putting on your slippers, shoes or boots, it was wise to give them a good shaking.

"Snakes caused plenty trouble in the rain and monsoon period and puttees were a reasonable protection. The cobra was a common and dangerous snake and the policy was to keep your eyes fixed on it and wallop it in a scythe fashion to kill it at first blow — if possible.

"We were permitted to have dogs 'on strength'. They were given a ration allowance. The airmen who kept them were dog lovers and we would often take them with us when out for a stroll. They slept on the beds or under as the case may be."

This is a first-hand account by Aircraftsman Ross who served in No. 28 Squadron, RAF, at Ambala and other places in the North-West Frontier Province, wherever the squadron of any of his flights or detachments was sent. He served in India from 1919 to 1923.

Chaz Bowyer, the distinguished air historian and himself an old RAF hand, adds:

"From an individual's point of view, life in India for the airmen was not too cheerful on the surface. The tour of duty was confirmed as a five years' stint after early 1924 and with the lack of necessary finance, accommodation and amenities for married personnel were severely restricted. It meant, for many married men, a five years' total separation from their families, while the bachelor had little in the way of off-duty recreation beyond that which he and his companions created for themselves.

"Personal clothing was outdated in concept, no officer or airman being officially permitted to venture into the blistering sunlight without sun helmet or spine protection pad. Khaki drill uniform was issued in relatively heavy-weight material 'in order to absorb perspiration,' while tightly bound cloth puttees were mandatory for work and parade, thereby cramping leg muscles in a vice-like grip of sweating, torture after any form of lengthy exercise.

"Working and relaxing in temperatures which soar to 112 degrees F in the theoretical shade or plunge to below freezing, especially on the forward landing grounds, high in the mountains of the Indian Frontier, life focussed on the aircraft of the squadron.

"And yet with traditional perverseness of the British serviceman, such conditions merely served to increase his determination to enjoy himself despite his surroundings. It is a truism that veterans of the years 1919-39 in India still regard their tours of duty as amongst the happiest and most satisfying they ever experienced.

"A spirit of comradeship was born which has never been surpassed in RAF history and both officers and men worked in the closest harmony in achieving a peak of efficiency in both duty and play. The tone of the period is reflected in the service songs born in those years. With a traditional flavour of cynicism and fatalism, these became part of RAF's folklore, and with their constant creed of 'roll on the boat' – the trooping ship which brought their replacements and then bore them home to kith and kin — the airmen created their own brand of humour and solace from stark surroundings and grim conditions."

— Chaz Bowyer, *RAF India.*

Trenchard's Brats

It was Lord Trenchard who spurred the British Government into training young boys in the repair and maintenance of aeroplanes, because they would form the real backbone of the new RAF both at Home and overseas in the farflung corners of the Empire. They were nicknamed "Trenchard's Brats".

One of them, in the RFC Boys' Section at Farnborough in 1917, was John Ross who did his tenure in India in the RAF. An account of India in the Twenties, through the eyes of Aircraftsman Ross, No. 28 Squadron, RAF, can be found in his diary.

It is a fact of history that practically all the literature that there is on the subject of military science and history has been written by officers of the three services. There is hardly any history or even a narrative written by a soldier or a sailor or an airman. The one exception that the author can recall is a privately published book entitled *Subedar* dealing with battles in the 19th century British India. That too was a narration by the Subedar, who knew little English, to his British officer, who penned down the Subedar's words.

At the end of the Great War of 1914-18 and during the inter-war period 1919-39, a number of books on the war appeared. This was the period when the new RAF was born as a separate independent service. It was the foresight of Lord Trenchard that built the RAF. In those days, most planes were bi-planes with fabric covering the wings. So, to ensure that the fabric stayed in place, a rigger was required. For the engine, a mechanic whom the RAF called the 'fitter' was needed. Thus, the single unit fighter/ bomber aircraft had the pilot, the fitter and the rigger. Folklore has dubbed the team as the "Trinity'.

John Ross had kept a diary and from it emerged a book which recalled his service in the RFC and later in India. When he served in places like Ambala, Kohat, Risalpur, Miranshah, he used to service and maintain a Bristol fighter in the No. 28 Squadron. The pilot was Flying Officer Hugh Pugh Lloyd, who later rose to the rank of Air Chief Marshal and has written a foreword to Ross' narrative. He writes, "The author was an air mechanic servicing the Bristol fighters and he flew with me on so many occasions." Ross himself was commissioned in the RAF VR on February 3, 1944, as a Flying Officer.

To Indian readers, the mention of No. 28 Squadron, RFC/ RAF, would bring back memories. In an earlier publication by the author, *Skyhawks*, mention is made of No. 28 squadron and its operations in Belgium, France and Italy. One of the four Indian pilots who participated in that war was Sardar Hardit Singh Malik of No. 28 Squadron, who after the war joined the Indian Civil Service (ICS). He had the pleasure of visiting the squadron at Ambala when he was the Deputy Commissioner of the district.

After the war was over, the country had so many aircraft which were not needed in peace-time. It became the policy to decide what the role and requirement would be of the new peace-time RAF. Certainly, so many squadrons would not be needed. The idea was to retain a certain number of officers, pilots and a small number for various other duties. Therefore, a good mixture of war veterans, pilots, administrators and others were kept serving. Included were some young pilots direct from flying training schools ready to enter the new peace-time RAF. To scale down the hugely expanded armed forces, a committee headed by Sir Eric Geddes was appointed to recommend the size of the peace-time services. The reduction resulted in thousands losing their jobs and placed on reserve. The men called it the "Geddes, Axe".

A small number of NCOs was retained and also a few air mechanics; only a few efficient NCOs who offered their services were retained. To fill in the void, many from Boys Section were at 18 years of age, fully trained to be placed along with the old heads to start their regular engagement in the new RAF.

"I was one of the pilots sent to India in early 1919 when we built the new No. 28 Squadron, taking over from No. 114 Squadron, RFC. We built new aircraft sent from England, erected by the old NCOs and the new young air mechanics. They did their duties very well under extreme difficulties, keeping the aircraft in fair trim and they helped to make good the flying achievements over Indian territory and over the North-West Frontier Province in aircraft just held together by bits and pieces and a few spare parts we could get.

"In the days of early overseas service from 1919, most of us in all squadrons were new to the tropical environment and the big change from BE2C and BE2E to modern aircraft operating at that time. This was the beginning of a new era," says Air Chief Marshal Sir H P Lloyd who served as a pilot in No. 28 Squadron on the North-West Frontier.

First Impressions — People and Work

When Ross landed with his colleagues at Bombay on October 1, 1919, and the small RAF party marched through the streets, it was with mixed feelings. India was new to them and it was strange and yet familiar. "There was a large number of natives, but the buildings and streets were similar to ours, transport was anything on wheels. One thing we could not understand, until informed, was the red splashes staining the footpaths in so many places. It was the spitting out by the natives of the remains of the betel nut they had chewed.

"One thing that puzzled us was the large number 'scissors' stacked on the canteen shelves in the Colaba transit camp where we were billeted. What do they want with so many scissors, we wondered and soon found out. They were special cigarettes securely wrapped in cellophane sealed for transporting by sea to tropical countries only. They were a popular brand of cigarettes smoked by troops and others in India."

After a 48 hour train journey, the group arrived at their destination — Ambala. To the newcomers, soon to join No. 28 Squadron, RAF, the sight of the airfield was reassuring that they had indeed reached their destination. The airfield was part of the huge cantonment known as British cavalry lines. Practically all officers, NCOs and men were DW (Duration of War) servicemen engaged for service after the war. Only a few of them were re-engaged to stay and they were of great help in advising the newcomers about the prevailing conditions. "They gave information on your bearer and his pay which was a few annas per week. The bearer knew his job serving airmen and soldiers and spoke English."

Carrying Arms on Church Parade

On January 1, 1922, a newly arrived Sergeant, A E Cowton, posted to No. 27 Squadron, who has left an admirable account of his own experience in India, described the church parade on that day at Risalpur.

"The parade assembled just before noon, at which time precisely, a Royal Salute was fired by the Artillery, the Union Jack was hoisted and the National Anthem played. The Colonel Commandant read out the Royal Proclamation and the whole parade then marched past, the band knew no march for the RAF — and accordingly, played 'D'Ye Ken John Peel.'

"One minor feature of the church parade was common to all service units, the carriage of rifles and side-arms. The primary reason for this apparent paradox was stated to be that troops should be ready at all times to go into action. But it is quite possible that the inherent native practice of stealing any item left unattended for more than a minute may have had a distinct bearing on the matter."

— Chaz Bowyer, *The Flying Elephants*,
No. 27 Squadron, RAF.

However, Bowyer wonders at the 'official reasoning' for the continued carriage of firearms on church parades in England in the 1940s and 1950s. In India, it may have been necessary, but why so in England in the Fifties?

There is more to it. Aircraftsman John Ross adds:

"When off guard duty, our firearms were kept in strong rifle racks under strong lock and key in the guard room. We had to keep the bolt with us often securely fastened to our body because they (the Pathan tribals) had difficulty trying to make a rifle bolt as good as ours. It was a serious offence to lose a bolt, but none was lost."

The Efficacy of Air Power

In spite of severe limitations imposed on the armed forces, particularly in the Frontier areas, the tribals of the unadministered territory, saw first-hand the efficacy of air power, which was used judiciously and even sparingly. Once experience was gained from 1916 to 1939, it was apparent that air power as an important element of combined operations had come to stay.

From 1923 until 1929, each of the six outbreaks of tribal unrest was dealt with by aircraft alone, while during 1930, out of 12 outbreaks, eight were settled by aircraft, without any assistance and four with the military in cooperation.

It will be futile to go into the details of the protracted controversy between the RAF and the Army regarding the extended use of air power on the North-West Frontier. A few facts, however, may be cited.

In April 1929, the Secretary of State for Air circulated a paper by the Chief of the Air Staff, suggesting the substitution of the Air Force in place of ground and naval forces, stationed on the North-West Frontier of India, the Persian Gulf area, the Sudan, and East and West Africa. The scheme included a proposal to place the combined forces at different places under the control of the Air Force.

It is hardly surprising that the Army authorities scathingly criticised the proposals. The Howell Committee set up to make recommendations on the proposals concerning the North-West Frontier of India, in particular, accomplished little up to January 1932, its work generating no less heat than light. The RAF emphasised the following advantages which the Air Forces possessed over the ground forces.

- That Air Forces are not affected by difficult terrain as found on the North-West Frontier.
- That Air Forces can strike at the seat of trouble even far from a military station, whereas ground forces would have to march to the place, giving time for the trouble to spread.
- That a single air squadron could operate over Waziristan on one day and over Bajaur, perhaps the next day, thus, affecting a great economy of force. The wider aspect of this flexibility was the possibility of flying strong air striking forces without loss of time to any threatened part of the Empire in the Middle East.
- That air operations cut out expected casualties suffered by troops through sickness and enemy action in expeditions against the tribes.

On the basis of the above, it was proposed by the Chief of the Air Staff in the UK that an augmented Air Force on the North-West Frontier should be given the responsibility of daily watch and ward duties and of bringing a hostile tribe to terms by air action.

By this means, some 25-30 battalions of infantry and about 10 batteries of artillery were to be reduced from the covering troops, while only five or six squadrons of the Air Force were to be added, thus, affecting an annual saving of about two million Pounds Sterling on a total capital outlay of only one million Pounds Sterling.

But those responsible for the defence of India did not consider the experiment free from undue risk and, thus, the scheme bore no fruit.

The disparity between the Air Forces of foreign powers and the air squadrons in India increased rapidly until it was feared that putting the RAF in India against the Japanese or the Italian Air Force, in trying to defend Singapore or Egypt would not only be useless but noxious as it would infallibly entail the unnecessary and profitless destruction of skilled pilots.

In 1938, the RAF in India consisted of four bomber squadrons, four Army cooperation squadrons and half 'A' Flight of bomber transport squadrons (two aircraft).

The Air Force's role was to control tribes on the North-West Frontier and for air transport, primarily for internal security, defence of the North-West and Eastern Frontiers and seaward reconnaissance, shipping protection and cooperation with the Royal Indian Navy. The number of squadrons required for the purpose was estimated to be seven squadrons for tribal control on the North-West Frontier, five squadrons for internal security, three squadrons for the defence of the North-East Frontier and 21 squadrons to form the nucleus for expansion in case of a major threat of war, a total of 36 squadrons altogether.

"It is important for the winning of the war that we should not only secure air predominance, but secure it on a very large scale. In World War II, it was done, but it took three years to get there."

— Air Vice Marshal S N Goyal (Retd), IAF,
Expansion of the Armed Forces and Defence Organisation,
1939-45.

Appendices

The Aviation Speak

Nomenclature in the armed forces has a history of its own and aeronautics or aviation or flying is no exception to it. Land and sea have been for centuries the arena, both in peace and war, for the sailors and the soldiers. When the third dimension made its initial feeble attempts to join the two senior stalwarts, the vocabulary began to expand and take on new meanings.

The sky, air, horizon, clouds, cyclones, waves were the words commonly used by the sailors, but as curiosity about the sky manifested itself in the work of scientists, engineers and inventors, what they first heard was aeronautics. It soon became aviation. "The word 'aviation' — you may pronounce it as 'ay-viation' or 'avviation' — is a 'convenient description of air travel in all its ways. "The word 'avis' means a bird, the word aviation may be allowed to include air-faring by balloons, and by machines which have rotating vanes or planes as well as such flying machines as have wings which remotely resemble those of birds," says C G Grey in his pioneering book *A History of the Air Ministry*. The first vehicle to fly became a balloon and the person who flew it became an aeronaut.

How did an aeronaut turn into a pilot? Not directly, but via the name aviator — a man who practices aviation. When the Montgolfier Brothers made history in 1783 by their first balloon flight in Paris, France, the aviator was unknown. Soon, however, the name continued being used until the beginning of World War I. By then, the balloon had been replaced by a heavier than air machine called the aeroplane. An interesting sidelight of it is when, during the late 19th century experiments on flying, someone named his experimental flying machine as 'aerodrome'.

Even before manned flight had become a reality in 1903, the age of airships had begun and strangely enough, the terminology for the air was borrowed from the sea. The flying craft was called an airship (ship of the air) and the man controlling it in the air was called the Captain, both nautical terms.

Grey explains further, "The word aircraft should be taken to mean all kinds of the vehicles of the air, balloons, gyroplanes, helicopters, autogiros, airships, biplanes, monoplanes, landplanes, and seaplanes. Seaplanes should include aeroplanes on floats, or floatplanes, as well as flying boats."

"Unhappily, certain intelligentia insist on using the word aircraft when they specifically meant the aeroplane." Further, he objects to the habit of abbreviating aeroplane to "plane and aerodrome to drome." Unfortunately, the 20th century that heralded the air age, also abbreviated the nomenclature and worse, a new language of acronyms emerged that seems to be gaining strength day by day in the 21st century.

It began with the aeronaut. With the coming of the space age in the Sixties of the 20th century, aeronaut for the Americans became an astronaut and for the Russians, keeping the cosmos in mind, became a cosmonaut.

The science and technology of military aviation has borrowed many words/names from the sea. Take the word 'pilot'. The earliest use of this word was made on the sea. Whenever a large warship or an aircraft carrier or an oil tanker has to come into port, it is the harbour pilot who guides it in and when the ship has to leave the port, it is again the 'sea pilot' who guides it out. Today, a pilot means a person who is fully trained to fly — take off, climb and fly at level, come down and land.

Between 1903 and 1914, the word was aeroplane. Only after World War I, when there was a tremendous expansion in civil aviation, did the word 'aeroplane' gracefully retire, being replaced by an equally compound word 'aircraft'.

When Zeppelin retired as a General from the German Army, he devoted himself to designing and building a craft based on the balloon which he called an air-ship. This craft had engines, controls and was airborne on the basis of a helium envelope. Since he was the inventor of this aerial vehicle, it got the name Zeppelin. Thus, even here, the traditional nautical link asserted itself — ship of the air.

During World War II, the newly set up Luftwaffe (the German Air Force), organised itself into Staffel (squadron), Jadgeschwader (literal translation — a swarm of aerial hunters) or a Wing. The highest echelon of the German armada was the Luftflotte (Air Fleet), the fleet indicating nautical origin. In the same vein, the Spanish Armada of ships that was once on its way to England has given rise to the expression 'an aerial armada' when a large number of aircraft fly together in formation.

When the Short Brothers of England designed and built the first seaplane, they called it a 'flying boat'. Sunderland flying boats became famous later both in peace and war. When aircraft began to take off from the decks of ships, the ships were called aircraft carriers, omitting the word ship.

However, before the era of the aircraft carrier came into its own, the French started naming such ships as seaplane carriers. And the aircraft that took off and landed on the deck of a ship was called a 'seaplane'. When the Allies were trying to defend the Suez Canal from Turkish attacks in 1914–15, the French seaplanes were also called hydroplanes in their official dispatches.

Long after World War II, when the Vietnam War was in full swing, the one current expression for armed helicopters was and is so even today — gunships.

Words associated with aeronautics, aviation, flying were also joined by other seemingly new words. When the Wright Brothers flew in 1903, all they had, apart from the flying machine, was a flat piece of ground. To take off and land, initially, was going up and coming down. Military aviation coined words like emplane and deplane as equivalent to embark and disembark (debark).

Later, it became take-off and landing. The ground on which the machine took off and landed was called 'a landing ground'. Today, we know that it is called a runway and the place is an aerodrome. Today, it is the airfield and the actual 'landing ground' is called the runway. And the entire structure, as with a railway station, is now called an 'airport'; the nautical link again. In addition, we have the word harbour — the planes were dispersed under the trees around the runway — harboured. Even an Army unit harbours for the night.

The earliest 'gadget' to represent the control tower was the wind sock that indicated to the aviator/pilot the direction of the wind. And it was always better to take off in the same direction as the wind, for it gave a push and helped the pilot and the machine get airborne quickly. Conversely, when landing, it was advised to check the direction of the wind and fly against it so that the machine would feel the brake and come to a halt faster. This was the era when aircraft had no brakes. During World War I, on the Western Front, a pilot would take out his handkerchief and hold it aloft by its corner against the wind to test both the direction and the intensity (wind speed) of the wind.

Once commercial flying started and the two World Wars witnessed the setting up of organised military aviation fleets, the need was felt for regulating the traffic in the skies. Thus, was born the idea of a control tower at every airfield. This also created in turn a new skilled job, that of an Air Traffic Controller (ATC). Just after World War I, wireless communication became widespread and a wireless operator became an integral part of the control tower staff for locating the position of aircraft in flight. With the coming of radar, an operator also arrived on the scene.

A number of changes came about during the Twenties — commercial aircraft companies (today called airlines) began to identify themselves and their nationality by painting the logo of the company and that of the country on the fuselage of the aircraft. Most of the airlines began painting their countries' flag to identify themselves visually. Rules and regulations for the proper conduct of flights across national boundaries as well as several rules for navigation were framed and they were also endorsed by an international body like the League of Nations earlier and the United Nations later.

Eventually, after World War II, when it became quite clear that aviation military and civil had come to stay, the International Civil Aviation Organisation (ICAO) came into being with all countries as members.

With regard to the physical characteristics of the aeroplane, again, one has to refer to the sea. On a ship, the left side is called 'port' and the right side 'starboard'. There is history behind these two names. When ships had no engines and used the sails and the wind for propulsion, navigation was difficult. In those days, astro-navigators used to stand out on a plank which was put on the right side of the ship to get an unobstructed view of the stars. This would help them to know their position and to plot future course of the ship. This was the starboard.

The left side was called the port side because that was the side you put in on at the port. In other words, when you came into the harbour, it was on the port (left side) that you turned on to the jetty.

The exterior of the forward end of the ship is called the bow and the opposite of this is called the stern. Forward is the front part and aft the rear or tail part of the aircraft.

All these names have been incorporated in aviation, both civil and military. If it is a single-engine machine, the left wing is the port wing and the right wing is the starboard wing. If the aircraft is a twin-engine machine, the left engine is the port engine, while the right one is starboard. In four-engine airliners, the pilot will call out port engine 1 on or starboard engine 4 on.

What used to be called the 'cockpit' being the front portion of the aircraft where the pilot sat and controlled the machine has now been changed, especially in big twin-engine or four-engine aircraft. It is no longer a 'cockpit', now it is 'flight deck,' the last word being from the sea — the deck of a ship.

The Air Force rank nomenclature is a happy blend of that the Army and the tradition-bound Royal Navy. We have the officer — Pilot Officer and Flying Officer — the first Navy and the second Army combined, and we have the Flight Lieutenant, Army inspired.

The next rank, Squadron Leader is again from the Navy. A collection of ships-carriers, cruisers, destroyers and frigates is a squadron. However, an innovation is the Wing Commander, wing being the operative word followed by the Group Captain — an exalted Captain from the Army.

With the next rank, Air Commodore, comes the prefix — Air, otherwise it is a naval rank. Then comes Air Vice Marshal — Marshal clearly being from the Army. Air Marshal is the next higher rank, followed by Air Chief Marshal.

What Admirals are to the Navy, Marshals are to the Air Force. Equivalence has been provided for Pilot Officer — 2nd Lieutenant, for Flying Officer — Lieutenant, for Flight Lieutenant — Captain, for Squadron Leader — Major, for Wing Commander —Lieutenant Colonel, for Group Captain — Colonel, for Air Commodore — Brigadier, for Air Vice Marshal — Major General, for Air Marshal — Lieutenant General, for Air Chief Marshal — General, for Marshal of the RAF/IAF — Field Marshal.

Comparing with the Navy, the similarity is stark:

For Pilot Officer — Midshipman, Flying Officer — Sub-Lieutenant, Flight Lieutenant — Lieutenant, Squadron Leader — Lieutenant Commander, Wing Commander — Commander, Group Captain — Captain, Air Commodore — Commodore, Air Vice Marshal — Rear Admiral, Air Marshal — Vice Admiral, Air Chief Marshal — Admiral of the Fleet, and the highest rank is the First Sea Lord.

What designates these new ranks that the RAF adopted? The badges of the ranks bear a remarkable resemblance to the naval badges. Beginning with the P/O, it is a thin tape in blue felt/cloth. The F/O gets a wider tape worn on the shoulder blades. The Flt/Lt gets two parallel tapes and a S/Ldr gets two parallel tapes with a quarter inch tape in between. The W/C gets three parallel tapes, while the G/Capt gets four. The Air/Cdre gets a wide one inch broad tape, while the AVM adds one tape to the wide tape and in the case of an AM, it is a wide tape and two thinner tapes. An ACM gets the wide tape and three such tapes parallel to it.

In the field of organisation, the smallest unit is the Flight, comprising roughly 4-6 aircraft. Next comes the Squadron comprising about 12-16 aircraft, divided into two or three Flights. Several squadrons are grouped together as a Wing and several Wings together as a Group. The next echelon in the organisation is the Command. During World War II, Britain had the Fighter Command, the Bomber Command, the Coastal Command and the Training and Maintenance Commands.

After World War II, when war planes become more complicated, expensive and lethal, the Group echelon was dropped and Wings were directly commanded by the Command Headquarters. In India, after 1947, we had No. 1 Operational Group which came directly under the orders of Air Headquarters. After some years, it was upgraded to the level of an Air Command.

There are also territorial commands as in the US Air Force, which at the height of the Cold War had the North American Air Defence Command (NORAD). In the Indian Air Force (IAF), air commands are distributed geographically, such as Western Air Command or Eastern or Southern Air Command.

RAF Commands in British Empire

As World War I was nearing its end, for the first time, the British Air Ministry started to publish annually details of the various domestic and overseas commands within the British Empire. This process, initiated by the Air Ministry, began even while the war was still on (August 1918) and ended in March 1939.

The first two years, the list covered only the commands within the British Isles. Only from March 1920, was a combined list of both the commands at Home and those overseas given.

The following is the first list of 1918:

- South-Eastern Area: Maj Gen F C Heath Caldwell
- South-Western Area: Maj Gen M E F Kerr
- Midland Area: Maj Gen J F A Higgins
- North-Eastern Area: Maj Gen Sir F Gordon
- North-Western Area: Maj Gen G C Cayley

The list for 1920, for the first time, covers overseas commands and for the first time includes the India Command.

In March 1920:
Northern Area: AVM J F A Higgins
Southern Area: AVM Sir J M Salmond
No. 11 Irish Group: Gr Capt I M Bonham Carter
Coastal Area: AVM A V Vyvyan

Cranwell: Air Cmdre C A H Longcroft

RAF headquarters Halton: Air Cmde F R Scarlett

Middle East: Air Cmdre W G H Salmond

India: Air Cmdre T I Webb Bowen

Mediterranean District: Air Cmdre Oliver Swann

From 1920 to 1939, the RAF India Command has appeared in the list regularly. Following is the list of such officers who headed the RAF in India:

March 1921: Air Commodore T I Webb Bowen

March 1922: Air Commodore T I Webb Bowen

March 1923: AVM P W Game

March 1924: AVM Sir Edward L Ellington

March 1925: AVM Sir Edward L Ellington

March 1926: AVM Sir Edward L Ellington

March 1927: AVM Sir Geoffrey H Salmond

March 1928: AVM Sir Geoffrey H Salmond

March 1929: AVM Sir Geoffrey H Salmond

March 1930: AVM Sir Geoffrey H Salmond

March 1931: AVM Sir John M Steel

March 1932: AM Sir John M Steel

March 1933: AM Sir John M Steel

March 1934: AM Sir John M Steel

March 1935: AM Sir John M Steel

March 1936: AM Sir Edgar R Ludlow Hewitt

March 1937: AM Sir Edgar R Ludlow Hewitt

March 1938: AM P B Joubert de la Ferte

March 1939: AM P B Joubert de la Ferte

It is interesting to compare the list of 1918 to the list of 1939 which shows a tremendous expansion of the RAF in the UK and overseas.

In March 1939:

Bomber Command: ACM Sir Edgar R Ludlow Hewitt

Fighter Command: ACM Sir Hugh C T Dowding

Coastal Command: AM Sir Frederick W Bowhill

Training Command: AM Sir Charles S Burnett

Maintenance Command: AVM J S T Bradley

Balloon Command: AVM O Boyd

Reserve Command: AM C L Courtney

RAF Middle East: AVM H R Nicholl

RAF Palestine: Air Cmdre A T Harris
British Forces in Iraq: AVM J H S Tyssen
Air Forces in India: AM Sir Philip B Joubert de la Ferte
RAF Mediterranean: Air Cmdre R Leckie
British Forces in Aden: AVM G R M Reid
RAF Far East: AVM J T Babington

All this expansion took place before the war which began in 1939. Thereafter, the expansion was phenomenal.

RAF Squadrons in India — Profiles

No. 31 Squadron, RFC/ RAF

Motto: "In Caelum Indicum Primus" — First in the Indian Skies

The decision to send No. 31 Squadron to India was taken in the last quarter of 1915, one newly formed Flight of the squadron set sail for India in December 1915 and arrived in Bombay on December 26 and proceeded to Naushera in the North-Western Frontier Province (NWFP) where it assembled its three BE2C aircraft.

On January 13, 1916, the General Officer commanding the Division inspected the Squadron, which was at that time, still short of two other Flights, that would make a complete squadron. This was the first inspection of any unit of the RFC in India.

The squadron was commanded by Captain C Y McDonald. This squadron's machine was the first military machine of the RFC to fly in the Indian sky when, on January 20, 1916, Captain McDonald made the first ever flight in history. Other 'firsts' were scored — Captain Colin Cooper and Lieutenant Gordon Dean flew for the first time and Lieutenant Hyghes reached a height of 7,000 ft.

On February 8, 1916, Captain Colin Cooper, Lieutenant Hughes and Lieutenant Gordon Dean looped the loop, the first time this had been done in India.

While the RFC squadrons on the Western Front were learning, by trial and error, skills of navigation in the air, recognition of troop concentrations of 'ours and theirs', locating enemy batteries and attempting air to ground communication for directing artillery fire and much later ground attacks on enemy targets, this lone squadron (No. 31) was doing very much the same in a different locale.

It was No. 31 that pioneered the method of cooperation with the artillery by trying out the old, crude wireless sets which were gradually becoming more reliable in terms of voice carrying, though the range was limited. One of the problems faced by the squadron was the ignorance of both the sides about each other. After the first not-so-successful attempt, Lieutenant Colonel L A Smith of the Royal Field Artillery laid down the basic qualifications for an Artillery Observer as:

"A successful observer of Artillery fire could only be an Artillery officer of some experience, who thoroughly knew what observations a Battery Commander required to utilise his Battery effectively."

Eventually, a compromise working formula was adopted which yielded good results for both the Artillery and the RFC crews.

By the middle of June 1916, Major C R Bradley took command of the squadron. He made a tour of the whole of NWFP to pinpoint and arrange a series of emergency landing grounds. He visited all the country around Kohat and Bannu and later went to Kurram district to Parachinnar. It was also decided to make Risalpur a permanent RFC station. All this was pioneering work which helped other squadrons that came to the Frontier after No. 31 had set up the initial facilities with the limited resources at its disposal.

The first time No. 31 went into action or as the staff called it, its 'first show', it operated air reconnaissance flights over hostile territory against the Kuki Khel Mohamands in October/ November 1916. Its pilots carried out bombing raids over Hafiz Kor, Gandab and Alikandi valleys.

On November 15, 12 wireless equipped machines flew and cooperated with the Army from Shabqadar Fort. They directed artillery fire at targets where they saw the enemy gathered in strength.

When the Jallianwala tragedy took place and rioting and disorder followed, No. 31 Squadron was ordered to restore order. In 1919, trouble in Kabul exploded and again No. 31 did its part in bringing hostilities to a close.

As other squadrons were formed or sent from Iraq or England, they benefited from the experience of the No. 31 air and ground crews. By the Twenties gradually for the Army more roads were built and for the Air Force, Risalpur, Kohat and Peshwar along with Bannu and Razmak became the main stations for training and rest. In Punjab, Ambala became the main hub both for training and as headquarters which later shifted to Delhi.

Every squadron rotated its three Flights on the Frontier for the crews to get to know the Frontier and gain practical experience.

During the Twenties, the squadron continued its Army cooperation work, while honing its skill that proved beyond doubt that the Air Force could independently conduct operations. Wing Commanders conducted operations that were closely watched by the RAF at higher levels, by the Army and by the civil administration.

In 1924, practice night bombing was commenced and good results were obtained, dropping from 1,000 ft on a target consisting of a bunch of flares to pinpoint the target.

In March 1925, members of the Legislative Assembly were taken up for flights from Delhi and they appeared extremely gratified at their experience.

This squadron can also take credit for having pioneered supply dropping in 1928 which eventually became a major part of their duties once they converted to transport aircraft during World War II.

In 1929, due to floods in the area between Quetta and Karachi, the squadron carried other supplies which later came to be known as 'aid to civil power' — a tradition that its successor in India, the Indian Air Force carries on even today (2010).

In 1933, experiments were carried out to judge as to how much time it would take to photograph an operational area. The task was accomplished in just several hours, another first for the squadron.

On May 31, 1935, at 3 am, a severe earthquake took place in Quetta causing serious damage to life and property. The RAF suffered 160 casualties, of which 52 were killed. The earthquake destroyed every building on the station. Rescue and repair work immediately commenced and three aircraft were airborne to assess the actual extent of devastation. The squadron was evacuated to Drigh Road, Karachi.

Operations and training continued side by side until in 1939, it was decided to convert the squadron to a bomber transport squadron. Valencia aircraft of No. 216 Squadron, RAF Meliopolis, Iraq, were flown from Alexandria to India whilst the remainder of the aircraft arrived crated and were assembled at the Air Depot, Karachi.

The squadron did its share of flying in operations against the Faqir of Ipi throughout 1940 and during this year, a complete Chitral relief was carried out by air.

The outbreak of hostilities against Japan in December 1941 found the Indian Command lamentably short of transport aircraft, for, with a detachment operating in the Middle East, only two serviceable DC2s remained with the squadron at Lahore. These were sent to fly between Calcutta and Rangoon carrying urgent stores and evacuating personnel until ultimately one was destroyed during a Japanese air raid on Mingaladon airfield.

Beginning April 1942, the Middle East detachment returned and the whole squadron was located at Akyab. Operations continued till the end of March, when the squadron was forced to move back to Calcutta. In the same month, the first DC3 aircraft arrived and later more of them. Operations continued.

By now, the US 10th Army Air Force were making regular flights over 'the Hump' from India to China and the Indian Command decided that Fort Hertz should be built up as an emergency landing ground and outpost.

In June 1942, the first two DC3s (named as Dakotas or Daks by the RAF), especially designed and built for troop carrying and supply dropping, were received by the squadron and soon put into commission. Fort Hertz was not the only place receiving attention from the squadron. Many other evacuee columns were also carried by air during the course of the war.

In early 1943, whilst the Japanese Air Force was engaged in tactical operations against our forces in the Arakan, the first Wingate (Chindit) expedition was launched in North Burma. Major General Orde Wingate, commanding the expedition, went from Imphal in an antique way with pack mules and bullock carts, but taking with him RAF Liaison Officers and radio apparatus, so that each column of the expedition could call for air aid and supplies when needed.

During the months of March and April 1943, the expedition was maintained behind the enemy lines by Dakotas of the squadron which had now moved to Agartala, assisted by Hudson aircraft of No. 194 Squadron, RAF.

It was during this operation that the squadron for the first time, dropped supplies by night as well as day. At first, fighter escorts were provided but when the bulk of infantry were beyond the Chindwin, this was impossible owing to the limited range of the fighters.

After the conclusion of the operation, General Wingate stated that he considered these supply dropping operations a brilliant and unexpected success.

In addition to the Wingate expedition the squadron's commitments were many and included continuous airlift for Army units in the Chin Hills and the maintainance of Sumprabum and Fort Hertz. The opening of the new campaigning season in the autumn of 1943 saw the squadron supporting the Army. In addition, several flights were made to China over 'the Hump' to Kunming. By this time, the squadron had been in operation non-stop for over a year.

In February 1944, the Japanese launched an offensive in the Arakan and cut off the 7th Division. No. 31, combining with other squadrons, carried out the air supply of the isolated 7th Division with great skill and courage. During the siege of Imphal, which lasted three months, the squadron was kept extremely busy carrying innumerable variety of loads to isolated spots.

In June 1945, the squadron moved to Kyaukpu on Ramree Island and though Rangoon had fallen in May, the lack of harbour and rail facilities and the effect of monsoon rains upon the dirt roads made it imperative that air transport should still be used.

In August 1945, the squadron moved back to Central India for training for glider and paratroop operations, to open the way to recapture Singapore. Soon after the Japanese surrender, the squadron was engaged in speeding up rescue and repatriation of Allied prisoners of war and internees.

During September 1945, another move was made to Kallang, Singapore, from where many sorties were made carrying essential supplies for POWs in Malaya (now Malaysia) and the Dutch East Indies (now Indonesia). By January 1946, the squadron was at Batavia where it was disbanded on September 30 and reformed at Mauripur, Karachi, in November.

By September 1947, the withdrawal of RAF units from India and Pakistan began and in consequence, this squadron moved to Palam (Delhi) from whence it detached 12 aircraft for refugee evacuation. It assisted in the centralisation of many RAF units spread over the country until it eventually returned to Karachi where it was disbanded on December 31, 1947.

The squadron was reformed in the UK on August 13, 1948, as a communication squadron. It had spent all its life in India since December 1915 to December 1947 — a period of 32 years that saw military aviation blossom and grow from a small enclosure of the Army to a formidable force in its own right. Its service in India and for India has been described in the foregoing paragraphs, for this was the first military aviation unit in Indian skies that prompted the members of the squadron to adopt as their motto: "First in the Indian Skies" — which has remained and is a part of India's military aviation history.

No. 27 Squadron, RAF
Motto: "Quam Celerrime ad Astra"

The history of this squadron is virtually the history of the Royal Air Force. Starting life as a fighter unit, No. 27 later flew in practically every major role open to a Service squadron. It acted as bomber, reconnaissance, Army cooperation, nightfighter, day and night interdiction, mercy rescue, transport, paratroop vehicle, conventional jet bomber (after the war) and missile delivery system.

Since its early dogfights over the Somme, its aircraft have operated among the baking mountains of India's North-West Frontier. During the disastrous Malayan campaign of 1941-42, over the steaming jungles of Burma, down the perilous air corridors to Berlin, across the arid desert wastes of Suez and Egypt; until its final tour of duty at an anonymous Strike Command dispersal aerodrome, with the devastating combination of the Vulcan/ Blue Steel missile.

Like many other squadrons of the RFC/ RAF, No. 27 Squadron dates its history from 1915. The first truly fighting squadron specifically designed for fighting as opposed to general duties, was No. 11 Squadron which was formed on February 14, 1915, and equipped with two-seater Vickers FE5s.

In the event, No. 11 came to be employed almost equally on reconnaissance and bombing duties. The first single-seat Scout unit to come into existence was No. 24 Squadron. On September 1, 1915, one Flight of No. 17 Squadron was detached. This nucleus became officially entitled No. 24 Squadron, RFC and on the 28th of the month, Major L G Hawker, VC DSO, arrived to his appointment.

Working almost non-stop, Hawker accomplished wonders, only to be thwarted in his efforts by receiving orders to detach one of his trained Flights as the nucleus of a newly forming squadron. On November 1, 1915, a simple handwritten order was placed on No. 24's headquarter notice board which detailed a list of some fifty men under the statement: "With effect from November 5, 1915, the undermentioned personnel will be known as No. 27 Squadron, Royal Flying Corps, under temporary command of Captain M Malcolm." Thus, a squadron was born and a tradition commenced.

By January 1916, the squadron was equipped with the Martinsyde G 100 Scout, a two-bay bi-plane having a wing span of 38 ft and powered by a 120 HP Beardmore engine. The aircraft carried a Lewis machine gun on a fixed mounting above the centre-section of the upper mainplane, firing above the propeller. Provision was made for the carriage of eight 20 lb or two 112 lb bombs under the fuselage.

It was at this time that the squadron carried the 'sobriquet' Elephant which was later to be painted on all the aircraft. In later years, the squadron was known as the 'Flying Elephants'; the aircraft began displaying the elephant symbol from April end 1916. In February 1916, the squadron was ordered to the Western

Front. It was allocated to the 10th (Army) Wing of 1 Brigade commanded by Colonel Herbert.

Operations began on a quiet note in March and April. Soon, a decision was taken by Lord Trenchard, then GOC of the Flying Corps to withdraw No. 27 from its original role of fighting due to the aircraft's limitations in that role. His intention was to utilise the Martinsyde's useful load-carrying capacity and long endurance in bomber and reconnaissance duties instead.

On July 1, 1916, the first battle of Somme commenced and the squadron was deployed, and operated on Army cooperation tasks. This was followed by the second battle and in September, the third battle. Flying operations continued long after October and April 1917 saw the start of the Battle of Arras in which the squadron also participated.

By September 1917, the squadron had been continuously deployed for 19 months in the field. It was now equipped with DH4 day bombers. The task assigned to the squadron was high level bombing.

On April 1, 1918, the Royal Flying Corps ceased to exist and passed into history, now being replaced by the Royal Air Force (RAF), an independent service on par with the Army and the Navy. By then DH9s had also been added to the stable of aircraft.

Throughout October 1918, the squadron mainly concentrated on bombing and strafing the retreating German forces. At 11 am on November 11, the Armistice came into force and the guns on both sides stopped firing. This applied to the Air Force as well.

In May 1919, No.99 Squadron, a DH9 day bomber unit, left its base at Aulnoye in France and flew by stages to Ambala (India) where it quickly became involved in operations against the Mahsuds. Soon it moved to Mianwali where on April 1, 1920, it was disbanded on paper and officially renumbered as No. 27 Squadron, RAF.

A few months later, along with No. 60 Squadron, No. 27 came under the command of No. 1 (Indian) Wing at Peshawar. Together, these two squadrons took part in operations against hostiles. On January 12, 1922, five DH9As of No. 27 accompanied by four DH10s from No. 60 Squadron conducted a bombing raid on Datta Khel, north of Dardoni where the tribesmen had taken refuge after ambushing an Army column in the Spinchilla Pass of North Waziristan.

On March 3, 1922, the Prince of Wales (later King Edward VIII) visited Risalpur and Nos. 27 and 60 Squadrons along with the Royal Horse Artillery provided a ceremonial Guard of Honour at the Naushera railway station.

During the early part of 1922, a decision was taken to garrison Razmak permanently and to construct a Central Waziristan Road linking the Jhandola Landa Road to the existing Bannu–Dardoni Road, North Waziristan.

In May 1922, Air Headquarters which had moved to Ambala became RAF Headquarters India, thereby, abolishing the old title of RAF India Group.

In January 1925, Nos. 27 and 60 made history by undertaking the first long distance formation flight from Risalpur to Calcutta and return. The Flight commenced on January 14 and landed at Calcutta on January 18, having completed 1,330 miles in fourteen and a quarter actual flying hours.

Early in 1925, bombing training was placed on a progressive basis to prepare for a competition inaugurated by Air Vice Marshal, Sir Edward Ellington, AOC-in-C, India, who had presented the Ellington Bombing Trophy for inter-unit competition.

In mid-December 1926, it was planned to have an air display in the new year — 1927. The display took place on February 21, 1927, on the Delhi Race Course. In November 1928, widespread revolt against King Amanullah Khan's rule took place in Afghanistan and violent mobs stormed Kabul in an attempt to dethrone him. News of the revolt reached Peshawar on December 27 and the British Minister there, Sir Francis Humphrys requested an immediate evacuation of the British population from Kabul.

At that time, RAF India did not possess any transport aircraft; the only aircraft available were DH9As of the Nos. 27 and 60 Squadrons and these were incapable of lifting a large number of passengers over any reasonably short period of time. The nearest RAF unit with proper troop carrying capability was No. 70 Squadron with its Vickers Victorias some 2,800 miles away at Baghdad, Iraq. This unit was immediately sent to Karachi.

In the meantime, all Ninaks (DH9As) of Nos. 27 and 60 Squadrons were stripped off military equipment such as gun and bomb racks in preparation for flying over Afghanistan, the crews being hastily issued with visas to their passports stamped as 'visitors'.

On December 18, 1928, the first aircraft took off and flew 150 miles to Kabul taking a Popham Panel to be dropped in the British Legation there in order that Humphrys could arrange for messages to be passed to the aircraft.

On December 23, 1928, the first phase of evacuation commenced and continued till January 1, 1929 by which date the last of the 134 women and children were taken out safely. From January 28 to February 25, 1929, the final phase of evacuation took place, surmounting the vagaries of the worst ever winter in Afghanistan.

This first ever air evacuation on any large scale resulted in 586 people including 41 tons of baggage being airlifted and involving 57,438 miles of flying.

In December 1928, came another first. Parachutes were issued to the air crew consisting of Irwin seat packs for pilots and lap type for air-gunners. After initial resistance by the pilots, regulations were issued making it mandatory for all pilots and air-gunners to carry parachutes with them on all flights.

No. 60 Squadron, RAF
Badge: A Markhor's Head Affrontee
Motto: "Per Adua ad Aethera Tendo" (I Strive Through Difficulties to the Sky)

The markhor (an animal) is found in the region of the Khyber Pass and the squadron first adopted the head of this animal as its badge when it was operating on the North-West Frontier in the early 1920s.

No. 60 Squadron, RFC, was formed at Gosport, Hampshire, on April 30, 1916, and a month later, crossed to France as a single-seat fighter squadron. Its work as a fighter squadron during nearly two and a half years' war service was outstanding. It claimed the destruction of 274 enemy aircraft and gained 49 decorations, including a Victoria Cross won by Captain W A Billy Bishop.

Disbanded in January 1920, the squadron was revived in India as a bomber squadron a few months later and in the years up to World War II, did a great deal of valuable work in helping to quell various tribal disturbances on the North-West Frontier. In February 1941, it left India for Mingaladon near Rangoon.

It was towards the end of 1927 that an almost legendary figure made his appearance on the North-West Frontier — Aircraftsman 1, T E Shaw known to millions of people as 'Lawrence of Arabia'. Posted to Miranshah in June 1928 as a clerk on the strength of No. 60 Squadron, Shaw performed all the normal duties of his rank and trade and never once left the confines of his trade during his short service there. He was a popular figure with the airmen.

Shaw's rare collection of books, many of them prized first editions, was eventually presented to the Miranshah Fort library. Eventually, due to ill-founded political pressures, it was considered expedient to remove Shaw from India and on January 12, 1929, he sailed from Bombay in the SS *Rajputana* bound for Plymouth.

No. 11 Squadron, RAF
Badge: Two Eagles Volant in Pale
Motto: "Ociores Aerioresque Aquilis"

Two eagles flying together is based on the idea that in World War I, this squadron did most of its fighting in two-seater aircraft. The eagles symbolise speed and strength.

No. 11 Squadron, RFC, was formed at Netheravon, Wiltshire, on February 14, 1915 from a nucleus of No. 7 Squadron, and in July of that year, crossed to France equipped with the Vickers FB5 ('Gunbus') two-seat pusher bi-plane; it was the first homogeneous two-seat fighter unit to join the Expeditionary Force.

The squadron was soon in action and at first the FB5 with its movable front Lewis gun was treated with respect by the enemy. Many notable combats were fought, and for a particularly determined and successful attack on an enemy aircraft on November 7, 1915, Lieutenant G S M Insall was awarded the Victoria Cross. By March 1916, the FB5 was outclassed by the Fokker mono-plane and the squadron was temporarily issued with some single-seat scouts — Bristols and Nieuports.

It was at this time that 2nd Lieutenant Albert Ball, regarded by many as the most heroic of all the great World War I fighter pilots, joined the squadron. It was with No. 11 that Ball achieved his early triumphs and won his first decoration, the MC. The squadron was gradually re-equipped with FE2Bs and the Bristol and Nieuport Scouts were transferred to No. 60 Squadron, Lieutenant Ball going with them. Photography and reconnaissance were the chief tasks of No. 11 during the latter part of 1916 and early 1917 and in June, it was re-equipped with Bristol fighters. From then on, the squadron was engaged in intensive fighting.

After the Armistice, No. 11 Squadron went to Germany with the occupying Army, but returned to England in 1919 and at the end of that year, was disbanded.

Re-formed at Andover in 1923, No. 11 Squadron was a Home-based day-bomber unit until 1928 and during this period was successfully equipped with DH9As, Fairey Fawns and Hawker Horselys. At the end of 1928, it sailed for India and by the beginning of April 1929, was established at Risalpur as part of No. 2 (Indian) Wing, for duty on the North-West Frontier. Here, during the inter-war years, the squadron, flying Westland Wapitis and later, Hawker Harts took part in many operations undertaken by the RAF in maintaining law and order.

Shortly before the outbreak of World War II, the squadron was reequipped with the Bristol Blenheim and sent to Singapore to reinforce the Far East Command. It returned to India in April 1940. This squadron was in India from January 1929 to August 1939.

No. 39 Squadron, RAF
Badge: A Winged Bomb
Motto: "Die Noctuque" (By Day and Night)

No.39 Squadron, RFC, came into being on April 15, 1916, during World War I, with headquarters at Hounslow. It was the first squadron to be formed especially for Home Defence. It gained distinction for its part in defeating the German airship menace. On the night of September 3, 1916, Lieutenant W Leefe Robinson shot down the Schutte-Lanz airship at Cuffley, a feat for which he was awarded the Victoria Cross. This was the first German airship shot down on British soil. Squadron pilots shot down three other airships.

During the Allies' final advance which began in August 1918, the enemy was forced to abandon the Belgian coast. This made it improbable that further airship or aeroplane raids would be made. In October 1918, it was decided to send this squadron overseas. No. 39 Squadron, equipped with Bristol fighters went to France at the beginning of November, but the Armistice intervened before it could be deployed.

On November 16, 1918, No. 39 was disbanded, but in 1919, its number plate was transferred to No. 37 Night-fighter Squadron, then at Biggin Hill. No. 39 now became a day-bomber squadron. Initially a cadre, the new No. 39 Squadron reformed for its formation flying at some of the early RAF displays at Hendon.

In the winter of 1928–29, the squadron went to India for service on the North-West Frontier and in early 1940, moved to Aden to reinforce the Middle East Command.

No. 5 Squadron, RAF
Badge: A Maple Leaf
Motto: "Frangas Non Electas" (Thou Mayest Break but Shall not Bend Me)

The maple leaf in the badge reflects the squadron's close association with the Canadian Corps (1917-18).

For most of its existence, No. 5 Squadron has lived and worked in close cooperation with the Army. It was formed for this purpose at Farnborough on July 26, 1913, and served on the Western Front in a corps role from August 15, 1914, to February 1, 1920 (at the end of World War I), having made history for the RFC by forcing down the first German aircraft. It was disbanded in September 1919 and reformed at Quetta in India by renumbering as No. 48 Squadron.

Here again, it served as an Army cooperation unit, on the North-West Frontier until June 1940, when it began to work up in the bomber role. It was not until February 1941 that it became a fighter squadron, although still equipped with pre-war Army cooperation aircraft (Hawker Audaxes) and stationed at Risalpur.

Two months later, ‘A’ Flight was sent to Dum Dum for the defence of Calcutta, whence the whole squadron moved in December 1941. In May 1942, a detachment was sent to Burma to join No. 146 Squadron, and metamorphosis took place later that month whereby the units at Dinjan became No. 5 Squadron and the units at Dum Dum became No. 146 Squadron.

On June 17, 1942, the first operational fighter sortie was flown with Curtiss Mohawks as equipment. From then, the squadron engaged in bomber-escort, standing patrols and close-support attacks and claimed its first enemy aircraft on August 20, 1942. In January 1943, the first Rhubarbs were flown, on the Imphal and Chindwin Rivers. These became an integral part of No 5’s operations.

In June, the squadron became non-operational to convert to Hurricanes II D’s and was not able to use these on vehicles until the following January. On the 8th of that month, 27 lorries and 14 bullock carts were destroyed. Later, the squadron transferred to Hurricane II C’s and returned to more normal bomber escort and interdiction sorties.

These consisted of escorts to supply dropping Dakotas, Rhubarbs and dive-bombing. In June, the squadron again became non-operational, retiring to Ceylon and after some anti-malarial spraying in August, converted to Thunderbolts in October, returning to operations at Nazir in December. These consisted of escorts to supply dropping Dakotas, Rhubarbs and dive-bombing with wing-mounted 500-lb bombs.

These were used on No. 5’s last operations which were bombing attacks in support of the invasion of Rangoon. With the war over, No. 5 returned eventually to India where it converted to Tempests and on August 1, 1947, the squadron was disbanded at Mauripur.

No. 20 Squadron, RAF
Badge: An Eagle in Front of a Rising Sun
Motto: "Facta Non Verba" (Deeds Not Words)

This squadron was formed as a fighter unit on September 1, 1915, during World War I at Netheravon (UK). It was equipped with FE2Bs and Martinsyde Scouts when it went to France in 1916 and flew offensive patrols. For a whole year, the squadron was flying from Clairmarais as a part of No. 11 Wing, RFC.

During 1918, the squadron built up its operations to a peak in May when it destroyed 56 German aircraft. By the end of the war, its claim was to 613 enemy aircraft destroyed.

Six months after the war ended, the squadron was at Risalpur in India, still with Bristol fighters but in the Army cooperation role. For over twenty years, the squadron was in and out of action on the North-West Frontier, policing the raiding tribesmen on this turbulent Frontier.

Flight Lieutenant Basil Embry (later Air Chief Marshal) while serving in England, always wanted to serve in India. He got his wish in 1934 when he was posted to the Wing headquarters at Peshawar and served in that capacity taking part in active operations. In October 1937, he was given command of No. 20 Squadron.

About six months after his taking over No. 20 Squadron, 'A' Flight of the Indian Air Force's No. 1 Squadron, was sent to Peshawar to operate under Embry's command and "I regarded it as a privilege to have them serving under me. It was the first time that the Indian Air Force had seen active service, but they quickly acclimatised themselves and built up a fine reputation. Among them was Flying Officer S Mukerjee, now their Chief of Air Staff."

Early in 1942, the squadron was in a low state being used to form No. 151 OTU at Peshawar. It was not until January 1943 that the squadron was really in business again when it reequipped with Hurricanes for tactical recce work. In March, the squadron returned to the fighter role at Peshawar and began to work up on Hurricane II for tactical recce work. It was not until December that the squadron became operational from Nidania, its first strike being against petrol tanks at Pauktaw in Burma on Christmas eve.

The squadron's first chance to use the 40 mm cannon came soon after when it sank a boat at Rathedaung. It continued its recce commitment in 1944 as well as strikes on Japanese motor and river transport. In May, the squadron had a detachment at Imphal for work against Japanese armour.

In November 1944, 'A' Flight converted to Hurricane IV's with rockets and in December, the squadron moved to Sapam to become fully operational once more. The fighting was intense and successful. In February 1945, it went on to 'cab-rank' operations for the Irrawaddy crossing and stepped up its activities in the following months.

One of its most successful operations was to blast open Fort Dufferin with rockets. By May, the pace was slackening and in June, the operations ceased. Conversion to Spitfires followed soon and in September, No. 20 went to Bangkok to show the flag.

Soon after, the squadron retired to India and converted to Hawker Tempest 2's at Agra. After that, the squadron moved to the UK.

No. 28 Squadron, RAF
Badge: In Front of a Demi-Pegasus
Motto: "Quicquid Agas Age" (Whatsoever You May Do, Do)

The demi-Pegasus represents the white horse on the downs near Yatesbury where the squadron first became an operational unit and the faces signify Italy where No. 28 Squadron served in World War I.

Formed at Gosport (UK) on November 7, 1915, from a nucleus of No. 22 Squadron, it spent 18 months as a training unit. In July 1917, it moved to Yatesbury where in September it reequipped with Sopwith Camels. These it took to France the following month.

Hardly had it bloodied itself in the Third Battle of Ypres before a movement order came through sending the squadron to Italy. It arrived in Milan on November 12, with all its aircraft crated and was flying operationally on the 14th, a tribute to the non-stop work of the ground crews. At first, the squadron flew escort to bombing raids but it was found by the New Year that there was such little enemy air opposition that it was more effective to sling 4x25 lb bombs under the Camels and use them in the fighter bomber role.

The first such operation was on February 19, 1918, against airship sheds at Casara and was a great success. However in April, the British troops were transferred and No. 28 Squadron remained on the Italian Front. It now turned to more offensive patrols and the summer of 1918 provided intense activity, the squadron destroying 53 aircraft in three months. In fact, it was not until October when the Austrian Armies were defeated, that there was a pause in No. 28's fighting. The squadron remained in Italy till February 1919, when it returned to Yatesbury.

The squadron was reformed by renumbering No. 114 Squadron at Ambala, India on February 1, 1920. It now became an Army cooperation squadron, working with British forces keeping the peace on India's North-West Frontier, flying Bristol fighters, then Wapitis and then Audaxes. With this machine, it entered World War II and did not reequip until September 1941, when Lysanders came. These it used unsuccessfully in operations on the Salween Front in 1942 and eventually received Hurricanes for its Army cooperation tasks in December. For the rest of the war in Burma, it flew tactical reconnaissance sorties for the Army with Hurricanes.

It was in this squadron that Lieutenant Hardit Singh Malik, of the Royal Flying Corps (RFC) served in 1917-18 during World War I, on the Western Front in France, Belgium and Italy.

Landmarks and Milestones

1884 — Formation of a Balloon Section attached to Royal Engineers that took part in the Bechuanaland Expedition.

1892 — Balloon depot and factory set up permanently at Aldershot, UK.

1894 — Balloon factory established at South Farnborough.

1901 — Aero Club of United Kingdom founded by F S Hedges and Hon C S Rolls.

1901 — Royal Engineers' Balloon Section comes to Rawalpindi.

1907 — Balloon demonstration held at Agra for the Amir of Afghanistan.

1907, October 5 — First successful flight of the Army airship Nulli Secundus over London.

1908, June 8 — Alliott Verdon Roe, first Englishman to fly an all-British built aeroplane.

1908 — Balloon Section sent to Bengal Engineer Group (Indian Army) based at Roorkee (UP).

1909, December 10 — Colonel H S Massey, President of the Aerial League of the British Empire, arrives in Calcutta. Its Indian branch opened and General Sir O'Moore Creagh, Commander-in-Chief, Indian Army, assumes the Presidency of its Indian branch.

1910, March 8 — First aviator's certificate of the Royal Aero Club of the United Kingdom granted to J C T Moore Brabazon.

1910, December — Crates containing two Bristol Boxkite aeroplanes unloaded at Diamond Harbour, Calcutta.

1911 — Crates containing one Bristol Boxkite sent by train from Calcutta to Aurangabad, for participating in Indian Army manoeuvres to be held in January under General Rimington, Indian Army.

1911, January 14 — Aeroplane was erected and assembled on site with Pilot H M Jullerot, who flight tested the machine in preparation for a flight the next day.

1911, January 15 — World's first military air reconnaissance took place near Jalna, Western India.

1911, January 15 — First aerial reconnaissance report in prescribed Army form written by the Observer of the flight Captain Sefton Brancker, RA, and submitted personally by him to General Douglas Haig, then Chief of General Staff, Indian Army.

1911, April 1 — Air Battalion of Royal Engineers was set up in Larkhill.

1911, December — Establishment of the first naval flying school at Eastchurch.

1911, December — Lieutenant C R Samson, RN, made the first successful flight from the deck of a British warship HMS *Africa*.

1912, March — Horace Short produced the first successful seaplane in England.

1912, May 13 — The Royal Flying Corps (RFC) formed by Royal Warrant. From April 13, 1912 to May 7, 1914, seven squadrons (No. 1 to 7) were formed.

1912, June 19 — Central Flying School opened at Upavon Downs with Captain Godfrey Paine, RN, as the first Commandant.

1912 — Intense debate and discussion on aviation within the Indian Army, the civil and business establishment and the English language press on the desirability of setting up a flying school in India.

1913 — Viceroy's Executive Council discusses plans for setting up a flying school in India.

1913 — The double-winged pilot's badge was approved in Order No. 40 of 1913 for use by officers and airmen whilst they remain efficient pilots.

1913, March 29 — Government of India earmarked and sanctioned Rs 2.33 lakh for setting up a flying training school at Sitapur in the United Provinces.

1913, July — During naval manoeuvres, two seaplanes were successfully flown off the deck of HMS *Hermes*.

1913, November 22 — Record long-distance flight of 445 miles made by Captain C A H Longcroft of No. 2 Squadron, RFC.

1913, December 1 — Captain S D Massey of the 29th Punjab Regiment appointed as the Commandant of the Sitapur Flying School with three other officers from the Indian Army as Instructors.

1914, January — Flying School set up with three aeroplanes. Plans made for the first course of instruction to begin in September 1914.

1914, March 27 — General Sir Beauchamp Duff, Commander-in-Chief of the Indian Army inspected the Sitapur Indian Flying School. After his inspection, he was taken in an aircraft on a flight round the school which was piloted by Captain Massey, the Commandant of the school.

1914, July 1 — Naval Wing of the RFC became the Royal Naval Air Service (RNAS).

1914, August 4 — Once World War I started, the flying school was closed, the pilots were posted to various active squadrons of the Royal Flying Corps (RFC) either in England or France or Mesopotamia (Iraq). At the end of World War II, the flying school premises were handed over to the United Provinces Government to set up a Police Training School to train drivers and mechanics. The original runway today (in 2010) is a track on which motor drivers are trained.

1914, August 8 — First ever air raid alarm in Eastchurch area of England.

1914, August 13–15 — RFC squadrons flew to France for service with the British Expeditionary Force (BEF) of which the Indian Corps was a part.

1914, August 19 — First air reconnaissance of the war made by Captain Joubert de la Ferte (later Air Chief Marshal) and Lieutenant G W Mappleback.

1914, August 22 — First RFC casualty caused by enemy action (Sergeant Major Jillings wounded in the leg).

1914, August 22 — First British aircraft to be shot down in war.

1914, August 25 — First enemy aircraft shot down in air combat.

1914, August 21 — Lieutenant D L Pitcher was the first aviator of the Indian Army to take part in an operational flight serving as an Observer on board an aircraft piloted by Lieutenant W G S Mitchell during a reconnaissance sortie in France.

1914, September — Wireless machines of No. 4 Squadron first used to observe artillery fire at the Battle of Aisne.

1914, September 28 — German aircraft adopt distinctive national markings. A black Maltese Cross painted on both sides of the tail and the wings and the fuselage.

1914, November 12 — Orders issued for all British aeroplanes on the Western Front to have national markings of the British nation flag (the Union Jack). The same introduced for RFC aircraft on the North-West Frontier, India from 1916.

1914, October — Captain S D Massey of the Indian Army was given command of No. 1 Reserve Air Squadron in UK.

1914, October–December — Although Indian Army officers (there were five of them) initially flew on attachment to the Royal Flying Corps (RFC), by the end of the year, personnel and equipment from the Indian Central Flying School, Sitapur was formed into an Aviation Detachment paid for by the Indian Exchequer and used to support Indian Army operations in Iraq and Egypt.

1914, November — In response to the Turkish threat to the Suez Canal, an Indian Army contingent was sent under the command of Major General Sir Alexander Wilson to the site.

1914, November — An RFC detachment from the Indian Central Flying School formed to protect the Suez Canal. Captain S D Massey sent from the UK to command this detachment. Three civilian mechanics and three airframes without engines sent.

1914, November 27 — The detachment flew its first reconnaissance sortie.

1914, December 21 — First aeroplane raid on England.

1915, January — First successful photographic reconnaissance of the La Bassee Canal.

1915, January — For the first time, the Clock Code System of artillery ranging from the air instituted.

1915, January 19–20 — First air raid on Great Britain by an Zeppelin airship.

1915, March 26 — Captain Philip W L Broke Smith, RE, a former commander of the Indian Army's first and only Balloon Section, was appointed Assistant Director of Aviation, Indian Army, with the rank of Major. His first task was to establish an aerodrome and a depot at Basra, in Mesopotamia (Iraq which he did).

1915, April 17 — Broke Smith returned to Bombay, set up an aircraft depot there and arranged for the dispatch of 'A' Flight of aircraft and crews to Basra.

1915, April 22 — First enemy gas attack in Second Battle of Ypres.

1915, April 30 — Broke Smith left for Basra along with Captain Reilly who had been transferred from Egypt to command the new Flight in the rank of Major. Along with them left four mechanics and two Maurice Farmans were also sent to Basra.

1915, April — A few pilots from Australia and New Zealand arrived in response to a request from the Government of India to join the new Flight and help in setting up the Aircraft Park being completed by volunteers from Territorial Battalions from India.

1915, April 26 — Action for which first Victoria Cross (VC) was awarded for gallantry in the air to Lt. W.B. Rhodes – Moorhowse.

1915, May — Two British officers, Broke Smith and Reilly, were joined by four British and five Indian mechanics. With the assistance of a few Indian pioneers, they set up camp next to an Arab cemetery and made a make-shift aerodrome.

1915, August 22 — In a telegram to the India Office in London, the Viceroy of India said that though the Indian Exchequer was paying for the air operations in Mesopotamia and Egypt, this unit of 'A' Flight should be expanded to a squadron, but agreed to the War Office demand that it (the Flight in Basra) would come under the control of the War Office and through it get absorbed and become part of the Royal Flying Corps (RFC).

1915, November — All officers and men of the Mesopotamian Flight at Basra were absorbed into No. 30 Squadron, RFC. The Egyptian detachment was later also merged with this squadron.

1915, December 26 — The first military air unit landed in India. 'A' Flight of No. 31 Squadron, RFC arrived at Naushera in NWFP and their 2C and 2E aircraft were the first RFC aircraft to be seen in the Indian skies.

1916, January — The War Office was against reviving the now defunct Flying School at Sitapur to provide trained pilots for the forces. This, in effect, ended the Indian Army's sustained efforts to have its own air arm. The insistence of making the Indian Army's small Flying Corps, a part of the RFC, was a clear indication of the hardening of the War Office's attitude against a separate identity for military aviation in India, although at that point in time, all the five Indian Flying Corps officers and pilots were of European descent.

1916, January — Formation flying introduced.

1916, March — 'B' and 'C' Flights of the No. 31 Squadron joined the 'A' Flight and the entire squadron moved to Risalpur.

1916, March — RFC operations begin in Northern Waziristan in India.

1916, April 15 — First use of aircraft for delivering food and supplies to beleaguered garrison at Kut-el-Amara.

1916, May 31— Battle of Jutland. First air cooperation in naval action.

1916, July 1 — Contact patrols first instituted at the Battle of Somme.

1916, September 15 — First aerial cooperation with tanks at the Battle of Flers Courcelette.

1917, May 7 — First night aeroplane raid on London.

1917, May 20 — First German submarine (U-Boat) sunk by aircraft in the North Sea.

1917, June 28 — General Sir E H H Allenby appointed to command the Egyptian Expeditionary Force, whose air component was the small Indian Flying Corps, later merged with No. 30 Squadron, RFC.

1917, August 2 — Sopwith Pup aeroplane landed successfully on the deck of HMS *Furious* by Squadron Commander E H Dunning.

1917, September — A second RFC Squadron No. 114 was formed at Lahore from a nucleus provided by No. 31 Squadron.

1917, October 5 — Formation of the Palestine Brigade, RFC, whose commander was Brigadier General Sir Sefton Brancker.

1917, November 29 — The Air Force (Constitution) Act, which created the Royal Air Force) received royal assent.

1918, January 2 — Air Ministry formed – the only country and the first one to set up a separate Air Force and a separate Ministry to control and regulate it.

1918, March — Both the Nos. 31 and 114 Squadrons were in action, bombing and strafing the Marri tribes area.

1918, April 1 — Royal Flying Corps and Royal Naval Air Service amalgamated as the Royal Air Force.

1918–20 — Two new gallantry awards to correspond to the Distinguished Service Cross (DSC) of the Royal Navy and the Military Cross (MC) of the Army were instituted. They were "the Distinguished Flying Cross (DFC) for flying in the face of the enemy and the Air Force Cross (AFC) for civil flying."

1918, September 19 — Final campaign in Palestine opened. Destruction by air attack of the Turkish VII Army in Wadi el Fara, Palestine.

1918, October 14 — RAF Handley Page bomber dropped the largest bomb used by the British during this war – 1,650 lb.

1918, October 30 — Armistice signed with Turkey.

1918, November 11 — Armistice signed with Germany.

1918, November 29 — First flight from Cairo to India made by Captain Ross Smith and two mechanics.

1918, November — Major General W G H Salmond, AOC of Middle East RAF, commenced the very first aerial inspection tour of India and arrived in Delhi on December 12.

1919, January 11 — Major General Sir Hugh Trenchard, who had earlier commanded the Independent Air Force during the last six months of the war, was reappointed as the Chief of Air Staff.

1919, February 12 — Winston Churchill becomes Secretary of State for War and Air.

1919, March — Air operations commence in the Third Afghan War and in Waziristan. In May, operations against Sheikh Mahmud.

1919, June 14–15 — First direct non-stop flight across the Atlantic by aeroplane. Pilot was Captain John Alcock and navigator, Lieutenant Arthur Whitten Brown.

1919, July 2–13 — British Airship R34 flew across the Atlantic and back.

1919, August 4 — Present ranks of RAF brought into use.

1919, November 11 — Paris-London Air Mail started.

1919, November 12 — Captain Ross Smith and Lieutenant K M Smith left England on a flight to Australia.

1919, December 11 — White Paper on permanent organisation of the Royal Air Force presented to Parliament by Winston Churchill, then Secretary of Air.

1920, January–February — Successful air cooperation in ground operations by the Camel Corps against the Mullah in Somaliland.

1920, February 5 — RAF Cadet College opened at Cranwell.

1920, April — Nos. 27 and 60 Squadrons were paired and came under the control of the newly formed No. 1 (Indian) Wing at Peshawar. At this time, the whole of the RAF in India was still organised on merely Group basis.

1920, July 3 — First RAF public pageant/ display held at Hendon.

1920, August 9 — Formation of the South African Air Force.

1921, January — RAF Airship Service disbanded.

1921, March 12–30 — Cairo Conference called by Winston Churchill to examine the proposed administration of the League of Nations mandated territory after World War I. It was here that the decision to administer the mandated Mesopotamia (Iraq), by giving the sole administrative responsibility to the RAF alone was taken, thereby saving the British Exchequer the expense of maintaining a large land force in the territory.

1921, April 1 — Formation of the Royal Australian Air Force.

1921, June 23 — Air route from Cairo to Baghdad opened, operating an airmail service.

1922, January 1 — Proclamation Day Parade held at Risalpur, royal salute fired, Union Jack hoisted and national anthem played. While the Army had its regimental songs, the RAF had no music for its band during the march past.

1922, March 3 — The Prince of Wales (later King Edward VIII) visited Risalpur and inspected Nos. 27 and 60 Squadrons.

1922, April 1 — Formation of the Royal Canadian Air Force.

1922, April 4 — RAF Staff College opened at Andover.

1922, May — For the RAF, the headquarters moved to Ambala and became the RAF Headquarters India, thereby abolishing the old title of RAF India Group.

1922, June — Air Vice Marshal Sir John Salmond arrived in India on a fact-finding visit to assess the poor state of the RAF in India and make recommendations to the Government of India for improving its service.

1922 — Salmond's recommendation that the rank of the Air Officer Commanding RAF in India be raised on par with Army Commanders and a new organisation and administration be formed with a definite stated policy for the air service. This was accepted by the Viceroy of India.

1922, September — Air operations in Kurdistan.

1922, October 1 — Military control of Mesopotamia (Iraq) taken over by the Royal Air Force. Air Marshal Sir John Salmond was put in the command.

1923 — Risalpur constituted as No. 2 (Indian) Wing RAF. Wing Commander R C M Pink appointed as its first CO on November 23.

1923, March — RAF action against Sheikh Mahmud in Iraq.

1923, March 15 — Unit identification markings standardised.

1923 — AVM Sir Philip Game replaced Air Commodore T I Webb Bowen as AOC-in-C India and the RAF Headquarters moved from Ambala to Raisina, New Delhi.

1925, October 22 — No. 1 Apprentices Wing formed at Halton to train future technicians for the Royal Air Force.

1925, January — Nos. 27 and 60 Squadrons made history by undertaking the first long distance formation flight from Risalpur to Calcutta and return.

1925, March — Nos. 27 and 60 Squadrons were the first air units to occupy Miranshah, each with eight aircraft.

1925, March 9 — An independent air operation was carried out under the command of Wing Commander R C M Pink, CO, 2nd (Indian) Wing without ground troops and was adjudged to be a complete success, "despite a certain amount of nit-picking by some Army authorities."

1925, October 25 — Long distance service flight from Cairo to Kano, Nigeria, and back completed by November 19. Three aircraft led by Squadron

Leader A Conningham. This officer, during World War II, commanded the RAF's Desert Air Force in North Africa and supported actively the operations and final success of the 8th Army headed by General B L Montgomery against General Rommel.

1926, March 1–June 26 — Four aircraft flown from Cairo to Cape and back and subsequently to England under the command of Wing Commander C W H Pulford.

1927, January 1 — Imperial Defence College opened.

1927, February 21 — First ever air display in which both Nos. 27 and 60 Squadrons along with other units took part in formation flying. Each formation consisting of nine DH9As took off together, turned outwards and then flew across each other over the centre of the Delhi race course in front of the VIP stand. First in V Formation and then in Flights astern. The display was adjudged as a grand success.

1927, September 26 — Schneider Trophy contest won for Britain by Flight Lieutenant A M Webster in a Supermarine S5.

1927, October 17 — Flight led by Group Captain Cave Brown-C, left England for Singapore in four Short Brothers built Flying Boats.

1927, December 10–11 — Nos. 27 and 60 Squadrons cooperated for the first time by providing an aerial escort to King Amanullah Khan of Afghanistan and his entourage and his train for the journey via Kandahar through Quetta and Jacobabad to Karachi.

1928, June — Aircraftsman T E Shaw, earlier known as "Lawrence of Arabia," posted to Miranshah as a clerk on the strength of No. 60 Squadron. After a short stay, he was posted back and sailed from Bombay on January 12, 1929, bound for Plymouth.

1928, February — Defence of Aden placed under the control of RAF.

1928, October — Further reorganisation of the RAF. Nos. 1, 2 and 3 Wings at Kohat, Risalpur and Quetta, with one squadron at Group Headquarters at Peshawar. Air Headquarters at Ambala, with one squadron. Aircraft Park at Lahore. Aircraft Depot at Drigh Road, Karachi.

1928, December — Two more squadrons arrived, taking the total strength of the RAF in India to eight squadrons.

1928, December 23 — Royal Air Force evacuated women and children during the Afghan rebellion.

1929, April — Squadron Leader A G Jones Williams and Flight Lieutenant N H Jenkins flew from Cranwell in the UK to Karachi in India non-stop.

1929, September 6-7 — Flying Officer H R D Waghorn in a Supermarine seaplane won the Schneider Trophy contest.

1930, August — Flight from England to Canada and back by the Airship R100.

1930, October 4 — Loss of Airship R101 on its proving flight from England to India. Lord Thomson, Secretary of State for Air, and Major General (Air Vice Marshal) Sir Sefton Brancker, first Director of Civil Aviation, and others killed when the airship crashed in a storm while flying over France and was burnt.

1930, April — Long awaited replacement for the Wapiti arrives. DH9A comes to No. 27 Squadron.

1930, June — Seven thousand strong Afridi *lashkar* advancing on Peshawar as a part of Frontier Gandhi's agitation bombed and strafed.

1930, August 15 — Martial Law was declared in Peshawar District and remained in force for the next 18 months. Daily reconnaissance flights and ground support to troops engaged by hostiles.

1930, September — Bi-annual relief of Chitral garrison. Nos. 27 and 60 Squadrons provide air cover for the relief column for their passage through hostile territory.

1930–31 — Air action against tribal disorders in South Kurdistan instigated by Sheikh Mahmud.

1931, May 13 — Sheikh Mahmud surrendered.

1931, September 29 — Royal Air Force won the Schneider Trophy outright (Flight Lieutenant J N Boothman in a Supermarine S6).

1931, September 29 — World air-speed record of 407.5 mph set up by Flight Lieutenant G H Stainforth, RAF, in a S6 seaplane.

1933, January — No. 28 (AC) Squadron carried out long-distance flight from India to Singapore to develop a landplane route for the purpose of possible reinforcement of the RAF Far East Command. After that, this flight was repeated annually.

1933, February 6 — Squadron Leader O R Gayford and Flight Lieutenant G E Nicholetts flew from Cranwell to Walvis Bay, South-West Africa – a distance of 5,340 miles covered in 57 hours 25 minutes without landing.

1933, April 1 — Formation of the Indian Air Force. However, the date of the birth of the IAF has been changed to October 8, 1932, the day on which the IAF Act came into force and the first batch of six officers received their commissions.

1933, April 3 — First flight over Mount Everest.

1933, May — Operations against Mohamands and Bajaur continued till August 10 with aircraft from Nos. 27 and 60 Squadrons bombing the stronghold of the Khan of Kotkai who submitted to the government on August 13.

1934 — RAF's forward landing ground at Razmak, adjacent to the fort, named Queen Alexandra Piquet.

1934, December — London to Australia air route opened.

1935, August — An old outlaw, the Haji of Turngzai, and his three sons raised the banner of revolt in the Mohamand country. On August 20, Khel and Isa Khel villages were bombed by Nos. 27 and 60 aircraft. After a pitched battle with the Army column which ended on September 29, the hostiles submitted on October 1. During this operation, lasting six weeks, 256 sorties were flown in support of ground operations.

1936 — Routine flights and training and reconnaissance flights for photographing and mapping of the Frontier territories. Also contact air patrols.

1936, May — Home Defence Force organised into four commands – Bomber, Fighter, Coastal and Training Commands.

1936 — Official notification of legal approval for the squadron badge given to No. 27 Squadron. This order No. 256/36 given by the Air Ministry also announced the cessation of the use of unit role being included in the squadron official title.

1936, November — Open rebellion/*jehad* by Mirza Ali Khan, the self-styled Faqir of Ipi.

1937, January 17 — No. 37 Squadron from Kohat and No. 11 from Risalpur flew on a round trip to Singapore and back as a form of reinforcement to the Far East Command of the RAF.

1937, February 6–7 — Two British officers killed during an ambush by tribesmen on an Army patrol in Mahsud territory. Tribe held responsible and fined. Mahsuds refused to surrender killers. Nos. 27 and 60 Squadrons carried ground support and reconnaissance and bombing. Conflict spread. By middle of April, 40,000 regular troops and 5,000 militia in Waziristan deployed. The air element, apart from Nos. 27 and 60, had No. 20 Squadron operating from Miranshah, Nos. 11 and 39 operating from Arawali, and the Bomber-Transport Flight from Kohat.

1937, April 1 — Formation of the Royal New Zealand Air Force.

1937, July 30 — Admiralty (Royal Navy) took over complete control of the Fleet Air Arm.

1937, August — Air Chief Marshal Sir Cyril Newall took over as the Chief of Air Staff, RAF. He was commissioned into the 2nd Gurkha Rifles of the Indian Army and later was one of the four Flying Instructors of the Indian Central Flying School at Sitapur, United Provinces, India.

1937, August–September — Western Mahsuds and Tori Khel tribes came to terms with the government and were fined.

1937, December — General situation gradually returned to normal.

1938, March — Operations commence again as the Faqir of Ipi was creating ferment among tribesmen of the Madda Khel area.

1938, June — Madda Khel submitted to terms and evicted the Faqir who fled to Kharre.

1938, June — The first modern aircraft, the Bristol Blenheim I came to India and No. 11 Squadron was equipped with it in July.

1939, August 28 — No. 27 Squadron, RAF, received its Mobilisation Orders which entailed splitting the unit into three separate formations. 'A' Flight with four Wapitis went to Juhu, Bombay, while 'B' Flight flew to St. Thomas Mount, Madras where they came to be known as 'Y' Flight. The third formation remained at Kohat. 'B' Flight at Madras was employed on anti-submarine and shipping patrols of the coast. These were the first operational sorties flown by No. 27 Squadron during World War II. On September 9, the Juhu Flight was relieved by a detachment of No. 60 Squadron and it rejoined the unit at Kohat.

1939, September 3 — Great Britain declares war on Germany. Mobilisation of RAF and Dominion Air Forces ordered.

1939, October 1 — No. 27 Squadron, RAF, was ordered to be converted from this date into the nucleus of a Flying Training School for the training of new pilots for the Indian Air Force, which had begun its life as a separate service at Drigh Road, Karachi, in 1933, and was crewed by Indian volunteers. All pupils for the IAF were, henceforth, to be recruited from the civilian sector including several airline pilots and the majority of the successful graduates would be enlisted in the IAF Volunteer Reserve. The school was located at Risalpur.

1939, October — To cope with most aspects of the training syllabus No. 27 Squadron was reorganised into two main Flights. The first was the Initial Training Flight (ITF) and the second was the Advanced Training Flight (ATF). Tiger Moths were used for the initial flying and for advanced flying training, six Wapitis and six Harts were used.

1939, October — One of the first pupils under the new flying training scheme was the Maharajah of Jodhpur, who was at that time already an Honorary Air Commodore in the RAF.

1939, November 11 — A total of 38 Indian pupils were inducted into flying training. Prior to this, existing Wapiti pilots were given conversion training on Hawker Harts.

1940 — The IV Course was begun which later produced many Air Marshals and senior officers for the IAF.

1941, January — Bristol Blenheim I bombers began to arrive at Risalpur, meant for No. 27 Squadron.

1941, February 13 — Thirteen Blenheims of No. 27 Squadron took off from Risalpur for Kallang airport in Singapore.

Bibliography

Ahluwalia, Gian Chand, "A World in Conflict (World War II and India)," 1949.
Air Ministry: Elementary Flying Training, 1943.
Aircraft Camouflage and Markings, 1907-1954.
Anwar, Mustafa, Captain, "Civil Aviation in India," 1954.
Baldwin, Hanson, "World War I — An Outlined History."
Bamm, Peter, Major Army Medical Corps; Der Wermacht, German Army, "The Invisible Flag."
Bouchier, C. A., Air Vice Marshal (Retd) RAF, "Excerpt from His Autobiography," 1980.
Bowyer, Chaz, Aero-Historian, "The Flying Elephants" (History of No. 27 Squadron, RFC/RAF), 1972.
British Aviation: The Pioneer Years and British Aviation, 1967-69.
Bruce, C. E., "Waziristan," 1936-37.
Bruce, J. M., "British Aeroplanes," 1914-18; and "Fighters," 1914-18.
Chaturvedi, M. S., Air Marshal (Retd) IAF, "History of the Indian Air Force," 1978.
Cole, C. C. H., "Royal Flying Corps," 1915-16; and "RAF," 1918.
Cole, D. H. and Priestly, E. C., Colonels, British Army, "British Military History 1660-1939," 1945.
Cross and Cockade, Journal of World War I Historians.
DC3 Arthur Pearcy, 1975.
Deighton, Len, "Bomber," 1970.
Duke, Neville and Lanchbery, Edward, "The Crowded Sky," 1959.
Durand, A. G., "The Making of a Frontier," 1899.
Dutt, K. N, "A Coin of Indian Metal," 1949.
Egerton, Hugh Edward, "A Short History of British Colonial Policy," 1897.
Elliott, J. G., Major General (Retd) Indian Army, "A Role of Honour — The story of the Indian Army, 1939-1945," 1965.
Elliott, J. G., Major General (Retd) Indian Army, "The Frontier 1839-1947," 1968.
Embry, Sir Basil, Air Chief Marshal (Retd) RAF, "Mission Completed," 1957.
Ferte de La, Sir Philip Joubert, Air Chief Marshal (Retd) RAF, "The Fated Sky," 1977.
Flight Commander, "Practical Flying," 1918.
Forbes, A. Seeley, "The Afghan Wars," 1892.
Forsyth, R. A., "Squadron Will Move," 1947.
Fox, Ernest F., Explorer, "Travels in Afghanistan — 1937-38," 1943.
Franks, Norman L. R., Aero-Historian, "First in the Indian Skies" (No. 31 Squadron, RFC/RAF), 1981.
Fuller, John G., Aviation writer, "The Airmen Who Would Not Die," 1979.
Funderbunk, Thomas R., "The Early Birds of War."
Gale and Polden, "Royal Air Force Year Book," 1938.
Gibson, Guy, Wing Commander, RAF Bomber Command, "Enemy Coast Ahead" (Introduction by Marshal of the RAF, Sir Arthur Harris), 1955.
Gidwani, B. S., "History of Air Transport," 1954.
Grey, C. G., Aero-Historian, "A History of the Air Ministry," 1940.

Gupta, S. C., Aero-Historian, "History of the Indian Air Force," 1961.
His Majesty's Stationery Office: Short History of RAF, 1931.
History and Encyclopaedia of the War (1914-18), Published by The Times, London.
History of No. 31 Squadron, RFC/ RAF (1915-1950), Naval and Military Press in association with The Imperial War Museum, London.
James, L., "Indian Frontier War," 1897.
Liddel Hart, "History of World War I".
Liddel Hart, B. H., Aero-Historian, "The Rommel Papers," 1953.
Macmillan, Norman, "Into the Blue".
Macmillan, Norman, "RAF in the World Wars — 1919-1945".
Macmillan, Norman, Wing Commander (Retd), RFC/RAF, Biography of Air Vice Marshal, Sir Sefton Brancker, first Director of Civil Aviation, UK, 1935.
Malik, Sardar Hardit Singh, Lieutenant, RFC/RAF (1917-1919), ICS, OBE, MBE, Excerpts from Autobiography, 1979.
Masters, David, Aero-Historian, "So Few — The Immortal Record of the Royal Air Force," 1941.
Masters, John, Lieutenant Colonel (Retd), Indian Army, "Bugles and the Tiger," 1956.
Masters, John, Lieutenant Colonel (Retd), Indian Army, "Fourteen — Eighteen".
Masters, John, Lieutenant Colonel (Retd), Indian Army, "The Lotus and the Wind," 1953.
Masters, John, Lieutenant Colonel (Retd), Indian Army, "The Road Past Mandalay," 1964.
Morris, Alan, "The Balloonatics".
Neville, H. L., "Campaigns on the North-West Frontier, 1849-1910".
Reynolds, Quentin, "The Story of the First War in the Air".
Reynolds, Quentin, "They Fought for the Sky".
Roberts, Lord, Field Marshal, "Forty One Years in India," 1897.
Robertson, F. A. de V., Major (Retd), Aero-Historian, "British Aviation," 1940.
Rolo, Charles J., "Wingate's Raiders 9 — Story of Chindits," 1944.
Ross, John, Flying Officer (Retd), RAF VR, "RFC to the RAF India, 1919," 1987.
Russell, W. W., Wing Commander (Retd), RAF VR, "Forgotten Skies," 1945.
Saigal, A.L., Air Commodore (Retd), Indian Air Force, "The Fledgling Years, 1932-45".
Saundby, Sir Robert, Air Marshal (Retd), RAF, "Early Aviation," 1971.
Saunders, Hilary St. George, "The Rise of British Air Power (1911-1939)," 1944.
Sims, Edward, "Fighter Tactics and Strategy".
Singh, Harjinder, Air Vice Marshal (Retd), IAF, "Birth of an Air Force," 1977 (edited by Air Commodore A. L. Saigal (Retd), IAF.
Singh, Rajendra, Brig. (Retd), Indian Army, "History of the Indian Army," 1963.
Slessor, Sir John, Air Chief Marshal (Retd), RAF, "The Central Blue".
Smith, P. W. L. Broke, "The History of Early British Military Aeronautics," 1972.
Sunderman, James F., "Early Air Pioneers, 1862-1935," 1961.
Sutton, B., "Jungle Pilot".
Taylor, John W. R., "Combat Aircraft of the World".
Taylor, John W. R., Aero-Historian, CFS, "Birthplace of Air Power," 1958.
Thornton, T. H., "Colonel Sir Robert Sandeman," 1895.
Warburton, Sir Robert, Colonel, "Eighteen Years in the Khyber," 1900.
Watson, W. A., Major General (Retd), Indian Army, "King George's Own Central India Horse" (The Story of a Local Corps), 1930.
Wragg, David W., "Flight Before Flying," 1974.
Young, A. J. and Warne, D. W., "Sixty Squadron".

Index